For ourselves

From women's point of view: our bodies and sexuality

Text: Anja Meulenbelt, Johanna's Daughter
Interviews: Ariane Amsberg
Drawings: Jolet Leenhouts
Photographs: Sjan Bijman – Bertien van Manen – Anja Meulenbelt, Johanna's Daughter – Marie An Schut
Planning: the Sara collective health group: Wiky van Rijssel, Ariane Amsberg, Joyce Outshoorn, Ria van Hengel, Ria Sikkes, Loes de Bruijn, An Luttikholt, Marjo van Soest.
With thanks to: Marie An Schut, Ellen Santen, José Uytendaal, Marleen Heeman, Marijke du Plessis, and the women who were happy to be photographed or interviewed or shared their experiences in some other way.
English translation: Ann Oosthuizen with help from Marij van Helmond.
English edition edited by: Jill Nicholls with help from Tina Reid.

Sheba Feminist Publishers – 1981

For ourselves first published in the English translation in Great Britain
in November 1981 by Sheba Feminist Publishers, 488 Kingsland Rd,
London E8
Copyright text © Anja Meulenbelt, Johanna's Daughter – Amsterdam
Copyright interviews © Ariane Amsberg – Oestgeest
Copyright photographs © The portrait series 1 and 2 are by Bertien
van Manen – Amsterdam. The other photographs are by Sjan Bijman
– Haarlem, except those on pages 28-60-114-202-250 (Anja
Meulenbelt – Amsterdam) and 27 (Marie An Schut – Amsterdam)
Copyright drawings © Jolet Leenhouts
Copyright English translation © Sheba Feminist Publishers
Designed by Hennie van der Zande – Amsterdam
ISBN 0 907179 01 0
Paste up by Sue Hobbs and Hilary Arnott
Typeset in Helvetica 10/11 by Frances, Julia and Lin at
Range Left Photosetters (TU), 01-251 3959
Printed and bound by
Goldcrest Press, Trowbridge, Wiltshire

Contents

I. For ourselves

1. Introduction

If someone had asked me ten years ago whether I had sexual problems, I'd have found it an odd question. Me, sexual problems? I was still young, independent, living in Amsterdam where I could do what I liked. Now and then I had a lover, without being secretive about it, and if I felt attracted to a man I soon let him know about it. I was a sexual counsellor with the Association for Sexual Reform and held discussions on sexuality with young male workers, a bag of condoms in full view. I changed my cap for the pill when it came into fashion, and the pill for the IUD when that was the latest thing. We were in the middle of the sexual revolution, I and other women like myself. Sexual problems seemed to me something for the unsophisticated, nothing to do with us.

Since that time a lot has changed. When women first met in consciousness raising groups, sexuality was a popular subject. And it gradually became clear that we had deluded each other and, above all, ourselves. When we went into how often we made love for our own pleasure, it didn't add up to much. Too often we went to bed with a man because it was expected of us, because otherwise he would find another girlfriend, because then we would get a week's peace, because it was the only way to cuddle up against someone else. None of us had an easy time of it; those of us who were married or in a permanent relationship had unknowingly given away a kind of season ticket to the use of our bodies when we had signed the marriage certificate. Those of us in the kind of throw-away relationships which were becoming so popular didn't have an easy time of it either. Sex for the sake of sex seldom turned out to be the erotic rapture about which we had such fine fantasies. And whether we had a permanent relationship or made do with what came our way, our need for warm skin and tenderness was not being fulfilled, or at best only occasionally. And we still faked orgasm. And we still felt guilty.

The first consciousness raising groups are behind us now. Not only did we talk about sexuality, we also tried to change it. Some women tried to change the way they related to the man they were living with, with all the risks that involved. Some relationships improved, others split up. A number of women learned to live alone, and discovered that there is more eroticism to be found in our daily living than from the odd fuck which used to have to satisfy all our needs. A love affair with ourselves, instead of waiting for The Other. Still other women noticed they were beginning to find their woman friends nicer, more beautiful and more attractive, until they realised their sexuality had shifted from men to women.

These new discoveries were great as far as they went, but we were aware that they had their limitations. We still live in a society which is based on inequality. The women who gave up a permanent relationship with a man saw that this did not only affect their sexual lives, but had financial consequences too. The women who tried to change the way they related sexually to their husbands found out that it was almost impossible unless they could achieve a more independent position within their marriage by sharing childcare, earning their own money. Women who discovered their own capacity for sexual pleasure found that, as women in their fifties, they were no longer considered attractive by men. Women who came out openly in a relationship with another woman discovered that liberal tolerance was only skin deep.

So on the one hand we claimed small freedoms and we are beginning to know our real needs. We are becoming brave enough to refuse to fuck unless we really want to, not minding if we're called prudish or frigid when our sexual needs are not what men want them to be. We practise a good relationship with ourselves and with other women. On the other hand we are aware that we can't change our sexuality without also changing the rest of our lives. We long ago gave up the illusion that we could create a small paradise of freedom in bed while in the rest of our lives we are underpaid, badly treated, despised and exploited.

Our experiences, those things we have learned about our sexuality, are in this book. Along with the difficulties we encounter when we try to find out what our real needs are and what we can do about them. There are no easy solutions. There isn't just *one* kind of liberated or emancipated sexuality.

2. Not another book about sex?

There are a lot of books on sexuality, but we need another one. In the last few years our ideas about sexuality have changed dramatically. We look at it in a different way.

● We don't experience sex as something you do exclusively with your genitals. Your erotic feelings depend on how comfortable you are inside your own skin. How you 'handle' your body. So it isn't just a question of 'technique' but of our relationship to our whole body.

● We believe that our sexuality belongs to us, it isn't something we get from someone else. We are sexual beings, not sexless Sleeping Beauties who must first be awakened by the prince's kiss before we discover what sex is. This book begins with the sexual relationship we have with ourselves. Only then do we look at our relationships with other people.

● We no longer take for granted that sex is about being attracted to the *opposite* sex. The line between homo- and hetero-sexuality isn't as easy to draw as we used to think. Most books

8 assume that sexuality is *heterosexuality*, with perhaps a separate chapter on homosexuality, the exception, a deviation or variation. But our sexuality is *our* sexuality, never mind who we experience a part of it with.

Perhaps, we now think, we would all love both women and men if the consequences of a choice for the one or the other weren't so serious. It shouldn't mean that we are all being divided into two completely different kinds of people: homo- and hetero-sexual.

That is not to say that it doesn't matter whether you have a relationship with a woman or with a man. Women and men live quite differently. They occupy different social positions. A relationship with a woman is viewed quite differently from one with a man. The problems are different. For this reason there are separate chapters on relationships with women and with men.

● Our sexual experiences are not separate from the fact that we live in a man's world. Economic dependence, with or without the marriage certificate; the limited possibility of building an independent life; the fact that women are still burdened with the greatest share of childcare, and the fact that as women we have little protection against sexual violence and battering – all this inhibits our sexual freedom. That's why this book discusses not only how to make an orgasm, but also how relationships between women and men in this society are organised.

● In a male-dominated world, the sexual rules take men as their starting point. There are still very few books on sexuality that are based on what *we* experience. And what we might *want*. Most books tell us what we *ought* to do and how we *ought* to feel. A few years ago the Boston Women's Health Book Collective wrote *Our Bodies Ourselves*. Then came *The Hite Report*. These were the first books on the sexual experiences of women by women and were best sellers. And for the first time we had the nerve to say out loud that we weren't too happy with the sexual rules.

In this book we are trying to develop these ideas a little further: not only to describe what we no longer want, but also to explore cautiously where to go from here.

3. Who we are writing for

This book is written for women, for ourselves. If men read it and learn something from it, that's fine. But in the first place it's important that we speak for ourselves, that we make it clear what *we* want. We don't want to make ourselves dependent once again on what others understand or think they understand about what is good for us. We hope that eventually men will begin to write their own books about sexuality, not the lying confidence tricks which have for so long frustrated us and them, but honest books, written without false pride and with tenderness. Written from their collective experience and not from bogus 'authority'.

This book is meant for women, but not all women are the same. One woman will find the chapter on orgasm important, for another it offers nothing new. Women who are living with women **9**

...and I still feel fucked up..

will skip the chapter on contraception; women involved with men may think the chapter on loving women is not about them. The possibilities we have to enjoy life differ as our social situations differ. If you are in your twenties, with an independent income, without children, living in a big city, and you are considered 'pretty' in the eyes of the world, your opportunities are different from when you're forty, size eighteen, with three kids, living in a small community with few women around you with whom you feel you can talk and without your own income. *That's why what one woman takes for granted is beyond another's reach. Those women who have no opportunity to change their sexual lives, or don't want to, won't want to read this book. Those women who live in situations where they have always done as they wished will perhaps find little that is new in this book. It is written for the women somewhere between these two groups: women who are thinking about sexuality, women who want to change.*

4. About the language

It's not easy to talk about sex. This is partly because it's not so long ago that women weren't supposed to be interested in sex at all. Another difficulty, however, is that we don't have a language of our own in which to express ourselves. The choice we've got is this: we can use the language of innuendo, which goes with the double morality: 'sleeping with someone, going to bed with someone, between my legs, doing "it" '. This is the kind of language which doesn't give offence, but it isn't very clear, and when we use it we continue to act as if making love is something shameful and that a whole part of our body is dirty. We can also choose medical jargon: vagina, coitus, or even worse: sexual intercourse, cunnilingus (. . . searching like mad in the dictionary). Words which are more suited to a visit to a doctor or gynaecologist than to our sensual experiences. Can you hear yourself saying: 'I'd love to have coitus with you, after a bit of cunnilingus'?

gosh, I used to have to wash my mouth out if I said dirty words

But what is there instead? Men's language? Cunt, fuck, prick? It's a hard unfriendly language. As long as people say 'you cunt' and 'fucking mess', it is almost impossible to use the words for pleasant parts of the body or joyous activities. In Germany a group of women are trying to introduce new words: shell instead of cunt, pearl instead of clitoris. It's well-meaning, but it sounds so artificial. The word vulva sounds friendly, but it's a word you read, not one that you use.

There is no sexual language that really suits us. That already gives some measure of the extent to which our sexuality doesn't belong to us and how our experience is dictated. As long as our sexuality is not really ours we will lack a language which we can use comfortably. Until then I'll muddle along using all the different words. Sometimes I'll be using words like cunt and fuck in the hope that they sound all right. Sometimes words like penis

and vagina. Sometimes friendly words like making love. One

new expression: instead of 'getting an orgasm', I write 'making an orgasm'. Because an orgasm isn't a present we receive from somebody else, but a possibility within ourselves, a happening which we actively create.

5. About the illustrations

Language is often inadequate when we want to express our emotions. In the interviews with Ariane included in this book we can recover something of the totality of our lives. Perhaps it is easier to write about our sexual experiences in a novel, but this book isn't a novel. We have chosen instead to use a lot of photographs and drawings to make some of our feelings visible. We have used only a limited number of technical drawings; cross-sections of wombs and ovaries are remote from what we feel, so they are in the book only if we really need them to understand how our bodies work. We have looked in particular for pictures which express pleasure in our own bodies – the pleasure of sitting contentedly in the sun, naked with your bum in the warm sand, or the soft hands of a woman friend massaging your neck. We also wanted to make pictures which show what we really look like, with wrinkles and warts and breasts that hang downwards according to the laws of gravity. That may be a bit of a shock because we are used to seeing images of slim women of about twenty illustrating accounts of sexuality. That shock tells us something about our alienation from our own bodies, and about how we need to learn to see ourselves as beautiful the way we are. We have printed a series of photographs of cunts. Perhaps the reaction to them will be: 'Was that necessary?' Would that have been the reaction if the book were illustrated with lots of photos of faces? When we took the pictures we learned how little we knew about the landscape between our

legs. We have lived twenty, thirty, forty years with our cunts, yet when we took the pictures, most of the women could only recognise themselves by their fingers in the photographs. We know our hands. But those various folds and hairs are strange to us. In the photos we think they look like friendly parts of our body, all of them different as faces are different. Part of ourselves. Other lips, nothing to be ashamed of.

The pictures are of women only. At the moment it is women who are celebrating their physicality much more openly than in the past; many of the photos were taken on islands where women spend holidays together or at festivals where we meet to celebrate. Perhaps one day we will see pictures of men which seem just as warm as the images of women in this book.

6. What the book does not discuss

This book could easily have turned out five times as long. You can't separate sexuality off from the rest of life, and once you begin to write about it, it seems to be related to everything else. But we didn't want to write an encyclopaedia, so even during the writing we had to make choices. We could have written much more about relationships, about love, romance, jealousy, and about sickness, health and growing older. There is nothing about birth and giving birth in the book. There is almost nothing about education, which deserves a lot more attention. To compensate for these shortcomings, at the end of each chapter under the heading 'Further reading', we refer you to more books on the subject.

7. How the book was written

Only one woman wrote the text of the book, but she could not have done so without the experiences of hundreds of other women. You hear their voices in Ariane's interviews and in the bits printed in italics; women friends, women whom I have met who talked about themselves. A lot of collective thought has gone into it, from the health group in the Sara Collective, who first published the book in Dutch, and from the women's movement as a whole. I have used scientific and medical material where it is useful. But our own experiences and ideas are central.

This book is a present we wish to give to ourselves and to other women. We hope that women will buy it for themselves, for their women friends, for their daughters and mothers. We hope that women will buy it as if it were a bunch of flowers, a new pair of slippers, a box of chocolates.

Because we deserve it, and not just on Mother's Day.

Further reading

I've mentioned a couple of books in which women themselves have described their own sexuality: the true ancestors of this book. *Our Bodies Ourselves*, originally written by the Boston Women's Health Book Collective, is now out in Penguin. It's been adapted for British readers by Angela Phillips and Jill Rakusen. *The Hite Report* by Shere Hite (import) gives extensive coverage of the experiences of women, which she collected by issuing almost 2,000 questionnaires. It is long, but a good reflection of what women feel. At times I felt I had heard it all, the answers go on for pages, but perhaps that will convince people who are sceptical.

An interesting book about 'the falsity of women's sex lives' is *I Accuse* by Mette Ejlersen (Tandem, now out of print). Full of interviews and anecdotes, particularly about 'the myth of the vaginal orgasm'. *Bitching* by Marion Meade (Panther) is worth looking at too – about the games women have to play and the resentment they feel, rather than about sexuality as such.

II. Your own best friend

1. What are sexual needs?

We are brought up to have such fixed ideas of what sexuality is all about that it seems silly to talk about it. Sexuality, that's something that happens between a man and a woman. Sexual needs are something you have, just like you need to eat, drink or sleep. Sex is 'natural'.

MMMMMMMMM Lovely cuddle !!

If sexuality were natural, we'd just do what we felt like, have no problems about it and not be so bothered about what is 'normal'. There is no 'natural' way for people to have sex. We need a specific form of sex in order to reproduce, but whatever other needs we may still have depend on our culture, on who we are. Equally there is no specific feminine or masculine nature: in some cultures, the women behave like men do here, and vice versa. There have been periods in history where women were not supposed to have any sexual needs, and others where women were expected to be more 'lustful' than men. There are societies where it is considered normal for people to have no sex for a year, others where a man who doesn't fuck every day is looked upon with pity. In short: sexuality isn't 'natural' but learned behaviour, and how we experience sex depends on the rest of our lives. For example, our assumption that a man should be on top when making love comes from the fact that in our society men are 'on top' in other ways as well. It's not that it's 'natural' that way.

If we were to make a list of what makes us feel good, then our first and most important needs are food, sleep and shelter from the cold. Next comes a real need to be touched, cuddled. Babies who don't have enough physical contact don't grow, they can even die. I think that is just as true for adults. People who are seldom fondled, old people for example, people in prison, handicapped people, often feel lonely because of a lack of physical contact. And really that is more or less true for everyone.

'When we were discussing relationships in my consciousness-raising group, we asked one another whether any of us felt she was getting the warmth she needed. Nobody did. There wasn't even a difference between women who lived alone and women who were in permanent relationships.'

Our other fundamental needs are: to belong somewhere, to receive attention, to be 'seen' and 'heard', to share sorrow, comfort, to be understood, to be close to people you like. There is a need for physical exercise, and for release of tension, for example when we make an orgasm. In our society many of these needs are bundled together and labelled 'sexuality'. And we **15**

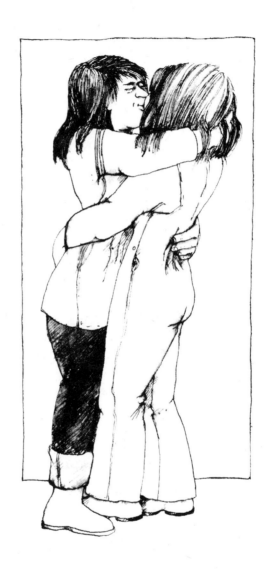

have only one way to express our sexuality, or only one correct way: in a relationship with a man, regularly, in the sort of physical gymnastics we call 'intercourse', 'coitus' or 'fucking'. The aim being to slide the penis into the vagina. And the ideal being to climax together.

For most women that's about it – there's hardly anything outside that prescribed behaviour. For women who don't have a permanent relationship there is even less. That's why women who live alone often think they need 'sex' when they feel lonely: it's almost the only thing you can expect to get. And women who do have relationships often complain that their need for tenderness or a good hug is never fulfilled because it always ends up in fucking, even if it's not what they want at that point in time.

'I have learned not to be physical with men. I am the kind of person who actually touches other people quite spontaneously when having a good conversation with someone I like. But that has led to a lot of misunderstandings. Men have become really angry because they thought I was seducing them and then didn't want to go through with it. Once I was nearly raped by a colleague at work who thought I was giving him the come on, and then changed my mind: he began to shout that I was a clever bitch, that I did it on purpose, that I led men on and was then too frustrated and neurotic to go through with it. "And she calls that emancipation", he added. The next day he came to apologise, said he had been a bit drunk and didn't really mean it. But all the same, you learn to keep your hands to yourself if you're not quite sure whether you want to go to bed with someone.'

'My husband won't just give me a good hug. If he suddenly stands behind me in the kitchen and begins to kiss my neck, I know exactly what he's after. Then we have to do it again. He doesn't kiss me because he loves me, but because he wants something from me.'

'I really enjoy eating out with friends or cooking a meal for someone. But I've had the most ridiculous misunderstandings about it. For some reason a man thinks you have given him an invitation to stay the night if you cook a meal for him. Then he asks: "What did I do wrong?" if after a while I say I want to go to sleep, but not with him. I lost a friend that way, at least I thought he was a real friend. Later on I heard he told someone what a difficult woman I was.'

It's no accident that many women find their needs fulfilled only when they make contact with other women, in women's groups, in the women's movement.

'I am appreciating women a lot more now. You can have so much fun with other women. I always thought you had sexual relationships with men, and just friendships with women. But now I'm beginning to understand that my relationships with women have actually something sexual in them too. Not that we have to do anything – it just feels so good to be appreciated, to dance together, to have my back stroked.'

It's important that we get to know our own needs and find out what we can do about them. We don't have to accept that we can't do anything to fulfil our needs because we aren't in a permanent relationship, or that women don't turn us on unless we happen to be lesbians, or that a fuck three times a month is all we can expect. Not all women have the same needs, there is no set pattern.

'I have a strong need for frequent orgasms, but I don't want to make love to someone regularly. I have discovered that these are two very different things. If I really want to make love to someone, then I enjoy an orgasm, but that isn't the main thing. I can just as easily make an orgasm on my own. For a long time I thought there was something wrong with me, that it was a bit perverted to want an orgasm but not to want to make love, even though I had a very good relationship. I had the feeling I was depriving him.'

'I don't have a need for regular sex. If I'm very much in love then I'm terribly randy, I hardly think of anything else. And then when I'm no longer in love, that disappears. I'm hardly interested, and can go without for weeks or months. I really detest these situations of "every other day". At first I thought I wasn't capable of a normal relationship because I didn't want to keep on fucking if I was no longer in love. It has caused a lot of conflicts and I've often carried on even though I didn't really want to, just so I wouldn't lose someone. Because I do have a need for constancy, someone to whom I belong a little.'

'I am terribly physical, I can lie in bed for hours caressing my girlfriend and spend a whole Sunday making love, but really coming is something we only do occasionally. That's when we suddenly look at each other in the car and think, yes now, and then we can't get home quick enough.'

It's important that each of us finds out what we really need to make us feel good. We have to work out what we need other people for, and *which* other people. We can make an orgasm with someone else, but we can also make it alone. Physical warmth – all your women friends can give you plenty of that, there is no reason why it should come from just one relationship. Perhaps you do still really need a permanent relationship as

well, but you might be less dependent on it because you

wouldn't have to get everything from one person any more. Whatever we choose, the most important thing is not to wait for someone else to make us happy, but to choose what we want for ourselves.

2. On your own, time for yourself

Fantasies of happiness in the arms of your prince or princess still flourish, even if the word Love has been replaced by Sex. With such high expectations, no wonder we experience disappoint-ments. We are disappointed in men, who because of their conditioning aren't always the sensitive, understanding, tender people with whom we would wish to form a relationship. If we choose a woman, we are disappointed if she cannot cope with the pressure from the world outside, or can't protect us from the pain we encounter out there in the big bad world.

We have learned to accept the idea that happiness means having a good one-to-one relationship and unhappiness the absence of it. So we have placed the responsibility for our own happiness on the other person, making ourselves more dependent and vulnerable than necessary. It makes it difficult for us to see what we can do for ourselves.

Most of us don't find it easy to live alone. Women especially are brought up with the idea that we will marry and look after a husband and children. Even if you don't marry, but live with a woman or man, the idea is that the relationship will be your life's greatest fulfilment. Men have more chance of finding their self-respect in their work. The lousy jobs women are offered make us even more dependent on a relationship. There is also the message that you're only a 'real' woman if you live for someone else. We all have to fight the voices in our heads which accuse us of being hard and egotistical if we do what we want, what we enjoy most. From babyhood we are fed with the idea that we should be undemanding and self-sacrificing, so that in the end we hardly know what we want.

the incomplete family

And then, the world is organised in such a way at the moment that it isn't easy to live alone. Going to a restaurant on your own, or to a film or a pub, seems more like an endurance test than a pleasure. It isn't any easier to go on holiday alone, or on a day's outing. Women without a relationship are often looked on as odd; there is something wrong with you, you can't communicate, you're pathetic. All the words which describe a woman who isn't in a permanent relationship with another adult have something negative about them: spinster, unmarried, single parent. You yourself may feel perfectly complete on your own, but for other people you're still only half a couple. A 'free woman' sounds immoral. The word virgin, which used to mean 'a woman who is of herself', now only means that you haven't (yet) been used by a man. An independent man is a bachelor, an independent woman is quickly an old maid. No one believes that you might have made a free choice. **19**

With all this pressure on us, no wonder it's difficult to distinguish our own needs from those imposed on us by society. You need to be very strong not to succumb to a feeling of failure if you don't have a permanent relationship. So we find ourselves in a vicious circle where we expect too much from the other person and don't develop a relationship with ourselves. Yet whether or not you share a part of your life with someone else, you are still the person you will be stuck with for the rest of your life, the centre of your own existence. 'The woman in your life', sings Lavender Jane, 'is you.'

'I stayed far too long with my boyfriend because I was in a panic about having to live alone. I often thought, I'll leave as soon as I find someone else. When it finally became too unbearable and I left, it was really difficult at first. I had to look for somewhere to live, I had lost a lot of my friends who obviously seemed to think they had to side with him. I realised that I had neglected my woman friends for years. Many of my women friends weren't particularly keen on listening to me complaining for hours on end. And justifiably so, I thought afterwards – if you drop them so easily when you have a lover, then you can't expect them to welcome you with open arms when he has disappeared. I've been living alone for a year now and it gets better all the time. I don't think I'll desert my circle of friends ever again for a relationship with a man like I did before.'

Living alone is something we can learn. It means organising everything ourselves, excursions, holidays. It means looking out for places to go to that we enjoy even on our own, so that we don't have to get that feeling of being shut in the house on Sundays while families walk by outside with flowers for mother-in-law. We have to make sure there are people around us whom we value. Luckily there are more and more places where it is possible to go on one's own even as a woman – women's centres, communal holidays. But it isn't just independent women who have trouble making friends and not feeling lonely. A woman living with a husband and children has hardly any time for herself. There's practically nowhere you can be on your own without the children coming in to tell you they're bored and that *you* must do something about it. You hardly get any time for yourself without feeling guilty about all the things you should be doing. To maintain a relationship with a woman friend is more difficult in a permanent relationship than when you are alone. Most couples go around almost exclusively with other couples. An evening out with a woman friend takes organisation and arrangements, while an evening at home with a lover or husband is no problem. Many women think it is odd to go on holiday with other women if they are in a permanent relationship.
Because we aren't used to keeping up a good relationship with ourselves when we have a relationship with someone else, and because we neglect our other friends, we make ourselves more **21**

dependent than we need be. More afraid of being on our own. And therefore more unhappy when we do find ourselves alone. And so we look for another relationship as quickly as we can to make us happy.

3. Loving yourself

Whether we live alone or in a more or less permanent relationship with husband, woman or children, the first task is to learn to love ourselves. An exercise: what do we do for others but not for ourselves? Do we only buy flowers and presents for other people? Do we think it's not worthwhile to open a bottle of wine unless we have visitors? Do we only use luxurious bath oils and put clean sheets on the bed if someone else is going to enjoy it with us? Do we make steak and a salad for guests, but eat bread and cheese when we are alone? Do we buy a book for Aunt Amy's birthday, but not for ourselves? Do we put that record on an endless list of things we'd like to be given, instead of buying it ourselves? Do we wait until we are invited instead of going for a walk on the beach by ourselves? Do we spoil our birthdays by running around with treats for other people instead of inviting ourselves to someone else's house for a change? Do we love dancing but feel too embarrassed to do it alone in the middle of our own room? Are we too scared to ask for an hour of warmth and attention when we need it? Then it's high time we started a romantic affair with ourselves.

'Now and then I take an evening for myself. I make a few preparations. I decide what I'd really like to eat and if I can, I prepare it the day before. Or I buy some good food at the delicatessen. A bottle of wine. And then flowers on the table and a pair of candles. Draw the curtains and unplug the phone. Turn on the TV, or a new book or a new record. Fantastic!'

'Before, when I was very tired, I used to climb back into my bed which was still unmade from that morning. I'd shut my eyes quickly so as not to see the mess. Now, if I'm really tired I try to put clean sheets on my bed, have a hot shower and get between the clean sheets all fragrant and warm. I sleep better too.'

'I know it sounds childish, but if I want to spoil myself, I put a hot water bottle in my bed, get a mug of warm milk and go to bed with a new novel. Sometimes I lie there really purring with pleasure.'

'If I want to do something really nice for myself, I plan a trip in the car. A village I've never visited. Getting out of the city is good for me. Eat a cheap meal in a village cafe. And then return home feeling very satisfied.'

'Once a month I'm alone for the weekend. My boyfriend goes to his parents and I've arranged not to go with him any more. I plan what I'm going to do long beforehand, an evening out with a couple of good woman friends whom I'd otherwise never see, a pleasant meal in the city with a few people.'

'I took up jazz ballet although I thought I was too old for it. The best thing was that there were women older and fatter and stiffer than me. We giggle a lot, and sometimes we swing the roof off.'

'I made a promise to my consciousness raising group that I'd take one hour for myself each day. In the beginning I didn't know what to do with that hour, I was so unused to doing something on my own. But now I notice that I become completely relaxed if I can just sit down peacefully and read the paper without anyone talking to me. Or spend an hour spoiling my body under the shower and then a rub with luxurious cream. Or put on music for half an hour and dance on my own without anyone watching.'

'Occasionally I join the children in the bath. I love the warm, fragrant little bodies. I have to make time for it, otherwise I get annoyed at the mess it makes.'

'Come summer time I rent a cottage somewhere with a couple of woman friends. A place where you can walk around outside without clothes on. Gossiping in the grass in the sun. Walking. Eating together. With an open fire. Hmmm.'

'If I have managed my money well, I take a couple of pounds or a fiver and buy a little present for myself. Something completely useless which I don't absolutely need.'

4. Eating

Loving yourself also means being good to your body and that isn't always easy. If we're very unhappy we tend to eat a lot of little snacks. If we're very unhappy we grab the sherry bottle too quickly. We forget too easily that we *are* our body, that it isn't just something we carry around with us. We know there is a definite connection between how our body is feeling and how we feel emotionally: if we're unhappy we seldom feel well, if we're in pain or we have habits which conflict with the needs of our body, we seldom feel happy. Respect for our bodies is the basis of a good relationship with ourselves. That means feeding ourselves properly, cutting down on harmful habits like smoking and drinking, taking enough exercise and taking our health seriously. In our Western society today, almost no one need go hungry. Yet for many people the memory of not having enough to eat during the war is still fresh. Or maybe we've inherited eating habits from 23 our parents, formed in a time when meat and sweets and white bread were luxuries. These now threaten to poison us: we eat too much sugar, too much fat, too much meat, too much salt and too many things like white flour and white rice. Junk like that fills us up, but has very little nutritional value. Nowadays there is sugar in everything, in bread, peanut butter, fizzy drinks, mayonnaise. And it hardly ever says so on the label. Fat is present in disguise in many products: ice cream, pork chops, crisps and savouries. Mince meat and sausages often contain mostly fat. Products like pizza, macaroni, white bread, cake and so on are made of white flour from which almost all the important nutritive ingredients have been taken out. There's too much salt in almost all ready-made snacks, in soups, even in babyfood and soft drinks.

The most delicious foods, the ones which don't take much trouble to prepare and with which you spoil yourself, are particularly bad: ready-made salads, sausage rolls, pies (even pasties, which some people think are nourishing, are full of sugar, fat and white flour). When we have nobody to look after except ourselves we tend to choose the easy way and live on food that is bad for us, but which doesn't require much preparation after a long day. We go for foods that look nice. Sometimes the biggest treat you can give yourself is *not* to have to cook. All the same it is worth checking that food not only looks and tastes good, but is good for us. And there are other ways of spoiling ourselves: not just fish and chips while we read the paper, but a carefully chosen varied meal, served up in a way that looks attractive.

'I used to think it was a special luxury not to have to cook for myself. I'd go to the Chinese take-away or open a tin of soup. Now I take special trouble to make an attractive meal for myself: a pretty dish, even if I'm not eating much, with a slice of tomato or a bit of lemon or parsley. A salad in a small bowl with a slice of egg on top. A napkin, and water in a wine glass. A pear for afterwards or a few grapes with a piece of cheese. Orange juice for breakfast and occasionally a soft-boiled egg. It takes more time, but it also gives me more pleasure.'

One problem about eating too much or badly is that we get fat. And that has everything to do with how we feel. There are different versions of 'too fat'. One is that we are fatter than is healthy for us, which means we don't have any energy and get sick more easily. The other kind of 'too fat' has to do with fashion: the idea that only extremely skinny women are attractive makes us go on idiotic and unhealthy diets to achieve this ideal – mostly without success. It is extremely important that we choose ways in which we can stay healthy, not overweight, but without falling into the opposite extreme of punishing ourselves with starvation diets and an ideal image that we are unable to reach. Most

women believe they're ugly, and most of us immediately

connect 'ugly' with being too fat. We are all familiar with the vicious circle of self-hatred: you feel unhappy, you comfort yourself with something to eat, and then you feel even more unhappy because you've put on another pound. It's very hard to break out of the circle. You can only begin by loving yourself enough to have respect for your body so you can find out what your real needs are. If you're lonely, or don't get enough attention, you can't fill the emptiness in your soul with a Kit Kat. It's important to find other ways of breaking your isolation or being appreciated.

5. Drinking

Alcohol is rapidly becoming the most common and dangerous drug. There was a time when a bottle of wine marked a festive occasion, it went with a special meal or a celebration. Now it's normal to have something to drink in the house and offer it whenever anyone comes round. Some people become addicted to alcohol, they're unable to do without it. And an increasing number of them are women, now that drinking has moved from the pub to the home. Alcohol is a problem not only for women who get so drunk they don't know what they're doing. Many women never get drunk, but without thinking about it have developed a habit of drinking more than is good for them every day.

'Since we've begun to keep something in the house because my husband often brings acquaintances home for a meal, I notice that I've started to take a glass of brandy with my coffee in the morning and a sherry while I'm cooking. In the holidays we tend to drink wine at every meal. And then in the evening brandy again with the coffee. And that's every single day.'

'Now that I have a good salary, I usually go out to lunch with the people at work and have a glass of wine. Then at five o'clock I have another drink. Sometimes when I get home I have another before dinner. And then at dinner and again in the evening.'

'I have slowly developed the habit of drinking a couple of beers while watching TV. I think it would be unsociable to let my boyfriend drink on his own, so I have some too. If we have visitors we get through quite a few beers.'

Drunkenness in unhealthy. But even if we never get drunk, too much alcohol often makes us feel tired and flabby. It makes us sleep badly, wake unrefreshed, become fatter than we should be. Alcohol is a poison which needs to be absorbed by the liver. If you drink too much, in the end your liver can't cope. Even if it doesn't get to that stage, too much drinking isn't good: your body is so busy digesting the poison that it doesn't have much energy left for anything else. With the exception of those people who **25** know that they can become addicted to alcohol, and for whom it is sensible not to drink at all, it's quite all right to enjoy a glass of wine with a meal or a drink at night. It helps to keep a check for a while on how much you consume. Sometimes you fill up your glass so automatically that you hardly notice it, and there isn't much pleasure in that. In company it's especially easy to drink without noticing how much you're taking. For someone to whom this has become a habit, it can help if you drink a glass of mineral water or orange juice instead. An advantage of not overdoing it is that if you do have a glass of wine, you really taste it, as it was in the days when wine was served only on special occasions.

If you notice you're developing a drink problem, it's important to find out the reasons why. When and why do you have a drink? Is it always to get rid of tension at work, or after a hard day when the children are at last in bed? Is it because you don't feel comfortable in the company you mix with? Is it when you are bored, or have the feeling that nothing you do is worthwhile? If this is so, you need to do something about it.

6. Smoking

.. cut down on harmful habits like smoking and drinking.

It used to be mostly men who got lung cancer. Thanks to the 'emancipation' of women, who are now allowed to smoke in public, more and more women get lung cancer. Smoking is a well-known way of getting rid of tension. It gives you something to do with your hands when you're in company, it gives you style. But in an enclosed space, if you smoke you force everyone else to smoke as well, and that can be torture, particularly for those who are trying to give it up. If you smoke when you're on the pill, it's twice as dangerous. This is the finding of recent research in Britain. If you're smoking while on the pill, the solution is to give up either the pill, or smoking, or both.

Just as with other forms of addiction, it's important to find out when you are most in need of a cigarette. If you smoke mainly to give yourself confidence, then training in self-confidence will help. If you don't know what to do with your hands, try to find something else to keep them busy. In Greece the men play with a chain of beads all day, which must make a big difference in the number of cases of lung cancer. I have two large double bedspreads as a reward for all the little squares I crocheted during boring or tense meetings. And what's more it is your right, if you don't smoke, to expect other people not to smoke in an enclosed space if it bothers you. Most women can hardly manage more than a friendly request for less smoking, or for the window to be opened – so that in addition to lung cancer we also get to freeze to death – but we're seldom brave enough to ask smokers to save their cigarettes until the break, or to go outside if they can't do without. A good exercise in assertion.

7. Exercise

Almost everyone has too little or not varied enough physical exercise. This is because most work is terribly unhealthy: you get tired out sitting behind a typewriter. Washing floors, standing behind a counter or doing piece-work overtaxes one part of your body while the rest gets no exercise at all. Men suffer from that too, but for women there are extra problems. Women have on average less muscular strength than men (although we have greater endurance power) and therefore it is assumed that women *ought* to have less muscular strength, that it is unfeminine and unattractive to develop your body. Many men, consciously or unconsciously, give off the message that they

prefer women if they are weaker, if they can't open a bottle of wine or have difficulty opening a window that has stuck. By making women's sport ridiculous, men often try to keep for themselves the territory where they prove their 'masculinity'. Women aren't allowed to be strong, otherwise they won't be attractive to men. (Which doesn't prevent many men from taking the car to work and leaving their wives to struggle with shopping and children.)

This message has stopped many women from enjoying sport when they were young, or from continuing to develop their bodies. Boys are under pressure to turn their exercise into competitive sport where they have to prove continuously that they can go faster, further and higher than other boys. Girls are expected not to be interested in that. So there are fewer opportunities for women gymnasts, especially if they aren't interested in competitive events.

Another restriction on women's freedom of movement is clothing. Luckily we no longer have to encase our bodies in stiff girdles, belts and corsets and spoil our feet with fashionable shoes in which we can only stagger along and keep getting our heels caught. We can, if we like, wear trousers, comfortable clothes, or shoes that enable us to stand, to run if we have to catch a bus or to take a walk without constantly tripping up. But you only have to open a fashion magazine to see that there is a change, that the tide will turn: the pencil skirt and high heels are back. You will look elegant if you drape yourself against a wall or a man, but don't try to *walk*! It's no coincidence that it is *women* who are told to wear clothes which inhibit movement, skirts so short you daren't bend down, shoes which make it harder to walk, not easier. Men's fashions change too, but they aren't expected to wear clothes which make it impossible for their knees to be more than ten centimetres apart, or that cut off their blood circulation with tight elastic.

One terrific way to get exercise is to cycle instead of sitting in a car or bus. Swimming is very good too. Some competitive sports are open to women, but there are other possibilities. Yoga is an excellent way to get exercise as well as relaxation. Self-defence, like karate, has a dual function: we get exercise and we are also less afraid of being attacked. Even if you never need to use it, the feeling of being in control of your own body is very good for your self-esteem. Karate, if it is well done, is an excellent way of getting into condition. And women can become very good at it precisely because it is based on suppleness and quickness rather than on muscular strength. Dancing, especially the types of jazz ballet which require training, is fun and, for many women, much more attractive than competitive sport. And good dancing schools also run courses for beginners.

For all these kinds of exercise it is possible, if you can't find a women-only group and don't feel like being in a mixed group, to make up your own group and then look for a teacher. It is possible to organise this through a women's centre, a **29** neighbourhood centre or your local authority. Running around outside or playing a game with a group of women is much nicer than doing it alone. Going to a sauna with other women is good for your body and will at the same time probably help you get rid of a few complexes, like: no one has such thick ankles as you and no one else has three bulges in her stomach when she sits down.

8. Staying healthy, being sick

On average women visit doctors more often than men do. That makes some unsympathetic doctors say that women complain more easily than men. I think it is mostly because of the kind of lives women lead that we are more often ill. Women who work at home, for example those who look after small children, do work that is never finished, their attention is divided, their work remains for the most part invisible and isn't much appreciated. On top of that, many housewives become isolated, they hardly see anyone during the day except the children and the milkman. We have evidence that this is enough to make someone ill. Women who work outside the home are doubly exploited and have a different kind of strain. Women who go out to work and have no family at home, have to look after themselves after work. In all these situations it is a fact that women have hardly any support. It's unusual if someone cooks for them or does their washing and it's not easy for them to relax. Almost all men have a woman to react against, their mother if not their wife, and a man's allowed to be bad-tempered after a hard day's work and not want to do anything but relax behind his paper. Women aren't allowed to behave like that. A woman who at five-thirty sat behind the newspaper, asked when the meal would be ready, asked her husband in a more or less friendly way why he couldn't keep the kids quiet, would be regarded as a virago, a monster of unfemininity. If you live alone, you don't have a man to make demands on you, but there is also no one to whom you can complain about what's happened during the day and how tired you are, or to make you a nice plate of food. Whatever the situation, women are less looked after and supported. So it is no luxury and not selfish to look after yourself better. It is good preventative health care to stay at home occasionally for a day if you aren't feeling too well, to develop a social life with other women, to allow yourself to be pampered by a woman friend or sometimes to shut the door on people who ask for your help, if, at that moment, it's too much for you.

It is part of your own health care to have a doctor who doesn't make you feel you're a hypochondriac. A doctor who immediately prescribes tranquilisers and sleeping pills without talking to you, or even examining you, is a bad doctor. You need to be able to go to the doctor at a time when you are dreadfully tired without having to be afraid that perhaps there is *nothing* wrong. Most family doctors are men. That's because it's a lot easier to be a family doctor if you have a wife who takes calls for you at home and organises the business in the background. Women don't have a wife behind them, so it's much more difficult for them. The disadvantages of a male family doctor are that, like all men, he is a man, with a man's prejudices. For example, most doctors find it easier to empathise with the stresses of a middle-aged businessman than with a woman going through menopause, because they themselves are men. There are gynaecologists who can't imagine why you don't like sitting with your legs in the stirrups and having a cold speculum shoved up your vagina. I think that doctors would have more understanding if they themselves took the trouble to sit naked in such a position with a couple of women touching them unsympathetically. Male doctors aren't *necessarily* unimaginative, but the chances of you getting someone who has an understanding of your tensions at home, or who will hold a speculum under warm water for a while, are greater if you can find a woman doctor. In some countries there are now some women doctors who don't only take on individual patients, but work with groups of women who can help and support them. You have a right to a doctor whom you can trust. You have the right to straight answers to your questions, to be taken seriously.

It is also important for us to learn to listen more to what our bodies are telling us. We've been taught to deny pain for as long as possible, to take pain-killers as soon as possible and, if that doesn't help, to go to the doctor so that he or she can do something about it. Sometimes a recurring pain can be a signal: if you always get a headache at the weekend, it's possible that the people around you at home are making too many demands on you, that you are giving too much and getting too little in return. If you get recurring backache, it perhaps means you are working too hard, giving yourself too little rest. If you suffer regularly from anaemia, it perhaps means that you don't look after yourself well enough. Perhaps you should say 'no' more often to people, sleep longer, be alone occasionally, get away sometimes, phone your workplace to say you are spending the day in bed *before* you are really sick. It's no coincidence that so many women are taking a new interest in forms of natural healing, like homeopathy, where we listen more to our bodies, strengthen our resistance instead of suppressing the symptoms. Without making a fad of it, we can learn from people who are intensely interested in physical health.

Finally there are two things you can do if you respect your body:
● If you are over thirty-five, have a smear taken by the doctor once a year to see if you have cancer of the cervix.
● Check your breasts once a month for lumps and changes.

Cancer of the cervix and breast cancer are not fatal if we discover them in time. But because we're afraid of cancer, we don't want to know if we have it and so we give ourselves much less chance of getting better. It's also a good thing to know more about it, not just when we're afraid we have it, but before that. **31**

9. Menstruation and menopause

We have also been told that it's a sign of weakness to have trouble with menstruation. Many women hate it because they are more irritable, more tired, have stomach cramps. Some women have found that they can make it a good time instead of a terrible one if they don't suppress their feelings and their needs. But that's very difficult if you are in a straight job, in which you can't easily take a day or two off when you most need it. In a job where constant achievement is valued, menstrual 'problems' are seen as a weakness and used as an argument against employing women. As if men don't have cycles in their energy flow too.

'I've noticed that I can feel very good during menstruation if I can give in to it. At that time I'm more sensitive, more emotional. If I fight against it, I become tearful and irritable. If I give in, I notice I am more creative. These are the days I enjoy being at home, doing something peaceful, reading a good book. I often use the time to write letters which I've left to one side for a long time, or to talk things through that have been in my head. Then I don't feel it as a weakness, but as another way of using my energy.'

We do get older. Not only once, but every time we move from one phase into the next. One such phase is called menopause, in which we stop menstruating and change our hormone pattern and in which we can have some physical problems. It's important to take it seriously. It's also important not to be totally unprepared for it, but to know beforehand what might happen so that we know what is just physical and what is due to our own personal situation. For many women who have spent their lives until this point looking after a family, there is an emptiness which is itself reason enough for depression, without counting hormone changes. No pills will help that. What does help is if we – before we get to menopause – understand that we still have a large part of our lives ahead of us which we ourselves must fill. That isn't easy in a world where older women don't count and are made almost invisible. But it is not impossible either: the rapidly growing 'Women in Menopause' groups in the Netherlands, with sixty different branches, prove that. Together we could get more recognition that growing older may mean slowing down, but doesn't make people useless. Women who work outside the home are less prone to menopausal complaints. This seems to be connected with their feeling of being valuable, of having a goal in life, even though it is also true that independent women who have to go out to work and to look after themselves become worn out more quickly. It is about time that people in this society stopped working themselves to death

32 until they reach sixty or sixty-five – only to be thrown away when they do. As we grow older we could *gradually* adjust to doing less work, or other work.

10. Breast cancer

One reason why women are so terrified of breast cancer is that we are afraid to lose a breast. Some women are more afraid of that than of the disease itself and sometimes it is a reason why we refuse to be examined for breast cancer, as if it will go away if we deny it's there. When actually losing the breast, many women have a deep fear that they are becoming deformed, repulsive and so have lost all right to eroticism for the rest of their lives. It is important not to suppress that fear, but to understand it. It is true that for those men who are accustomed to seeing women as composed only of legs, breasts, bum and cunt, we are less valuable with only one breast. But what are those men worth to us? We ourselves couldn't imagine loving someone less if a part of their body had changed. Then that is what we ought to expect from someone else. Luckily people are now more open about breast cancer than they used to be. There are more women who dare to say that they have only one breast. This fearlessness is an important example for other women. Those who have had the operation can help women who have just gone through it to work through their pain at the loss of a beloved part of their body.

It's not only women who have had a breast removed who are unhappy about their breasts. Almost all women are dissatisfied, and one reason for this is that we are continually bombarded with images of unreal breasts, lemon-shaped and lifted up high, in advertisements and films. Almost all women try, with the help of bras, to adapt their breasts to the ideal and so we continue to make ourselves and others unhappy, each woman thinking on her own that she is the only one with such small breasts, or with breasts which droop a mile. Some women become so unhappy about their breasts that they have plastic surgery. Perhaps a few feel better for it. But it is bad that we resort to mutilating our bodies and letting surgeons get rich by adapting them to an ideal image, rather than adapting our own images of what is beautiful to fit in with our real bodies. And the risk that after the operation we'll be left with strange, hard, deformed breasts, which we still don't like, is much greater than is generally made known.

Breast self-examination

The first rule for examining your breasts is that you must do so regularly. It's good to do it once a month after you have menstruated. You don't need to do it more frequently, otherwise it becomes obsessive. Your breasts are less full just after a period than before, so you are able to discover unusual lumps more quickly. After you have done it for a time, you will get to **33**

Breast Examination

know your breasts well and that's also good when the doctor examines you.

Examination

- Stand in front of the mirror with your arms hanging at your sides in a relaxed way and look carefully at your breasts for changes in size and shape. Look to see whether there are wrinkles or dimples or bumps in the skin or if the nipple has changed or if there is a discharge of blood coming from it.
- Stretch both arms above your head and look again. Look to see if there is any change since you last examined them. Look to see if one of the nipples is hard or if they look asymmetrical. You should show the doctor each small sore even though it won't necessarily be any form of cancer.
- Lie on the bed. Put a cushion or folded towel under your left shoulder and place your left hand under your head. Press down firmly but softly with the fingers of your right hand so that the hand is open, but the fingers together. Make a circular movement with your hand over the inside of your breast beginning at the breast bone in the direction of the nipple and look for a lump or thickening. Do the same in the area around the nipple.
- After that, touch the inside and underneath of the breast. Sometimes you can feel stiff muscles in this area, but don't be worried, it is completely normal.
- Place your left arm next to your body and, still with the open hand, feel under the armpit for a lump or thickening.
- With the same soft pressure, touch the upper top outside of the breast from the nipple to the side of the body.
- Finally examine the underneath outside, from the most underneath part of the breast to the nipple.

Repeat with the right breast. When you examine your breasts, anything which seems different from usual is a sign to go to the doctor for an examination. (Fuller breasts, pain or sensitivity are normal feelings around the time of ovulation and before menstruation.) If you find a lump or thickening, there's no need immediately to fear the worst, it can also be a cyst or any other benign swelling.

Taken from *Our Bodies Ourselves*

11. Appearance

If we feel good, we feel beautiful. If we feel ugly, we also feel bad. In a survey done by a Dutch women's magazine in 1978 half the women in the Netherlands were said to be dissatisfied with their appearance. I think the number is greater than that. In my first consciousness raising group, we talked about what we didn't

like about our appearance. One said her calves were too thick. No one else had noticed, but every time she put on her boots she had to squeeze her calves in and then gave up trying – it made her feel like a clumsy cow. Another woman thought she didn't look good because of her thin hair. We hadn't noticed that either. We all had something. Too fat (most of us), too thin (a couple). Too tall, so that you were always left out at dancing class because the boys didn't like dancing with tall women. Too short, so everyone overlooks you and no one takes you seriously. And a bulging stomach which only looks reasonably flat after two days' starvation. A double chin. Pimples. Hair on your legs. And breasts, especially breasts: too small or too big or drooping. Not one of us was really satisfied with her body. We were so shy at that time about our genitals that we didn't even talk about them. And yet we were all between twenty and thirty, which is considered an attractive age, and none of us was especially different from other women.

Appearance matters to women. Psychiatrists knew that long ago, only they decided it was a kind of inherent feminine trait, that vanity was part of woman's nature. The most important reason why we can't forget our appearance – even if we want to – is that, more than men, we are judged by how we look. We are constantly reminded of it by remarks on the street. We are constantly bombarded by advertisements which reinforce an image of the unattainable, ideal woman and by using this artificially created uncertainty they persuade us to buy a product which promises us that it will make every attractive man faint at our feet.

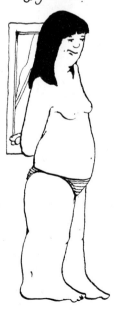

I just don't look in the mirror any more!

Small wonder that we stay awake at night worrying about what we look like, and that we hate parts of our body; that we put ourselves on starvation diets or hold in our stomachs and hitch up our breasts. Just as pictures of naked women suggest to men that sex is for the taking, so we, from an early age, are indoctrinated with the fiction that Love will come of its own accord if we can just manage to look like whichever filmstar is in fashion at the time. Of course Love isn't just a heavenly rose-pink cloud with violins playing in the background. The man who 'falls' for us determines what will happen to us in the future. We live in a world where we are kept dependent on men for our livelihood. We are dependent on our bosses who underpay us because we are women, on our husbands who keep us 'under' while supporting us in exchange for our servicing them. And men do judge us by our appearance. For example, in women's work, where appearance is an important factor – like for a saleswoman, a receptionist, or a stewardess. And in private life most men choose partners who are just a little inferior to them, not too intelligent, not too well-educated, not older, not taller, not too self-confident. And a good-looking wife is always a credit to you, so appearance is more sexually attractive than, say, intelligence. It is the only quality we are allowed to cultivate and have to cultivate in order to be in demand. That is the message **37**

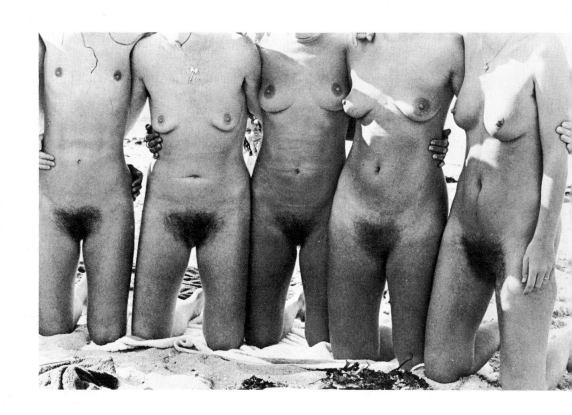

we receive. And even if we aren't interested in marriage, even if we don't want to be dependent on a man in any way, the message keeps whining on in our heads; it's hard to get rid of.
Our sexual attractiveness to others doesn't always correspond to our sexual needs. Many women discover their ability for erotic pleasure only as they grow older. But that doesn't mean that they can share this eroticism with many more people. People say hypocritically that life begins at forty, while at the same time pictures of attractive women constantly make it clear that you are old after thirty and therefore less attractive. It is accepted that a woman of twenty can take the initiative and let someone know that she finds her or him attractive, while if a woman over fifty did the same, it would be considered ridiculous and repulsive. How others see us has little to do with *our* own sexual feelings.

'When I lie in my warm bed, I like to think that I have a lovable body. A smooth skin, softly rounded body, it smells good too. I enjoy lying in the bath, looking at my breasts bobbing up and down in the foam. I powder myself with talcum powder. I love swimming naked, the cold water along my legs, the sun on my skin. I discover that I am a fantastic lover. I orgasm like mad. I have never had so much pleasure from my body. But when I look in the mirror I feel terrible. I am forty-seven. My neck is becoming old, I have stretch marks on my stomach and thighs. I am too fat. I am no longer attractive.'

It's hard not to be affected by the image of what is 'beautiful' which is imposed on us. The first time I looked differently at myself and at other women was when I was on Femø, an island where there's a holiday camp just for women. I saw naked women all around me of all sizes and ages. I realised that I now considered a woman beautiful whom I would have thought too fat if I had seen her in town with her clothes on. She fitted so comfortably into her skin, she had so much pleasure when she danced, it was infectious. I also noticed that I began to like the character of different bodies, the parchment skin of an older woman, the curve of a stomach which belonged to a woman who'd had a lot of children.
It helps to be naked amongst other women, not just because of what you *don't* like about yourself, but also because of what you *do* like. You wouldn't love your children less if they had big ears or long arms. It should be the same for ourselves. We can learn to value ourselves more, and other women as well, the way we are, not as 'they' decide we should look. In relationships between women, ageing isn't as important as in relationships between women and men. I consider qualities in women beautiful, which men would not find beautiful: strength, self-confidence, pleasure in her own body, those are the 'appearances' which draw my attention when I find another woman attractive.
Some women no longer choose to live up to the expectations of **39**

'feminine' looks. Clothes, make-up, the way you do your hair are signals, the way we tell other people how they should see us. If we don't dress in the way women are expected to dress, we are confronted with aggression. We can choose not to dress to please. No tight jumpers to show the curves, no shoes built to make your legs look longer but in which you can't walk. No more attempts to look like filmstars. In the early days of the women's movement many of us tried not to concern ourselves with making ourselves attractive to someone else – this was a reaction to the exaggerated emphasis placed on the 'ideal' body. Now we are returning to individual style, individual forms, but still wearing clothes we feel comfortable in: no dresses which stop us from bending because they are too short, or in which we can't run because they're too long. This gets us accused of trying to be men. As long as ignorant people think that loving women and 'masculinity' are one and the same thing, and as long as women are still afraid of being 'accused' of being lesbian, we remain silent and try to look like 'real' (read 'artificial') women. We don't have to accept their idea of what a woman should be. It's no coincidence that men's clothing doesn't inhibit their freedom of movement, and it's nonsense to leave the monopoly on that to them. If we think long hair is a nuisance or not beautiful, we'll cut it off. If we feel more comfortable in trousers, we'll wear trousers. And shoes in which we can walk. If it was really unfeminine to walk in flat shoes, then we would have been born with high heels on our feet. Attractiveness doesn't have to be equated with artificially created helplessness. The first feminists knew this when they changed their clothes. They put up with accusations of being 'unfeminine'.

12. Making love to yourself

A good relationship with yourself also means a good sexual relationship with yourself. Many women have never discovered how to make love to themselves and have never heard how to do it. Some women discovered it at an age when they had no idea it had anything to do with sex and keep on doing it very happily. Most women have experienced a time in their lives when, with or without words, it has been made clear to them that it is dirty to touch yourself. They still did it, but felt guilty, or else they repressed their sexuality completely. You come across peculiar things in old-fashioned sex manuals. It is no longer generally believed that you can get brain-damage or tuberculosis of the spine from touching yourself, but a generation ago there were plenty of authors who considered 'self-abuse' or 'masturbation' a necessary evil, which could, if practised excessively, lead to a weakening of the will and an inability to experience sexuality with another person. In modern books you often come across the

attitude that if children discover something sexually pleasurable, you should quickly distract their attention with toys or a game and that a lot of sport and fresh air will see to it that children don't get too many obsessive thoughts about it. In more progressive books it's more positively handled, but making love to yourself is almost always seen as a passing phase when you are still too young for 'real' sex, or if you are without a partner for a while. With the exception of feminist literature, I know of no books that see making love to yourself as part of a good relationship with your own needs, irrespective of whether you also share a part of your sexuality with someone else. Even if there is now less of a taboo on making love to yourself as an emergency measure, you are still supposed to prefer making love to a man. Most people still don't realise that making love to yourself is not just a substitute for sexual contact with someone else – just as making love to yourself isn't a substitute for contact with other people.

Many women discover their ability to make an orgasm themselves more or less by accident, or through someone else.

'I wasn't keen on gymnastics. Except when I discovered what a fantastic feeling I got when I climbed the ropes. The time I arrived at the top was the best. I sat up there with a red face and had to do my best not to fall down. Only later did I realise it was an orgasm.'

Almost every orgasm, even if you experience it with someone else, is in fact an orgasm you make yourself. There's always the bit which you yourself contribute to your arousal: your own fantasies, your own emotions, your own movements. And one of the most important factors which inhibits a woman from making an orgasm is the feeling that an orgasm is something you must wait to be given, not a potential you already possess in your own body and that you yourself create.

What makes it difficult for us to make love to ourselves? Thousands of things. The feeling that you are depriving someone if you just come on your own. The feeling that by doing that you are saying something derogatory about those with whom you do make love – saying she or he isn't a good lover. Because you are put off by your own body and especially that place between your legs. You have no time or space during which you can feel unobserved and can't be caught out. Because you are scared that you will become addicted to it and like it more than making love to someone else, because you are scared to let go. Scared that your clitoris will grow bigger and a doctor will be able to see that you 'do it' (which isn't true). Or you think that it is selfish, or a little ridiculous, or childish.

When we become conscious of these blocks, we are able to overcome most of them. Making love to yourself is no more egotistical than eating alone; we wouldn't think of starving just because there was no one to share a meal with. And 'being addicted' to it is only a bad thing if you think of it as a sickness. As **41**

for the fear that you won't be able to make love with someone else if you are too used to doing it alone, that's not a good reason. It has been shown that women who regularly make love alone achieve orgasm more easily with someone else than women who hardly ever make love to themselves. In the end, finding out for yourself what you enjoy is the only way to be able to tell someone else what you want. The woman or man with whom you make love won't just *know*, unless you say. The idea that sex is so spontaneous that the other will just be able to guess what you like has generated a great deal of misery.

Further reading

Diet for a Small Planet by Frances Moore Lappe (import) is still about the best book around about the rubbish we eat every day, and the causes of world hunger – 'the way in which economic factors, rather than natural, agricultural ones have determined land and food use'. Complete with high-protein, vegetarian recipes.

The Politics of Health Group has brought out a good pamphlet on the food industry, *Food and Profit* – you can get it from BSSRS, 9 Poland Street, London W1. They argue that ill-health is socially rather than individually produced.

Of course for many women the immediate problem is eating compulsively, and being conned by all those 'wonder diets'. Susie Orbach's *Fat is a Feminist Issue* (Hamlyn) is good because it analyses why women become addicted to eating and gives guidance on how we can kick the habit by becoming more aware of ourselves, and more confident. It's been the inspiration for a theatre group – Spare Tyre – and for a network of compulsive eating groups (see useful addresses).

There is, unfortunately, nothing quite like it on drinking. There have been some good articles in *Spare Rib* (issues 22 and 89), written from the point of view of women who have difficulty handling drink. *Women and Alcohol* by the Camberwell Council on Alcholism (Tavistock) is much more sociological, but has some useful information. On women and smoking there is Bobbie Jacobson's excellent book *The Ladykillers* (Pluto).

Getting Clear (Body Work for Women) by Anne Kent Rush (Wildwood House) is a lovely book to help you embark on a journey of exploration of your own body. Lots of exercises and experiences. You need not accept everything, nor do you need to use everything.

Women and Medicine by Joyce Leeson and Judith Gray (Tavistock) looks at women as both providers of health care and users of the health services. It also shows how women are getting organised to change their subordinate position – through trade unions and through women and health groups.

Lesley Doyal's *The Political Economy of Health* (Pluto) is pretty hard-going, but an interesting analysis of how things got this bad **43**

– particularly how the capitalist system has shaped medicine, here and in the Third World. *For Her Own Good* by Barbara Ehrenreich and Deirdre English (Pluto) asesses 150 years of the 'experts' advice to women. A devastating feminist critique of 'specialists' who have told women what to think and do in the fields of health, housework, childbirth and childcare.

The Hidden Malpractice by Gena Corea (import) is a contemporary expose of how American medicine mistreats women. Another American import with excellent essays on the politics of women's health is *Seizing Our Bodies*, edited by Claudia Dreifus.

If 'normal' people feel oppressed by images of ideal bodies, then people with disabilities must feel it even more. *Not Made of Stone* by K Heslinga (Woodhead Faulkner), about sexual problems for people with disabilities, suggests men be given artificial penises to help them regain their 'psychological potential'. Other ways of making love are considered only when coitus is impossible. A typical male point of view, daring to say that women can be satisfied with the artificial penis 'in the normal way'. *Entitled to Love* by Wendy Greengross is much more friendly (Malaby Press). *Let There Be Love* by P Gunnel Enby (Elek) gives the personal experiences of a young Swedish woman, paralysed from the waist down – about isolation, and the repressive attitudes of institutes for the disabled. Jo Campling's handbook *Better Lives for Disabled Women* (Virago) is full of practical advice covering among other topics relationships, sexuality and self-image, menstruation and menopause. Clear that 'traditional genital intercourse' isn't necessarily the most satisfying thing for able-bodied women either. Jo Campling has also edited *Images of Ourselves – Women with Disabilities Talking* (Routledge & Kegan Paul).

Breasts are best dealt with in two books, both American – *Breasts* by Daphna Ayalah and Isaac Weinstock (import), a large format book full of pictures and interviews. Women speak out about their breasts in relation to their whole lives and their identity as women. *Why Me?* by Rose Kushner (import) is both personal history and investigative research into breast cancer. Very informative, and not too distant. Not quite so good, but easier to get hold of, is Carolyn Faulder's *Breast Cancer* (Pan) – a guide to early detection and treatment. *Spare Rib* issue 37 had a good article on the experience of breast cancer – 'To Lose a Breast Seemed More Terrible than Dying' by Lin Layram. And *Spare Rib* issue 57 had a very moving account by Ann Scott of her mother's last months, with terminal cancer – 'Joan Scott – Living her Dying'.

In general still the best book which covers all aspects of our body is *Our Bodies Ourselves* (Penguin). Be wary of imitations – some are just attempts to cash in on the growing interest in women's health. *From Woman to Woman* is one such, by Lucienne Lanson (Penguin). The title gives the impression of

women together, but it isn't – it's a book by a doctor about us.

Bad information about sex. We are again told to have orgasms from sexual intercourse if the gentleman is kind enough to spend twenty minutes in 'foreplay' and at least fifteen on the Act Itself. However, the *New Women's Health Handbook*, edited by Nancy McKeith (Virago) is fine – covering most things from self-examination to smoking. And *The Well Body Book* by Mike Samuels and Hal Bennett is strong on self-diagnosis, preventive medicine and diet.

I think the best of many books on breastfeeding is Sheila Kitzinger's *The Experience of Breastfeeding* (Penguin). A good beginner's book on massage is *The Massage Book* by George Downing (Penguin) – straightforward, not specifically feminist, combining technical information with some sense of what massage is all about.

On menopause, try *Menopause: a Positive Approach* by Rosetta Reitz (Harvester). It talks about the experience of ageing as well as the science, and is an easy read.

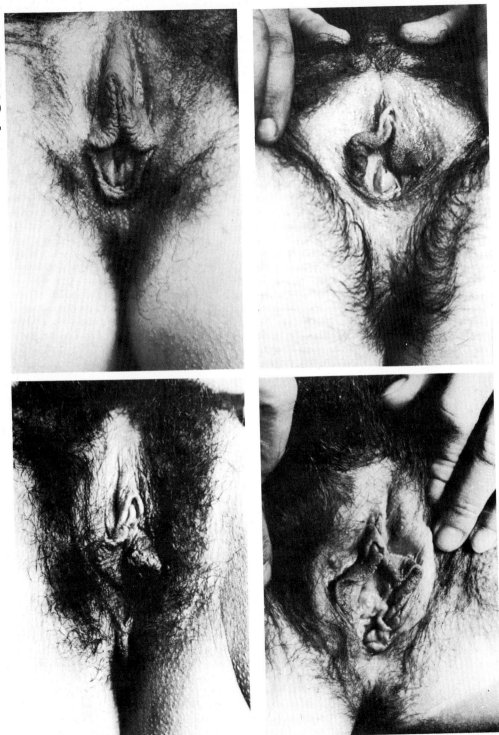

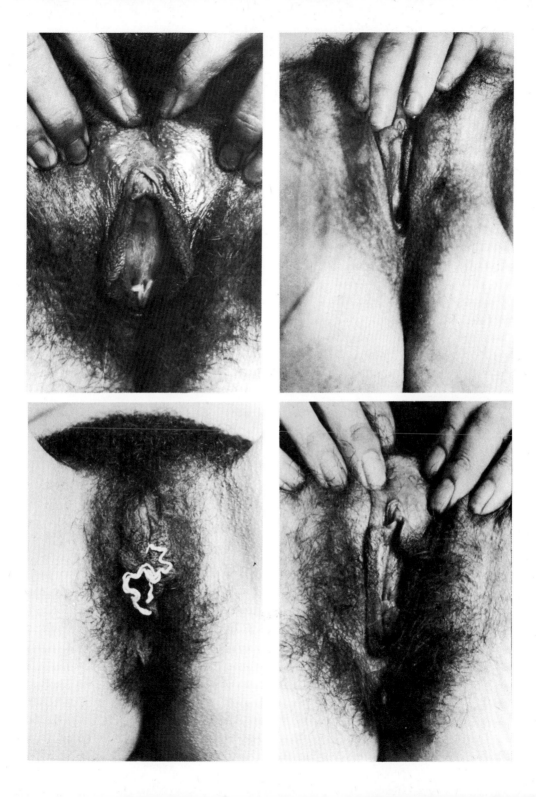

III. The blank space on the map of our bodies

Not all sexual problems can be traced back to our ignorance about an important part of our bodies, but it certainly doesn't help that we are so unfamiliar with that area of our bodies we call our cunt.

From the very beginning almost all of us have been given the wrong instructions about sex, *if* we are told anything at all. The first message is always: this is how babies are made. Daddy puts a seed in Mummy's tummy and a little baby grows there. From the beginning the emphasis is on reproduction, not on pleasure, while in reality we spend very little of our time making babies. The message transmitted at the same time is that the way we make babies is also the way we ought to make love. Real love-making is when a penis is put into a vagina, 'penetration' to use a dirty word, and all other possible ways of having pleasure, if we ever hear about them, are called 'foreplay' or 'variations' or actually unnatural or perverse. We will discuss later how oppressive this message is for women.

Another wrong message we have received is that little boys have a willie and little girls have a hole or a split. Many women also see their own cunt as a kind of a hole, not as a complicated part of our body with multiple possibilities. You can best compare your cunt to your mouth, which is not only a hole, but a complex organ. Men have only one organ with which they urinate, ejaculate and with which they can have an orgasm – their penis. Women don't have only one organ, a hole, but three: an opening with which to piss, a vagina which is an entry to the reproductive organs and a clitoris which is very useful for giving sexual pleasure. By treating this all as one entity we have created an endless series of misunderstandings.

'I used to wash myself very quickly and carelessly all the time trying to think about something else, because my mother had told me that my children would be born handicapped if I touched myself too much there.'

'I knew when I was very young that girls had a hole to pee with and boys had a willie. Peeing is dirty, so I only touched my cunt with a flannel or with toilet paper. Later when I heard that babies came out of that hole, I imagined that a baby was peed in by a man and then peed out by a woman when it was big. That seemed to me a dirty business. I heard about my clitoris much later, long after I was married.'

Although little boys aren't allowed to investigate their bodies either, they are still able to get to know them more easily. A boy **49**

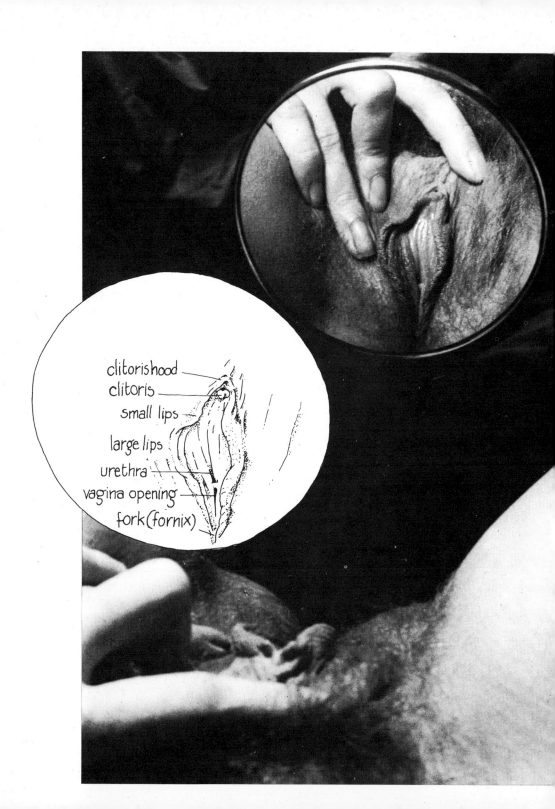

clitoris hood
clitoris
small lips
large lips
urethra
vagina opening
fork (fornix)

can see his willie more easily because it sticks out more than a cunt does. A little girl can try to look over her round tummy to that place from which she gets such a nice feeling, but she has to try really hard and then she sees only half of it. And then, boys, who have to learn to urinate standing up, are encouraged to hold their willie while doing so. Parents also pass on the unconscious message that a penis is a valuable possession. On the other hand a little girl is more likely to get the message that her cunt is not an organ, that it is the *absence* of an organ, a hole. In addition boys are usually allowed to pee in public, against a tree or in a urinal where they can see each other and so, in their first years, boys have the experience of looking curiously at each other, comparing, having competitions on how far they can piss and so on. And while they are mostly punished if they show too great an interest, in the end men are much more familiar with their bodies than women are with what is 'between their legs'. (It is true though that men are in other ways much more alienated from their bodies – they often see it as a machine, a tool, separate from their emotions.)

'Actually I didn't find out anything until my big sister began to menstruate and I was told that that the blood came out of her bottom.'

'I used to think of my cunt as a peculiar sort of cave, which gave off a strange damp smell, and now and then blood. I knew you had to be careful that boys didn't get in there because then dreadful things happened. I even felt that if I touched it I might hurt something.'

'I was brought up with the idea that my vagina was a kind of closed off hole, which had to be uncorked by a man sort of like a bottle of wine. I didn't dare put my fingers into my vagina because I thought I might damage something and my husband might notice and not want me any more. I was very surprised that I noticed so little the first time, I had really thought that there was a kind of tight skin pulled across that he had to get through. I expected a lot of blood and pain.'

'When I was little I did once try to put my fingers inside. I thought: the penis will never get in there. I'm much too narrow. I'll never be able to have children.'

'I always knew that I had a place which gave me a marvellous feeling if I caressed it with something soft. Mostly I did it with my doll's hair, my first sex object, although at the time I didn't know that my good feeling had anything to do with sex. I know my mother expressed surprise that my dolls became bald so quickly, and I was terribly embarrassed, so I must have had some idea that what I did was naughty. Later I forgot about it.

the happiest day of my life was when I discovered my clitoris

51

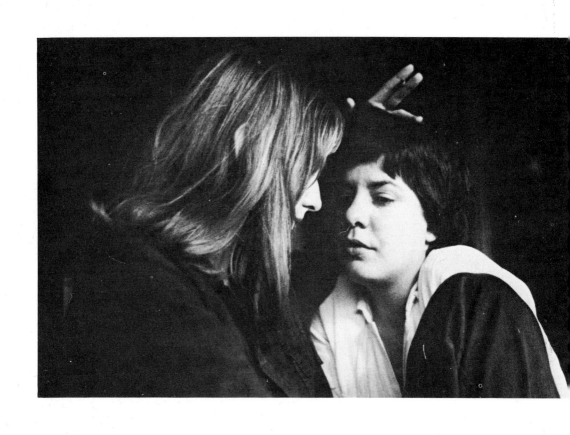

When I made love the first time it wasn't pleasant, it was actually many years before I had even a little pleasure in fucking. Only with my second husband did I learn to orgasm. Then I suddenly remembered the bald dolls.'

1. Voyage of discovery to your cunt

We wash our cunts, we stick tampons up them when we menstruate, or we change sanitary towels. Few women have taken the trouble really to get to know their cunts.

You can't get to know your cunt simply by looking at pictures in books. Cunts are just like faces, each woman's is just a little bit different.

Touching: having a bath or a shower offers a good opportunity to feel exactly how the large and small lips fit together. If you put your finger in your cunt you can feel that it isn't just an open, hollow tube, but that the sides touch each other and enclose your finger. The inside of your vagina is bumpy and mostly moist. If you sit on your haunches, you can probably feel your uterus at the end of your vagina. For women who haven't had children, it will feel more or less like the point of your nose; for women who have, like the point of your chin with a dimple in the middle. If, when you have your finger in your vagina, you move your muscles as if you were holding in a wee, you will be able to feel your fingers being softly gripped, held. These are the same muscles which pull together with an orgasm.

You can *smell* your fingers when they've touched your cunt. We have learned to think that body odours are dirty, but if you wash regularly, the smell can be pleasant and familiar. It is also useful to know how you smell when you are healthy because it will help you to know when you have an infection. Some women can tell from a change in smell that they are about to menstruate.

You can *lick* your fingers. The inside of your vagina is cleaner than tap water and has a beautiful self-cleansing system. Spit, if you examine the bacteria in it, is actually dirtier. The cleaning system ensures that the inside of your vagina is slightly acid, and you can taste that. If you are familiar with your taste and smell, it is also easier to be less inhibited when you make love to someone; you don't have to be so afraid that your cunt is repulsive.

Looking: you need a mirror to see your cunt properly but also you have to feel that you won't be disturbed while you are looking. A good time is after a shower when you are clean and warm in a warm room. The first thing you see is the hair. One woman will have a whole lot, another just a few curls which it will be easy to see through. Almost no one has a precise triangle of hair like you see in the drawings. Many women have hair growing on the tops of their legs and inside their buttocks. If you pull apart the outside lips of your cunt, you can see the inside lips. Many women worry because their inside lips stick out, and are longer than the outside ones. This is true for most women. It is also quite 53

ordinary that one is bigger than the other, just like our breasts which are also never exactly symmetrical. If you're not familiar with your cunt, you think at first that you are looking at an untidy collection of folds, but if you open them out you can see the clitoris, the little hole through which you urinate, and the opening of the vagina. Every woman's lips and the parts in between are different in shade, soft colours between rose and red, sometimes almost violet, sometimes brownish. As you get older the inside lips become thinner and a bit greyish.

The clitoris can be located where your inside lips meet. Because we have read in books that the clitoris is a miniature penis, we look for something like that and can't find anything. With most women the clitoris is hidden in a fold of skin, you can only see a small pink pimple – something smaller than the nail on your little finger, sometimes like the rubber on the end of a pencil – if you pull back the little hood. If you pull the inside lips upwards, it will usually appear. If you can't see it, you can usually find it by feeling. It is the most sensitive place, where the most nerve endings come together. Sometimes you notice your clitoris becoming bigger when you touch it and you can feel a tightening under the foreskin. What you see of your clitoris is like the tip of an iceberg. Inside is a whole system of blood vessels and nerves, all participating in an orgasm. Underneath, where the inside lips end, you can see the opening to the vagina. You can't see far inside without the help of a speculum because the sides touch each other. Sometimes you can still see little folds which are the remains of the hymen, a stretchable skin which is stretched open by women who've put their hands in their vagina, who have fucked or used tampons. With some women that skin is practically absent. Except in very exceptional circumstances there is always an opening to let out menstrual blood. It isn't always painful when something enters the vagina for the first time and if it is, it may be because you are tense and holding the

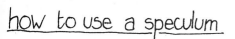

how to use a speculum

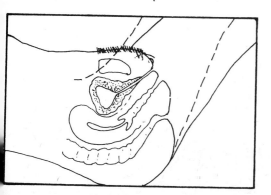

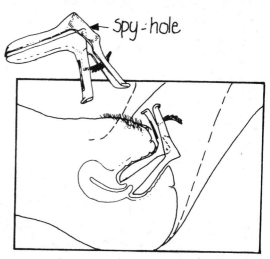

spy-hole

muscles of the vagina tightly together. Somewhere between the clitoris and the vagina is your urethra, sometimes just a hole, sometimes with a little bump next to it. The distance beween clitoris and urethra and vagina can differ from woman to woman. Also the shape of the lips and the clitoris are different with each woman. One has a shaft of about a centimetre between the place where the inside lips meet and the tip of the clitoris, in another the clitoris is an almost invisible rosy spot. This has nothing to do with how good the orgasms are which you can create.

You may be able to get a speculum from your local women's centre – it is a kind of plastic beak, the same as doctors use, which you slip into your vagina and then open out. You can see the inside of the vagina and the uterus with a mirror and a good light or torch. Many women have no idea how shiny and rosy they are inside, a view we keep for doctors only.

Women who practise self-help and regularly use a speculum can tell from colour changes whether they are about to menstruate or whether they are pregnant. You can see whether you have an infection and look out for erosion, red spots which sometimes bleed when you touch them. They might go away of their own accord or might need treatment. The inside of the vagina is just like a face – if you aren't well you get pimples and spots more easily, which disappear when you feel better. You can see and feel that your uterus – a muscle about the size of a pear with the narrow end pointing downwards – is moveable, sometimes tipped forward, sometimes backwards. If you examine yourself regularly, you have the advantage of being able to notice more changes than the doctor who looks only occasionally. The easiest way to learn to use a speculum is in a women and health group. It can be quite an experience to look at another woman's cervix; in doing so you will explode yet another taboo. After the first time, looking at your own cunt or another woman's becomes just as ordinary as looking at bare feet.

2. A healthy vagina

Normally your cunt keeps itself clean and all that's needed is to wash yourself daily. It is only when the normal bacteria have been in the open for some time that your own smell can become too strong. The skin between the lips is rather tender. Too much soap can be irritating. If you scrub your cunt as if you wanted to sluice it out, you could graze the skin and get exactly what you want to avoid: irritation, itch and possibly infection. You can use a clean cloth, but your fingers would do fine too. Now and then pull back the skin over your clitoris to make sure it's kept clean.

Your vagina is like your mouth – anything you wouldn't put into your mouth doesn't belong in your vagina. Clean fingers in your vagina are fine – when making love to a man you don't sterilise him first. But the bacteria from your intestines can become a
56 source of infection if they land up in your vagina. When you wipe

yourself on the toilet always wipe from front to back. The same is true for your flannel, which you shouldn't use for too long. When making love in a way that involves putting fingers or penis into your anus, you had better make sure that they don't then go into your vagina without being washed first. It is nice to wear clean knickers every day, and cotton is much better than synthetic rubbish. Trousers that are too tight can irritate. Vaginal deodorants are absolutely terrible and should be banned. Your own natural balance is disturbed by the chemicals which could cause an infection – so you achieve exactly the opposite of what you intended. Moreover, your cunt doesn't stink, and we're crazy if we let ourselves be talked into spraying away our own ordinary smells.

Another important thing to know if you make love to a man: there are indications that cancer of the cervix has something to do with penis-hygiene. In cultures where men have been circumcised – that is, had the foreskin, under which dirt can collect, removed – cancer is rare. And nuns hardly ever get cervical cancer. It isn't yet proved conclusively, but it won't do any harm if your lover cleans himself regularly.

There is no need to douche the inside of the vagina if you are healthy. Don't use vaseline as a lubricant; it doesn't dissolve in water and is therefore less easy to remove. If you use a cap, powder it with cornflower rather than talcum powder. Cornflower dissolves more easily in water and so is better for your cunt.

Your vagina 'sweats' inside and is therefore almost always wet. A little discharge is normal. Just as your nose will run when you've got a cold, so you are likely to have more discharge when you are tired or sick or when your resistance is low. It also often happens when you are pregnant. It can be a sign that you should look after yourself better. If you have an acute infection you often notice it by a different smell or by the colour. Sometimes it itches. There are two common kinds of infections:

– A yeast infection (candida or thrush) causes a discharge like cottage cheese and smells a little like yeast. It itches. What you can do to combat it is to keep your vagina acid. You can do that by douching with water to which you add a little natural vinegar, or with natural yoghurt. If you put a tampon carton filled with yoghurt into your vagina, then push it up and use a sanitary towel to stop it leaking, and go to sleep like that, there's a good chance that after a couple of times the thrush will clear up.

– Trichomonas smells differently, it has a sharper smell and gives off a yellowish or greenish foamy discharge. It also itches. The doctor can prescribe tablets for it. If you are making love to a man, he will need to be treated as well, otherwise you will keep passing the infection to each other.

If you know your own smell, you can tell if it is a yeast infection, or trichomonas or something else. A doctor can easily tell by taking a swab. There are also tablets which contain medication for both infections, manufactured for doctors who don't like to do an examination. The idea is that if the one doesn't help, the other will. You don't need to accept that. It's nonsense to swallow medicine if you don't need it, and the medicine for trichomonas is strong, so you're better off not taking it unless it is really necessary.

Discharge and itching can also be symptoms of an illness you have caught from someone else. Syphilis and gonorrhoea are easy to cure but are dangerous when neglected. It is strange that we are still ashamed of illnesses we catch from making love and not of a cold, which you can also catch from someone. A lot has been written about sexually transmitted diseases. Unfortunately they rarely tell you *how* you catch something. Mostly they assume that all women fuck with one man and always in the same way. You have to guess what you could get if you made love to a woman, or what you can carry via your mouth and hands.

One disease that many people don't realise has anything to do with making love is bladder infection, or rather urine tube infection or cystitis. An infection can be caused by foreign bacteria or by irritation. Because the urethra is so close to the vagina it is quite possible to catch an infection when fucking, especially if you are very sensitive there and make love violently. Sometimes you notice it the next morning by a burning pain and the urge to urinate a lot, but actually only doing a small amount each time. Sometimes this occurs a little later on. The thing to do is: urinate before and after making love, drink a lot of water to flush it out well. If that doesn't help: try different ways of making love, or make love more gently. You shouldn't leave a urine infection unattended. A neglected infection can affect your kidneys in the long run.

Tampons are useful if you don't like sanitary towels between your legs. If you menstruate for a long time, you might notice that your vagina becomes dehydrated from the tampons and you may have difficulty putting in a fresh one. There is also a chance of irritation or of pieces of cotton wool staying behind. If you suffer from dehydration use sanitary towels at night – or instead of tampons. It is also a good idea to feel around with your fingers after the last tampon to make sure nothing is left behind. A tampon can't disappear. So if you can't find it, keep looking!

Further reading

The best book for information on sexually transmitted diseases is still *Our Bodies Ourselves* (Penguin). Onlywomen Press is doing a pamphlet on vaginal infections, and has an illustrated guide to self-examination, *Down There*. Write to Onlywomen Press, 38 Mount Pleasant, London WC1. Self-examination is also covered in the *New Women's Health Handbook* (Virago). Santa Cruz Women's Health Centre in America has produced a book called *Lesbian Health Matters* (import) – very sympathetic

and informative on lesbians and VD.

Angela Kilmartin's *Cystitis: a Complete Self-Help Guide* (Hamlyn) is a good cheap handbook by a cystitis sufferer.

There are several good books around now on menstruation.

Why Suffer? by Lynda Birke and Katy Gardner (Virago) is an excellent handbook covering pre-menstrual tension, irregular periods and period pains. For a longer read, there's *Female Cycles* by Paula Weideger (Women's Press), exploring the science, the experience and the mythology of menstruation. *Have You Started Yet?* by Ruth Thompson (Piccolo) is a very reassuring introduction to periods for young women – not patronising, plenty of drawings and quotes.

Since this book was written, tampons, once seen as *the* answer to sanitary towels, have been found to have certain health problems. You can get lots of information about this by writing to Cromer Street Women's Centre, 90 Cromer Street, London WC1. In *Spare Rib* issue 65 there was a good article about using natural sponges instead.

'I do nothing I don't like and am quite firm about that'

— We made this appointment to talk about sex a long time ago. Since then have you thought of any special things you want to talk about?

— Yes, about my first lover. Naturally I've also thought about all the men I've slept with since and I counted eleven. But my first lover is the most important. I still see a lot of him, although there are long stretches in between when we don't see each other because he lives so far away. Since we were first lovers he has been married, and divorced.

— How old are you now?

— Thirty-two.

— You live alone. Has that always been the case?

— Yes. I only lived with my first lover for a few months and again for a few months with my most recent lover. My first lover was the only one I knew for a very long time before we actually went to bed together. I was twenty-four then. Before that there was a long period of physical affection and tenderness. We used to sleep together, I mean that literally. With all the others I made love as soon as it was clear that we were sexually attracted to each other. With them affection and physical contact were followed within a few hours by coitus, but the long lead-up seems to me to be actually more pleasant. I'm glad I've experienced that at least *once* in my life. I wasn't so forward then as I am now, and I let him decide how far we should go. We used to visit each other, but we always phoned first and then we'd sit for hours talking; we often played games – monopoly, master-mind, cluedo. Occasionally we'd buy new games together. Sometimes we'd smoke a joint. Occasionally the evening ended with us lying stretched out together on the floor making love, and the best way was to do it simply and just to enjoy kissing and touching, the excitement of slowly undressing each other without it having to end in fucking. He never went too fast or too far, and that peaceful feeling that he wouldn't press it – it was complete bliss. My other boyfriends were just not prepared to spend so much time beforehand, and perhaps later on I wasn't that interested any more either. Because after that I began to experiment with what you call free sex; I would go to bed on the spur of a moment with a boy I had met at a party, for example. Sometimes a relationship has grown from such a contact.

— Did it hurt the first time you made love?

— Yes. The first time my boyfriend tried it, it was very difficult and he couldn't get it in. He also promptly lost his erection. Then we drank a glass of wine, ate some toast and talked a bit. I would have been quite happy if it hadn't happened again that night, but later on he got another erection and we tried again. It was really

60

pushed through, and I felt nothing but a dull pain. I didn't bleed, it was just painful. The next morning we did it again and that was very painful too. After that it was fine.

— *Has fucking never been painful since?*

— Well, if I haven't fucked for a long time, and then, say, after six months I fuck vigorously, it can feel sensitive afterwards. My first lover also hurt me when the penetration went on for too long.

— *What do you think of as being too long?*

— Twenty minutes seemed long.

— *Did he need twenty minutes to orgasm?*

— No, he could come in five or ten minutes. But if he wanted to make it go on longer for my sake . . . then afterwards I'd feel sore.

— *I can imagine! My god. I've sometimes counted the thrusts and when I got to a hundred, it seemed really too long.*

— I didn't know that twenty minutes was abnormal. Don't people talk about going on for hours?

— *I usually come first and then I like it best if he doesn't pump for too long. The quicker the better.*

— I've never come with a man, but I can't imagine that I would want to have a penis inside me afterwards in any case. When I have masturbated all I want is to lie peacefully or turn over and fall asleep.

— *Why did your friend want to go on thrusting for such a long time for your sake?*

— He wanted me to have an orgasm.

— *How?*

— From the penetration.

— *Did you, at that time, still think that that had to be possible?*

— Oh yes! Certainly. And sometimes I was really close to it. It was always pleasant, sometimes very pleasant and then I really had a feeling that I was on the point of orgasm, but I never managed it. I knew it was very important to him and I thought it was OK him wanting it so badly, but I felt under a lot of pressure because of it. I would rather someone left me to look after myself, otherwise I'm too conscious of trying to get an orgasm – and naturally it's completely unsuccessful. Anyway it isn't necessary for me to come with a man any more since I know I can give myself an orgasm if I need one. I don't find orgasm during intercourse so important, but penetration on its own gives me a very nice feeling and that's enough for me.

— *When and how did you discover that your clitoris had an important function?*

— I knew that from when I was eighteen. I think I read it somewhere. Feminism also had something to do with it. In 1969, at least a year before I went to bed with a man for the first time, I came into contact with feminism. A woman I worked with was in a women's collective which organised lectures and set up courses, and she invited me to a series of lectures. At that time I thought, oh feminism, I don't need that, that's not for me, I'm fine, I can manage fine by myself. But I was immensely **61**

pamphlets and material home with me and there was something in them about making love and the clitoris. My first lover also knew about it, I didn't have to tell him. He did it very well with his fingers and his tongue and he used to go on just as long as I wanted him to. He enjoyed it too, I didn't get the feeling that he just did it for me.
– *Do you believe that?*
– Oh yes, I was convinced of that. He always wanted to lick me, I didn't have to ask him. At first I was shy and a bit embarrassed. Sometimes he went on for twenty minutes, he liked doing it. I cquld smell it on his fingers if he had caressed me and sometimes, if he had put his fingers in my vagina, he licked it too. I liked that.
– *Do you like your own taste and smell?*
– Yes, I also smell my fingers when I've masturbated. I'm not sure if I've tasted my fingers, but anyway I've tasted it from his mouth when he'd been licking me for a long time and we kissed each other afterwards. I like that very much, the combination of taste and smell.
– *Yes, so do I. My first boyfriend had a moustache, and the smell stayed on it for a lovely long time.*
– How funny, my first lover also had a moustache! I was amazingly at ease with him when we made love. We could tell each other what excited us, or how it felt. I could be as explicit and obscene as I liked; I can't do that with everyone by any means. With other men I'm scared I'll put them off and that they'll be disgusted if I'm so open. If a man I didn't know so well were to say those things to me while we made love, I wouldn't like it.
– *What kind of things did you say then?*
– Oh, something like: 'Your prick feels so good inside me', but I find it difficult to say it now because it comes out of the excitement and passion of the moment and it also contributes to it.
– *Did you say that while he was licking you as well?*
– No, he was too far away for that, perhaps I'd make little sounds. It was much easier to say it while we fucked and his ear was right next to my mouth. We both lived in flats and so in no way could we afford to scream or make too much noise.
– *But if he knew how a woman's body worked, why did he still try to thrust as long as possible to get you to orgasm?*
– I became terribly excited when he did it, I liked to feel him inside me. From my reading I know that orgasm doesn't take place in the vagina but through stimulation of the clitoris, but it is also possible that the clitoris is stimulated indirectly during coitus. I felt this indirect stimulation when we fucked. Also, I didn't get an orgasm from twenty minutes of licking, you know.
– *How did you know that you didn't experience orgasm? Had you already had one?*
– No. I once read a story in which a woman asked: 'How do I know when I have an orgasm?' and someone answered her:

'Don't worry, you *know* it when you have one', and I didn't yet have that certainty. I reached a very high peak of excitement but there was no explosion, no relief of tension which I assumed ought to follow. I felt as if I was building up to something, but that I never quite reached it.

– *Were you perhaps afraid of an orgasm? People do describe it as an 'electric shock' and that is really the last thing I'd want to happen to me!*

– No, I didn't have that kind of association. On the contrary, I was convinced that it was very pleasurable, and I really wanted to know what it was like and how it felt. I think that I can't let myself go enough, because I'm too conscious of the presence of the other person. The only way I can get an orgasm is through masturbating, only then can I go deep into my own fantasies and into what I am feeling. Then I'm not distracted by someone else and what he's doing and how far he's got.

– *Have you ever had an orgasm in the presence of a partner?*

– Only once, but that was completely unexpected. It happened with my last boyfriend. I met him at a conference, and later he came to live with me. We slept together in my bed on the first night, but neither of us was intending to make love. I felt very much like it and took the initiative, because then the tension of shall-we-or-shan't-we would also be out of the way. A short relationship grew from that. After a few weeks of sexual contact he proposed that we remain just friends. He was going to leave soon and was scared he would become too involved with me.

– *Did you believe that?*

– I think it had more to do with his freedom. I am terribly jealous and can't bear it if someone shares the same intimacy he has with me with someone else. In the first week he said that he hoped that I didn't think that he wouldn't sleep with other women, and I made it very clear what my limits were and said that that was precisely what I expected, although I wouldn't forbid him to do anything. Anyway, as soon as we had agreed not to make love any more, he got randy and wanted sex, and when I refused he became very loving and tender and said: 'Oh come on, just one more time.' I didn't feel much like it as you can imagine and was actually furious that he had so much power over me; he could do what he liked and still get his way. And then, during that so-called last fuck, I felt that liberating climax I sometimes feel when I masturbate, although it wasn't such an intense orgasm as I sometimes get during masturbation. It may well be that at that point I couldn't have cared less and that I was only concerned with myself without paying attention to him. I didn't *do* anything either, I just lay there peacefully enjoying what was still to be enjoyed.

– *Did you let him know that you came?*

– Yes. He wasn't very impressed.

– *And you?*

– I was surprised and very happy. I could hardly believe it and began to talk about it enthusiastically. In the beginning of our **63** relationship I had told him emphatically that I would rather he didn't ask me whether I came or not, because I wanted to take that pressure off myself. He never did ask me, except just once. I had made love ecstatically and apparently had been a bit noisy, groaning and making noises, moving a lot and so on, so that he thought perhaps I had had an orgasm after all, but it was just pleasure.

— *Did you ever masturbate in front of him.*

— Oh yes, once when I thought he was asleep, and once when I asked if I might see him masturbate to orgasm because I had never seen it, and then he wanted to see me do it too, but I couldn't with him there although I did try. It seems I can only do it on my own when no one is watching me.

— *Have you ever tried to use your own hand as well?*

— No, because that also gives me the feeling that I'm being watched. I don't like being on top either. I like it best if I can feel his whole body against mine and then it is very difficult to move my hand in between us. But I think that the main reason I can't do it is because I can't lose myself in fantasies if there is someone with me.

— *Can you say something about the fantasies?*

— Yes, I'm willing to do that, but they aren't very feminist and I feel a bit embarrassed about that. To orgasm, my fantasies always involve being fucked, preferably by a stranger — a not very attractive man who wants to have sex with me and to whom I put up a little resistance. There is nothing about love or relationships in it, it's pure sex. Sometimes I'm the one who wants sex and I pester the man until he can't stop himself, sometimes I don't want it and he seduces me, but I'm never forced or raped. Occasionally things like that happen to me in real life, and then they are extraordinarily unpleasant, but later I can use such a situation in my masturbation fantasies. Then, naturally, I have complete control and everything happens exactly as I want it to and I can summon up men and let them disappear at will. I'll give you an example. I once got a lift from two lorry drivers. But as soon as I climbed into the cab I regretted it because I had been manoeuvred into a very vulnerable situation. I had to sit between them and there wasn't the slightest chance that I could jump out, we were much too high up for that. After a while one of them asked me exactly why I was travelling with them, women don't usually accept a lift if there are two men in the car. I kept the conversation on a friendly, humorous vein, and said: 'Well, because of your honest faces.' But they still carried on the conversation in that direction, asking whether I lived alone and travelled alone, if I got turned on by smoking hash, if I wanted to go for a drink with them, saying I could sleep in the truck and so on. But I said I had to be back in the youth hostel at a certain time and let them know that I clearly wasn't interested. Luckily it ended all right, but even while it was happening, I had the thought that this, if I could get out of it alive,

64 would become an interesting masturbation fantasy. And so it has . . . There are lots of these difficult situations. If a man is too nice or too helpful towards me, I am always suspicious, because I'm always scared he'll ask something in return, even if it's just a kiss. And often that happens. In particular, if someone does that when he has done me a favour, I feel I have been taken for a ride. For example, a man carried a kiln up to my flat for me, and when he left he grabbed my hand, pulled me to him and wanted to kiss me. I managed to limit it to a quick kiss on the cheek, but I even found that disgusting. I remained polite to him though, and refused him in a friendly way, although I wanted to hit him. He still had to connect the kiln for me, and I didn't want to offend him because I had already paid for it, and I was scared that he might keep me waiting, or not connect it properly, or not connect it at all. If I ask someone for something, I don't want them to take extra trouble just because I'm a woman, because then they force me to be grateful to them. If they do something for a man, they do it because they want to. Things like that usually happen so quickly and unexpectedly that I can't avoid them and I'm always in a situation in which I can't make a fuss. Last week I was sitting with a friend in a street cafe and a friend of his came to sit with us. When he said goodbye, he bent over me and gave me such a dirty, wet kiss, with a half open mouth, right on my mouth, I was furious! But I didn't want to make a scene. Things like that are usually done in a situation where it is difficult or impossible for a woman to say anything.

— *Did your mother ever give you any good advice about men?*

— She taught me not to run after boys, but to make them run after me, that you had to smile and be sweet and charming. The indirect messages she gave me were much more important, for example in the way she behaved towards my father, always soothing him, satisfying him, sacrificing herself. She always took the piece of burnt toast for herself, the smallest slice of cake . . . I wasn't allowed to get into a car with a strange man. When I was ten I was playing on the street with two girlfriends, and a man in a car asked us the way. When I went up close I saw that he had his penis out of his trousers. I was terribly shocked and we ran away. While I was getting a lift once, a man took out his penis and began to masturbate. Luckily we were driving through town, and I got out of the car at the next traffic lights. But I haven't hitched a lot. Three years ago I had a nasty experience in the South of France. I had been riding and took my horse back to the stables. I had to wait for a bus, and the owner asked me if I would like to see some photos of his horses. And what did they turn out to be? Photos of one of his stud horses being castrated, men holding him down, blood everywhere . . . I didn't want to see them, I walked off. But he said: 'No, no, don't go away yet, here are some more', and he jumped on top of me, he was much stronger than I, I fought back, but I couldn't throw him off me and so I began to scream. Then he stopped. He said: 'Oh, I'm sorry, I didn't mean anything, you'll come again next week to ride won't you? Publicise my stables to the students a bit.' And I wasn't able to say angrily: 'No, you prick, of course I'm not coming back.' I just said: 'Yes, yes', thinking all the time, how do I get out of this without being hurt? If I had started to scream at him, he might have hit me, I didn't want to make him angry. Then he told me how much I owed him for the ride, and I was such a dummy, I even paid him!

– *What did you actually like about your relationship with your last boyfriend?*

– He was very tender and loving, in bed and outside, and we found it easy to talk to each other, he was good company, he got on with my friends, he was seldom angry or irritable, he was very patient and stable in temperament, and I like that. If we had conflicts, we could talk them through, he never walked away, and if I was in a bad mood, he could get me out of it. All the qualities my first boyfriend didn't have. He never wanted to talk things through. If there were irritations, he shut himself off and withdrew. He also didn't like talking about his deepest emotions. If we had an argument, he always disappeared until it was 'forgotten', but he is still the best lover I ever had. My last boyfriend had a very romantic attitude to sex, he had his best experiences with a very innocent and virginal girl and I believe he was sorry I wasn't more prudish and inexperienced, but was curious and wanted to find out and try everything. He didn't like talking about feminism, even though he held very emancipated views.

– *Has feminism influenced your sexual behaviour?*

– I was a feminist long before I had sex! And I'm sure that this is expressed sexually. I do nothing I don't like and I'm quite firm about that. When I was travelling I met a man I wanted to go to bed with, and I thought, god, I'm sexually experienced, he is attractive and seems to want it as well, why shouldn't we? So I went to bed with him, but at one point I no longer enjoyed it – I wasn't wet enough, and I didn't feel very excited and so I asked him to stop. I said it hurt and I didn't want to go on.

– *Was he already inside you?*

– Yes. Then he asked if he could still sleep in my bed, but I said I preferred to sleep alone and he went back to his own room.

– *That's another proof that such things are possible. Was he angry?*

– No, why should he be? Sex should be enjoyed by both people.

– *Has it ever happened that someone asked: 'Was it good', and that you then said: 'No, I didn't enjoy it much'?*

– Yes, that is difficult. I have done it once, though, but it is easier to say so later on.

– *When do you actually decide to go to bed with someone?*

– For a while I liked going to bed with men I had just met. Just out of pure curiosity and for fun. Perhaps also because I wanted to make up for lost time, since I began to have sex so late. Now I have satisfied this curiosity, and I only go to bed with someone I **66** care for, otherwise it isn't worth it. The other day I could easily have gone to bed with a good-looking fellow, but then I thought, oh, I want Sunday morning to myself, I don't want to have the trouble of thinking how to get the man out of my house if he hangs around. There must be more to it than just sex, not just a pretty face but a friendship, or at least a fascinating person. Once I went to bed with a boy who was still a virgin. He was nine years younger than me, but he didn't realise the difference in our ages. I knew how old he was. We had met at a party and been out a few times, to an exhibition, to the market, had drunk beer together. He was on his way to North Africa and asked if I wanted to travel with him, but I couldn't get away because of my work. We just liked each other. One evening he dropped by, stayed for a meal and we began to make love. When we got into bed he lost his erection and he told me it was his first time. I tried to get him stiff again, by putting his penis in my mouth, and he came immediately. Later on he had another erection, and then we really got it together. He was terrifically loving, soft and a bit innocent and in addition was very tender and affectionate, which made it extremely pleasant. Even though he had had no experience, he really knew how to kiss and caress and touch, and I found that heavenly. He was young and handsome, had a terrific young body, almost without hair, and he was just a very nice person. The next day when I told him how old I was, he was astounded, even shocked and I believe it changed his feelings for me a bit.

— *When, as you put it, you feel like sex, what precisely do you want?*
— Affection, touching each other. I want my whole body to be touched, and stroked and kissed. And if it is someone I like, I find it so extraordinary that we can express our mutual liking and tenderness for each other in a physical way. I want the sense of being vulnerable as well, the vulnerability I feel in myself and in the other when we are naked together, and the sexual feelings, the excitement I feel when someone puts his hand between my legs, or strokes me and then comes inside me.

— *Have you ever faked orgasm?*
— No. I've never lied about that.

— *Do you find it difficult to be honest?*
— Yes, because saying no isn't enough on its own. It seems as if they think my orgasm is the barometer of their accomplishment in bed, and so I always have to pacify them and tell them it isn't their fault.

— *If you get very excited from love-making, don't you then need to masturbate afterwards?*
— No, the excitement dies away. I don't get nervous or irritable from it. It has also happened that the man with whom I make love didn't come. One man used to drink a lot, and when he didn't manage to come, he just took his penis out again. My first boyfriend sometimes didn't come and that wasn't a problem for him, he wasn't bothered by it at all. It's good to see that a man

sometimes can't come, and that in spite of penetration and in spite of excitement, he can't have an orgasm either.

— *Did you go to bed with your first boyfriend during the time that he was married?*

— No. Only again after his wife had left him.

— *Have you ever been the 'other woman'?*

— Actually, no. I don't want to make love to married men or with a man who is in a serious relationship, because either he does it merely to have a little diversion and I don't mean anything more to him than that *or* I will be hurting his wife. And if I knew her, I wouldn't be able to be friends with her unless she knew about it and approved, but I don't fancy that at all. It's too easy for men to play two women off against each other. And if he says: 'My marriage is bad already', then I'm just giving him a chance to escape from it. Then they don't have any need to work at their relationship, or to change themselves.

— *Are there certain times or periods when you have more or less need for sex?*

— Yes. For example, I mostly feel like masturbating late in the afternoon or in the early evening. Two and a half years ago, when I had just learned to get an orgasm, I masturbated every day, sometimes three times a day. It was wonderful! Gradually I did it less often. Now even three weeks may go by without my needing to masturbate, and then again I might feel like it three or four days in a row. Before I learned to masturbate, I once went for a whole year without feeling a need for sex. I didn't make love at all. In fact I don't know the need for just sex. And if I do feel like masturbating, it isn't such a sexual urge, it's more because I feel so relaxed afterwards. It is so useful and easy that I can do that now, and that I don't need anyone at all, and afterwards I can do what I want without having a man hanging around me.

— *How did you actually learn to masturbate?*

— From a woman friend in my consciousness raising group. I told her that I had never had an orgasm. As a child I sometimes used to put the blankets between my legs, because that was a nice feeling against my clitoris, but I had no idea what I was doing. My mother told me not to do it! Anyway, this woman advised me to try with the hand shower, and just to find out what temperature and what pressure of water was the best for me. I did that. There wasn't a drop of water left for the other people in the house but I succeeded, and it was an extremely intense orgasm. My legs began to tremble and I didn't manage to keep the stream of water on my clitoris all the time. It was a very intense feeling, almost too much to bear. So I quickly learned to do it with my hand. That's easier for me and I like the feeling I have *before* the orgasm best. It isn't so sharp that way, and I have more control over it.

— *How do you do it?*

— I rub myself over the whole area with three or four fingers **68** because my clitoris itself is too sensitive to touch directly.

– *Do you like to take a long time over it?*
– Yes. If I think it's going too fast, I keep it back by consciously relaxing my thighs and stroking more slowly, and then I get to a sort of high plateau feeling, which I try to stretch as long as possible, and when I do eventually fall off, it's over. My clitoris is then too sensitive to touch any longer, but if I have had a big orgasm, I sometimes lie motionless for about ten minutes savouring it afterwards.

– *What contraceptive do you use?*
– I took the pill for a while, but I got a lot of nasty side effects from it – biliousness, dizziness, often headaches and later on even migraine. I went to a lot of doctors about it, and they all said it was from the pill. My breasts got heavier too, although I didn't have any objections to that. But the headaches, they were really intolerable. I tried four different kinds of pill. I also tried a cap, but found that too unspontaneous. You always have to know beforehand, or you have to stop when you are already busy, to put it in. I didn't want an IUD either, because my sister had fallopian tube infection from it, and a friend got infection of the uterus for which she had to have an operation. They both complained to the doctor about the pain and were told it was normal. Another friend told me she had been sterilised, and I went to her doctor, but he didn't want to do it, said I should wait and asked if I had a boyfriend. That was with my first boyfriend.

– *Did you both not want children?*
– He did. He always said that was why we couldn't marry, because he wanted children. That was long before I had myself sterilised. I always knew that for that reason our relationship couldn't last. I've known for a long time that I don't want children. Three or four years before I was sterilised, I realised it was possible not to have children. In my women's group, one woman said that that she didn't want children and said how she wanted to live. I realised at once what freedom such a decision would give me. I had always expected that I would marry at twenty-five and have children, and so I had to make sure that I had experienced all the adventures and done all the travelling that I wanted, because after that I would be tied to my family and wouldn't be able to get away. But that evening in the group I realised that I could choose, that my life didn't have to be like that. I would be able to go on living as I chose without a time limit or a limit of any kind. It was a relief not to have any children. I suddenly realised that I had an alternative. A second doctor led me to believe he would do the sterilisation, after first having treated me rather theatrically as if I were his daughter. We even set a date for the hospital, but then I was told over the telephone that I first needed the permission of a psychiatrist, because the doctor-director didn't want to take the responsibility. Eventually I found a doctor who would do it. He thought it was entirely my decision. I was operated on in the morning and could go home again in the afternoon. I felt so well **69**

that I could actually go to work again the next day, although I had taken time off.

– *Do you ever feel sorry about your decision, when you hear all your friends talking about their children or their longing to have children?*

– Oh no! I always think they don't know what they're letting themselves in for. The trouble, the time, the energy . . . I know more than enough about the practical side of it because I'm the oldest of six children, so nappies, feeds, being woken in the middle of the night, baby-sitters – I really know it all! I have no romantic illusions about motherhood and don't want the responsibility. I'm glad I've had the operation – my body hasn't been changed by it, I don't have any headaches any more and I need the freedom. I can come and go when I want, travel when I like, change my job. I'm not tied to any time or place.

– *Up until now, have you been satisfied with living alone?*

– Yes, I've always liked living alone, having privacy, shutting the door behind me, and if I want to see people, I know where to find them. For a couple of years I lived with a group of people in a house where I had my own room, a sort of communal life where you eat together and share the sitting room and kitchen. Now, for the first time in my life, I have a space which is entirely my own and I like it a lot – to come home at night and be able to read a book or go to bed or make music and eat what I feel like. Naturally now and then I miss someone with whom I can share my impressions about a book or about something which has happened to me. I can share a lot with my friends, depending on their interests and sex, but when it gets cold and is dark early, I sometimes long to come home to a brightly lit home and the prospect of a meal being ready. If you live alone, you have to arrange everything, ring up people, make plans, while if you live together with other people, there is always someone to whom you can say: 'Hey, let's go out tonight.' It just takes less energy.

– *Do you think you'll continue to live alone?*

– Sometimes I see myself as an old woman still living an independent life, travelling and doing what she wants, and sometimes if I meet someone I like, I see myself living with him. But these thoughts are always followed by all the things I would have to give up and that would be a lot! Then I get that feeling of being hunted again, that I would have to do and see everything before he moves in with me or me with him. We would have to make careful arrangements about individual freedom and about travelling alone. I have a lot of reservations about throwing myself into a couple. The times that I did live with someone it seemed so easy to give up everything, because we had such a good time together, but when they left I was always relieved, because I got back time of my own and could spend the evening as I wanted, could visit people I wanted to see.

– *What do you find difficult about living alone?*

– When I have to make a decision, I always have to take it all on
70 my own. Sometimes I do wish there was someone to share the

responsibility with: should I buy a house, shall I buy a car, where will I spend my holidays, how long shall I stay there . . . you name it. Sometimes I get into trouble because I make decisions in the mood I am in at that moment, and that mood depends on all kinds of outside influences. But up till now I haven't regretted any of the decisions I've made. I take total responsibility for everything, and at times that is a heavy burden. Sometimes I miss that 'homey' feeling. I have to make my own home, completely on my own – sometimes that's a very comfy, safe nest, and sometimes I think I should look for somewhere else to be.

– *Do you find it difficult to travel alone?*

– No. Theoretically I am alone, but in practice I always have people around me. When I went to the Middle East, I met a whole lot of people and I was hardly ever alone. I only felt lonely there on days I didn't enjoy myself, or when I felt ill or didn't like a place, or when they tried to browbeat me into buying rubbish. When I am somewhere very beautiful, then I want to share all that beauty with someone else, especially if it's familiar, not if I see it for the first time.

– *I've never travelled alone, it seems really scary. How do you manage?*

– I usually know roughly where I'm going, and when I arrive in a place I go to the youth hostel or look for a small hotel, and then go out from there to look at the town, make trips into the country, walk for a whole day.

– *How do you feel when you are out walking?*

– Oh, that's wonderful, I love it. I walk at my own pace and rest when I feel like it. I can enjoy the country very much when I'm alone.

– *When I'm out of doors, I get the crazy idea I need to share my joy with someone else and I want to call out: 'Look, how beautiful!'*

– Yes, I feel that too, and while I'm walking I notice that in my thoughts I'm writing a letter to someone. Once I took a friend with me, but I had to think about it for a long time beforehand, because I didn't know how much it would mess up my plans. But it went very well, and I could also do quite a few things I would never have been able to do on my own, like for example, picnicking on a huge rock next to the sea. I often meet people in youth hostels with whom I do things, like last summer a woman of fifty-nine, who was hitching through Scotland on her own. She told me how easily she got lifts, while I was having a hard time. I admired her, she was an exceptional woman. She had travelled all over the world and worked when she needed money. When I heard that, I hoped that I would also dare to live like that later on, and rejoiced at all the things that are still waiting for me when I'm as old as she.

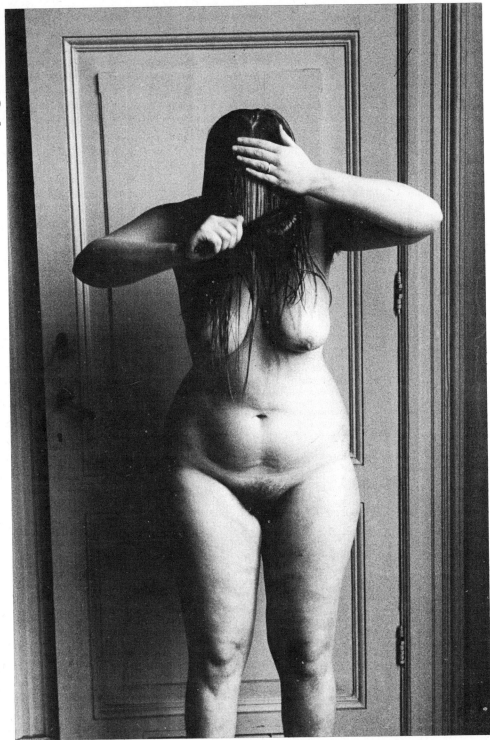

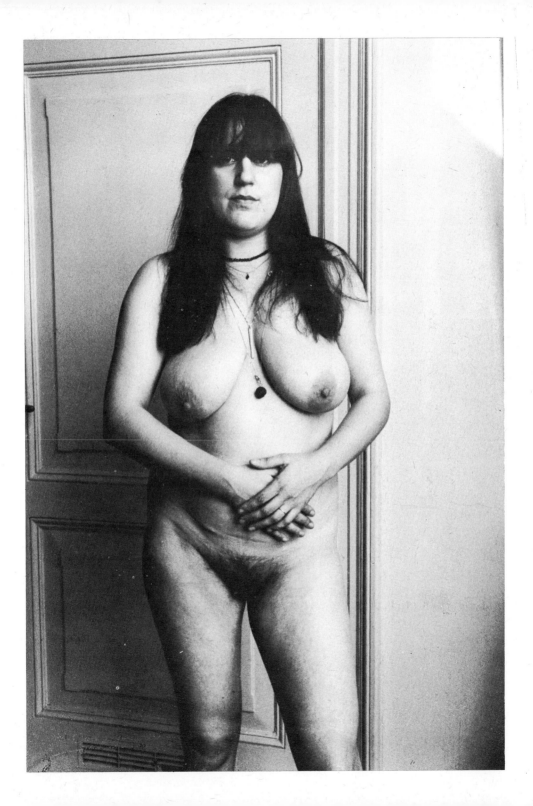

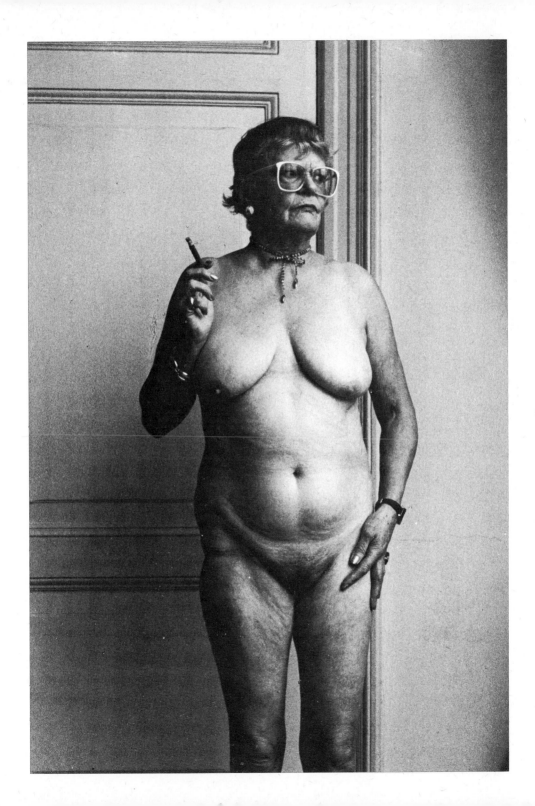

IV. The big lie and the 'sexual revolution'

At a women's conference we asked all the women there how many of them had ever faked an orgasm. Those of us who were organising the conference knew from our own experience how often we ourselves had done so. Because we thought it would be so terrible for him if we didn't orgasm, because we didn't have the courage to tell him that 'ordinary' fucking hadn't made us come, because we thought we were abnormal, or too demanding. Or because we couldn't believe that he would enjoy trying to make love differently in such a way that we *would* have an orgasm. We had acted out sham orgasms by starting to moan or moving more violently or even, the most accomplished actresses amongst us, by pulling in the vagina muscles so that it seemed just like the spasms of a real orgasm. Not that this art was appreciated by men, most of them believed us anyway, and there were dozens of men who just assumed that we came when they came, or who simply didn't seem to be interested.

Not one of us was proud of our deception. We were ashamed, and it was a long time before we dared tell each other. It made us unhappy because if you do it once you can't ever again turn the clock back and say, after so many times, that that wasn't a good way to make an orgasm. We also clearly understood that the fact that we didn't dare to be honest had everything to do with our powerlessness in our relationships with men, yet we still felt uncertain. And during the discussion we also realised what we did to other women with our big lie, because each time a man came across a woman who faked it, he would be less likely to ask again whether it was going well, and it would be even more difficult for the next woman to tell the truth.

When we asked the women at the women's conference how many of them had faked orgasm too, we got this answer: one hundred and four women said yes, seventy-two women said no. More than half! And when we took into account afterwards that there were many lesbians at the conference for whom pretending was less of a problem (see the chapter on women and women), it seemed safe to say that the great majority of heterosexual women have participated in the big lie at least once, if not more often. And this in a time of sexual revolution in which we are free and easy, use the pill and don't need to be so scared of being pregnant any more – a time in which it is at last being recognised that women are sexual beings too. It gave us quite a shock.

'I faked orgasm for thirteen years. I felt I couldn't bear to tell him that I didn't enjoy it very much – it was the only thing he really 79

enjoyed and I didn't want to deprive him. It would have hurt him, especially after all those years.'

'When my daughter brought a book home which said that women could have not just one orgasm, but many, one after the other, I was dead scared my husband would read it. I thought, at the moment I just have to pretend one orgasm, but to be fashionable I'll have to have more. Luckily he wasn't interested.'

'I haven't enjoyed it since I got married. But then, you are married and it's part of it. So once a week it had to happen. Mostly you could sense it coming, and I'd think, there we go again. Afterwards I was always happy, because then I wouldn't have to do it for a few days. I think my husband always regarded my relief as sexual satisfaction. He'd ask: "Do you feel good?" and I could honestly say that I did. But it was relief.'

1. The battle for the orgasm

Most of us have grown up during the era of father Freud. Even without having read his difficult books, we have been influenced by his ideas on female sexuality. Most doctors are influenced by them, sexual counsellors too, and his ideas are reproduced in books about sex. Briefly, his opinions are that men have an active 'libido', sexual drive, and women don't. That women are jealous of a man's penis, and that an adult, healthy, mature woman has shifted her sexual feelings from her clitoris to her vagina. He says that when a little girl of around three to four years sees a little boy's penis for the first time, she is immediately overwhelmed by intense jealousy which she can never quite overcome. As a result, she realises that her own clitoris, with which she loves to play, is a poor substitute for a boy's penis. She will have the feeling that she has been 'castrated'. The shock, says Freud, means that for the rest of her life the woman suffers from 'penis envy', she is more vain, more conceited because she lacks that amazing organ and she will long for babies. Naturally she will prefer baby boys, who will make up for her own deficiency. And she will shift her love for her mother, her first 'sex object', whom she blames for her lack of a penis, to her father, the proud possessor of The Organ. And on the way to adulthood, she will shift her erotic feelings from her childish 'penis substitute', the clitoris, to her vagina, so that a man's penis can become the instrument of her erotic satisfaction.

We don't have to look very hard to see how much hot air there is in such a theory. There is no reason on earth why a little girl should experience her own clitoris as a second-class organ. Many little girls enjoy caressing their cunt, sliding down the banisters or rubbing it against a blanket in bed. It is pretty far-fetched to imagine that little girls think that little boys have a

nicer feeling because they have a willie, or that they think that their lovely little place is a miniature penis. You could much more easily imagine that boys, who see that women have breasts from which milk flows, and a belly from which children grow, are jealous because they will never be able to have that. But the scholarly gentlemen have never come up with the idea of 'uterus envy'.

It is much more likely that girls soon realise that boys possess a number of privileges that girls don't have. They see that boys are much more encouraged to be strong, that they are allowed more freedom and may play outside more often. The fact that girls are 'protected' may quickly give them the feeling that they are weaker than boys. And children who live in a traditional family where mother looks after father when he comes home from work – where they see, for example, that little girls are expected to do more of that kind of service than little boys – will take on those roles. In addition, girls will get the feeling that the possession of a penis means you have more power over others than if you have none. It clearly means that you don't have to wash up, that you have more money and that you don't have to tidy up when you make a mess.

So it's no coincidence either that more girls want to be boys than the other way around. If 'penis envy' does exist, it is caused not biologically, but socially: those who own penises are the bosses in this world. Yet there is no good reason why you can become powerful only if you piss standing up. The idea that a mature woman ought to shift her sexuality from her clitoris to her vagina is one of the most barbaric ideas of the patriarchal culture created by male society. Thousands of women have been made deeply unhappy by it, and we are still busy clearing up the devastation which this misconception has created.

The idea that a healthy woman ought to have a vaginal orgasm is not just a technical misunderstanding. It has everything to do with the way women and men are being perceived. For a long time it was not known that women had their own sexuality. Those were the days when women were expected to stay patiently at home and accept their husbands' decisions in all important matters. That is slowly changing now, and because women aren't automatically considered to be dependent, ideas about female sexuality are changing too. But we are stuck for a long time with the experiences and ideas with which we have been brought up. For that reason, I've had a look at the books with which our mothers, and sometimes we ourselves, were brought up. The books we often found hidden behind the 'respectable' books or put away in a drawer. Books which went into many editions and were read over and over, but which almost no one kept on the open bookshelf.

2. Mister van de Velde

If there was *one* book which was read in the Netherlands until it fell apart, it was *The Ideal Marriage* by Dr van de Velde. The copy I have, printed in 1959 (it was first published before the war, in 1923), is full of stamps from the public library and seems never to have stood on the shelves for long before someone borrowed it again. Without doubt van de Velde was very modern and progressive for his time, and many people must have been delighted that there was at least one book which didn't talk in vague terms about 'melting together at the peak of love' or of the 'unity of true lovers who have found each other for ever', but which told in detail exactly what sexuality was all about. It's a pity that van de Velde wasn't able to see through the prejudices of his time.

Van de Velde's starting point is that the differences between women and men are biological and should be maintained. In short, he says that for the creation of a new person we need an egg and a sperm, and you can already see the qualities of female and male in the qualities of the egg and the sperm. The woman is passive, she asks to be aroused: the man is active, he makes the movements. But the egg-woman doesn't just wait passively, no, she waits passionately, trembling for her sperm-man. From the fact that sperm cells seek the egg (he forgets for the moment that the egg makes a long journey too), he deduces a whole series of qualities: men are natural leaders, they must conquer their wives lovingly. Because even if she resists him, a 'true' woman won't respect a man who doesn't overcome her with 'gentle force'. What's more, sperm cells are in competition with each other, so this quickly explains male aggression. So women are by nature emotional, vulnerable, irrational, and, especially, maternal. It is therefore logical to take the next step and say that men should work outside the home: women will find their main task in child bearing and looking after their offspring: 'It is thus not an exaggeration to conclude: the body of a woman is fit by nature exclusively for the survival of the species, the production of children.'

Men who do not naturally dominate, or women who don't get much pleasure from being dominated, are simply 'unnatural'.

But it isn't so 'natural' for men to dominate, otherwise van de Velde wouldn't be so worried that people might do things which could affect the 'natural' dominance. He is scared, for example, that the leader role in men will be affected if men don't lie on top when fucking. Occasionally the woman may get on top, but it mustn't become a habit: 'An injurious side effect of the unlimited application of this would be the complete passivity of the man, and its replacement by the complete activity of the woman, which must be seen as in conflict with the natural relations between the sexes, and which will in the long run work against them. For this reason alone it is not encouraged that this manner of union should be made the rule.'

Wanna fight,
mister,
Dr van de
Velde???

It is to be expected that in this world view the woman's sexuality is totally adapted to the man's. As a doctor, van de Velde knows that women have a clitoris, an organ which is exclusively for 'sexual arousal', comparable to a man's penis. He does not conclude from this that for a man, a certain way of making love is more pleasurable for his penis, while for a woman another way is more pleasurable for her clitoris. No, there is only *one* real way of making love: 'By normal sexual intercourse, I mean the intercourse which takes place between two mature people of different sexes, with the direct or indirect intention of sexual satisfaction, and which reaches its climax with the crossing of a certain threshold of sensation, the release of male sperm into the female vagina, with more or less simultaneous orgasmic satisfaction by both parties.' And with those words is laid the foundation of years and years of misunderstandings, which we can trace in almost all sex manuals to this day. Only attraction between opposite sexes is normal. Only penis-in-vagina sex is normal. And women and men ought to climax together during fucking.

Van de Velde also knew perfectly well that it isn't always so rosy, otherwise he and the other 'authorities' on sex would not have had such busy practices. But it is less important *how* women feel, than what they *ought* to feel. Women *ought* to orgasm when their men orgasm: 'It is certain that during natural union, the ejaculation of the sperm is the most important factor for the orgasmic satisfaction of the woman.' The clitoris may participate, during foreplay it may be caressed, and hopefully during sexual intercourse it is rubbed enough to heighten the stimulation, but if that doesn't happen, then the love-making isn't incorrect, but there is something wrong with the woman: the clitoris is too high up, or too small, or the organ has remained in a childish state of development. A woman who doesn't get an orgasm from 'normal' sexual intercourse is frigid.

In a great many books written before and after the war, we find this kind of nonsense. We can ask ourselves why people would try so hard to saddle women with a kind of sexuality which didn't satisfy them. It certainly has to do with the oppression of women in general. There has always been a fear of the dormant sexuality of women, and what might happen if it were to break out. If one were to recognise that women have their own sexuality, in which they are not dependent on male 'leadership', then one would also recognise that they have a will of their own, that they do not willingly subjugate themselves to the wishes of men, either sexually or in any other areas of their lives. For this reason many male 'authorities' have thought it necessary to remain silent about the clitoris, or to assume that it is diseased or childish if women have their sexual feelings there. Because the recognition of the clitoris as the sexual centre of our body is at the same time a recognition that we don't *need* a penis for our satisfaction – and that is something that most men don't want to admit, even now. Attempts to suppress our sexuality by forcing **83** us to accept ideas of what is 'normal' were just as effective as the clitoridectomy, literally the cutting away of the clitoris, that is customary in many Arab and African countries to this day. What the 'authorities' did was to castrate us psychologically.

Women have not always been silent about this oppression. Even at the time when doctors and psychiatrists wrote those dreadful books, there were still women who knew the theories didn't fit. I have recently found a book by Alice Rühle-Gerstel, written in 1932, which says that for women, the act of reproduction and the way in which we experience sexual satisfaction are not one and the same. The actual source of sexual pleasure is the clitoris, she wrote even then. And in her analysis, she found that women's so-called 'frigidity' had much more to do with the fact that women were forced to make their sexual needs subordinate to the needs of men, rather than that women have, by nature, fewer sexual needs. Her ideas made hardly any impression, and it is easy to understand why. Very few women could claim enough freedom *not* to make their own sexuality subservient to men's. It's no accident that ideas like these were to gain acceptance only when women were making demands for more independence in other areas of their lives.

Various research projects have shown that the most traditional 'feminine' women do not necessarily experience the most pleasure in sex. Sexual pleasure goes with being able to stand up for yourself emotionally, so you must be in a situation where you can allow yourself to do that. In spite of the popular misconception that feminist women are sexually frustrated, actually the opposite is true: women who are struggling to be emancipated are also struggling for what they want sexually. That they don't always succeed without conflict, or that it doesn't

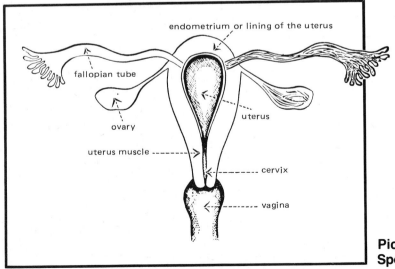

**Picture puzzles:
Spot the clitoris?**

always result in behaviour which men find 'feminine' or 'attractive', is another matter.

When Kinsey got a lot of publicity for his research, it began to dawn on people for the first time that the vaginal orgasm was a fairy tale. It is still true that something is only taken seriously when a man says it, even if women have been saying it for ages. For example, feminists have been saying for years that housework makes an important social and economic contribution, but it was only when a male professor said it that it made the headlines. Kinsey published his report on female sexuality in 1953, in which he said that the small lips of the vagina and the vaginal cleft and the clitoris contain nerve endings comparable to those in the male penis. Kinsey noted that a woman could achieve orgasm just as quickly as a man – if she masturbated; in other words: if a woman can choose for herself how she is stimulated – but Kinsey didn't make quite such far-reaching conclusions.

A little later the laboratory research of Masters and Johnson was published. This investigated, by means of all kinds of technical apparatus, how female and male orgasms are created. Their conclusion: there is only ONE female orgasm, and that orgasm always occurs through direct or indirect stimulation of the clitoris. The only real difference between female and male potential for orgasm was that about half the women were capable of multiple orgasms, that is, many orgasms close together.

The knowledge of the clitoral orgasm should have put an end to all the tricks played on 'frigid' women: operations to remove the clitoris, shock therapy, years of lying on the psychiatrist's couch if they had husbands who could afford to pay the bills. But it is still true that men would rather pressurise women into conforming to

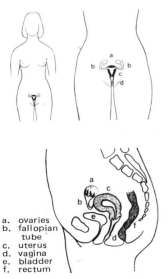

a. ovaries
b. fallopian tube
c. uterus
d. vagina
e. bladder
f. rectum

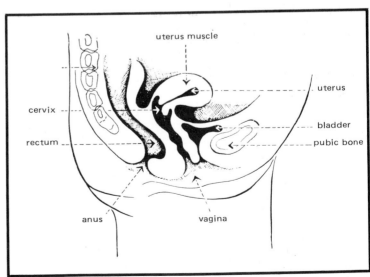

their fantasies than adapt their fantasies to women's reality. A really terrible example is an American gynaecologist, one Dr James Burt, who has entered the market with a new discovery. When women have babies in America, they are cut as a matter of routine, because that makes the birth easier, especially for the doctor. When this doctor stitches it together, nice and tight for the husband, he at the same time practises shifting the clitoris so that it can be reached more easily during 'normal' intercourse. Dr Burt now specialises in this: he operates on women so that the clitoris lands up closer to the vagina and he tells us that it is now less trouble to give a woman an orgasm during fucking. By the way, he has also provided his own wife with the ideal cunt. Luckily he is an exception and has been criticised by therapists, who are afraid their livelihood will be affected, and by the women's movement.

Anne Koedt was the first woman in the new wave of the women's movement who had the courage to write that the myth of the vaginal orgasm is a way of keeping us down. It is due to her and to women who came after her, like Shere Hite, who interviewed thousands of women, that gradually more people have come to understand how oppressive it is to force women to accept a sexual pattern which has nothing to do with our needs.

3. The sexual revolution, another lie

It was at the end of the last century and the beginning of this one, that the first 'sexual revolution' took place. In the Victorian age which preceded it, women were regarded as sexless mother figures or oversexed whores. Now it was generally accepted that sexuality wasn't the expression of animal and low desires or lusts, or merely a means of reproduction, but that it was something beautiful between women and men. (Homosexuality still remained in the closet with the other base lusts; it was still 'bad'.) So it was said that women had just as great a need for sexual satisfaction as men. The first public propaganda for birth control was made around that time. The Netherlands was the most progressive, having the first clinic for birth control,

**Picture puzzles:
Spot the clitoris?**

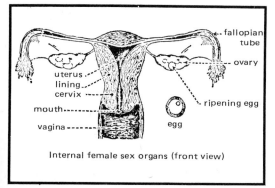

Internal female sex organs (front view)

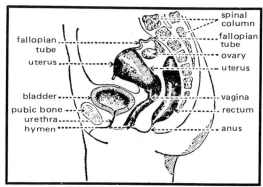

established by Aletta Jacobs in 1882. Even at that time, there were feminists who understood that this sexual liberation for women wasn't a simple question of awakening our passions. The taboo on sexuality between women and men was lifted, but that on lesbian relationships became even heavier. At that time, there were many friendships between women, and it was assumed that it was normal for women to write letters to each other full of passionate feelings for each other. They could also sleep with each other, without anything special being said about it. But friendships between women, as compared with a 'real' sexual relationship between a woman and a man, were regarded as childish and second-rate. In addition, although the new sexual freedom spoke of communication between two equal souls, women were not equal to men. Women then were even more economically dependent on men than they are now; they had very little freedom in public life and so very little freedom to satisfy their sexual needs. The double standard of sexual morality had not disappeared, and the same man who called a woman prudish when she didn't want to go to bed with him outside the protection of marriage, could also slander her to his friends as a slut if she did. Except for those women who succeeded in building an independent career for themselves, the sexual revolution still meant that a woman had to do her best to please a man. *Before* the time of the sexual revolution, she had to keep herself chaste and suppress her own sexual needs. Now the new 'Bohemiennes' were expected to discard their old prudishness. It was still the wishes of men which dictated what would happen. It seemed as if the sexual revolution of that time was mainly a way of liberating men from the trouble of paying for their sexual desires, either with prostitutes, or in a marriage. Female sexuality was now openly available, but without the economic position of women having undergone any significant change. No wonder many feminists of the time would have nothing to do with it. A story written around 1916 by Meridel le Seuer, who moved in libertarian writers' circles in America, describes how an American writer pursued her, and when she refused to satisfy his sexual desires, announced that she would never become a good writer if she couldn't get rid of her prudishness. A modern argument. That many women didn't care much for 'free love' meant that the image of early feminists we now come across in books is almost always one of a sour, prudish old maid, instead of realistic women who sometimes preferred to do without a sexual relationship rather than let themselves be exploited.

Meanwhile we have just experienced a new wave of the sexual revolution. The pill, a more lenient approach to abortion, fewer taboos around extra-marital sex, a less blatant oppression of homosexuality, less censorship on pornography, a recognition that women are also sexual beings – it seems as if it has become established that sexual liberation is for women too.

88 But unfortunately, many of the patterns of the previous wave are

if I don't want to make love to him, I'm frigid and if I do, I'm a slag..

still recognisable. Women still aren't really equal to men, even if it is assumed that they are. The vast majority of women are economically dependent on their husbands and their bosses. Modern women are under pressure to enjoy sex, but they aren't consulted on what kind of sex. Attitudes do change, and we are now expected to experiment with different 'positions', but the relations within which sexuality occurs are still largely the same. We now have more technical knowledge of female sexuality, but too many doctors, counsellors and sexologists just continue with the old nonsense or fit the new knowledge neatly in with the old prejudices. For example, having acknowledged that the clitoris is the sexual centre of a woman (they can scarcely deny this since science has shown it to be true), they come to no other conclusion than that the man should caress the clitoris during foreplay, or should choose a position which stimulates it more. Sex is still fucking, other forms remain trimmings. Not to enjoy fucking is a deviation. Not being able to orgasm during penis-in-vagina contact is called either frigidity or, in a more friendly way, an 'incapacity'. That many women still don't care too much for this kind of sex has been accepted by a large number of scientists, but the explanation for this is still seen in the traditional prudishness of women, in our 'frustration', and not in the fact that the way we make love is still dictated by men, and that women are seldom in the kind of relationship where they can actually find out what their own needs are. It occurs to hardly anyone that there is perhaps also something wrong with the way men go about having sex. Therapists are trained to help women over their 'anxiety about sexuality', but the end-point is always the same: she will be fucked.

'When I went with him to a party, I went mostly out of curiosity. I thought he was sexy. Wanted to see what it would be like to fuck with him. That happened. On the bed, on the floor. Standing up wasn't so successful, we kept falling down, but he kept on trying. From behind. We went right through the whole catalogue of positions. I participated partly because I wanted to experience it at least once, partly because I felt that I couldn't say I had had enough since I had let it happen in the first place. But it all left me ice cold. When I left he asked: "Will you come again tomorrow?" I said: "No." Then I saw him get a bit annoyed and he asked : "Didn't I do it right? Did you want something different?" '

'During the period that I had no permanent relationship, I experimented quite a bit with one-night stands. After a meeting or an evening in the pub. It was part of the style of the crowd I was going around with then. But it didn't suit me very well. If I enjoyed being with him, I fell in love and became attached to him which was very unfashionable in those circles. And if I wasn't in love, then there I was lying with a strange body in bed and thinking, jesus, how will I ever get rid of him?'

frustration ??

89

'He was the kind of man who had learned exactly how to do it. Extended foreplay, proper attention to my clitoris, polite questions about whether I had come. After all the trouble he had taken, I couldn't bear to tell him that I had the impression my cunt was made of plastic, completely without feeling. He looked so radiant, as if to say "Haven't I learned what women like beautifully?" He just needed my orgasm as a reward.'

We aren't just *allowed* to have orgasms, we *have* to. If not for our own pleasure, then at least for his. An extreme example of how we still have to fuck for his benefit, not for our own, was provided by the trial around the 'frigidity' of a thirty-eight-year-old French woman. She had been so maimed in her pelvis by a car accident that she had too much pain afterwards to take pleasure in sex. The Judge gave damages of around £2,000 to be paid to the husband because *he* was now so deprived. (*Liberation*, 21-9-1978)

With the 'sexual revolution', we are expected to divorce sex from emotion, as most men do. The idea that making love is much better if you love someone, or even offensive if you don't care for someone, seems to be an old-fashioned point of view. We used to be looked at askance if we enjoyed sex, now we are blamed if we don't follow the male pattern. It is difficult and confusing to find a way between the old role of the chaste woman and the new role of male-defined sex, the 'easy lay'. We still have few examples of what our sexuality would really look like if we were free to do what we wanted. Women who make love to women are more likely to express their sexuality in a more equal way. And if we want to have a relationship with a man, it is clear that not only do *we* have to change, but men too have to do something about the roles they take for granted. There are men who are beginning to say out loud that they aren't satisfied with acting the great seducer either, but they are the exception, and for the moment they need not expect much support from other men.

Further reading

Van de Velde's book, *The Ideal Marriage: its Physiology and Technique*, was published by Heinemann in 1928 and republished until at least 1957. The Women's Research and Resources Centre (see useful addresses) has a copy dated 1957. Or you might find a copy of it or something similar sitting forgotten behind the books in your parents' bookshelf.

Masters and Johnson's main books are *Human Sexual Response* and *Human Sexual Inadequacy*. They're probably in your local library, if you want to have a look. *Understanding Human Sexual Inadequacy* is a good explanation of their work by Belliveau and Richter (Coronet).

There are critiques of Freud in many feminist books – Simone de

Beauvoir's *The Second Sex* (Penguin), Kate Millet's *Sexual Politics* (Virago) and Mary Ellman's *Thinking about Women* (Virago), for instance. Anne Koedt's essay 'The Myth of the Vaginal Orgasm' (in *Voices from Women's Liberation*, now out of print) was a real rallying cry, written in 1970.

Juliet Mitchell's *Psychoanalysis and Feminism* (Penguin) is very informative and interesting on Freud and Reich. Another man who worked on sexuality, Reich was pretty progressive for his time. She's much more respectful of Freud than I am though, and doesn't criticise his masculine point of view enough.

V. Coming with an orgasm

It doesn't matter how we make an orgasm, so long as it feels good – that's the only reason why we bother with it. But because we have been so worried about getting an orgasm exactly as the books tell us we should, some of us haven't ever got close to finding out how we ourselves can make an orgasm. So this chapter is about how we can make an orgasm, and what can stop us from having one.

Making an orgasm is one of the best ways of giving our bodies pleasure, no more and no less than that. One woman needs an orgasm more than another; for one it is a wonderful experience, for another just a pleasant event. Depending on how you are feeling, it can be at one time an incredibly important event, at another a mere side-effect.

You can feel an orgasm quite differently at different times. Sometimes it is a good way of getting to sleep easily, or of releasing tension if you have just read an exciting book. It can be a little present to yourself, or a happening you share with someone you care about a lot. Very occasionally, for example if you are terribly in love, it can truly seem like ecstasy, the fireworks and heaven of pleasure you hear about in books and films. But this is hardly ever so, and isn't what everyone feels.

Very many women have problems or have had problems making orgasms. An important reason is that in our society, women aren't taught to participate actively in their sexual pleasure, and many women simply don't know how an orgasm is made. In addition, most women have learned to make their sexuality dependent on a man. Often men know even less about how women 'tick' than women do, because they are also indoctrinated with the penis-in-vagina idea, a sort of plug-in sex: when you put in the plug, the lights go on automatically. The films which show women panting to a climax as soon as a penis is waved in their direction don't help: neither do books where a woman inevitably explodes into orgasm as soon as the man 'penetrates' her. These are mostly male fantasies and, unfortunately, women writers have often adopted them. Perhaps because they too think that 'normal' women feel like that.

We shall explain why 'ordinary' fucking appears not to be the best way for most women to make an orgasm. Certainly if a woman doesn't know how to make an orgasm – by making love with herself or with someone else in a different way – it seldom succeeds with 'ordinary' fucking. The strange theories about how women *ought* to have orgasms, put out for years by psychiatrists, doctors and other 'authorities' have done dreadful damage and made many women uncertain and unhappy. Before we discuss that sad inheritance, we will look at what we know about orgasms, how they feel and how they are made. **93**

1. What it feels like

'I find it terribly difficult to describe what a orgasm feels like. I used to think I had had an orgasm when, while making love, I felt very good and excited, but I now know that that has much more to do with emotional excitement than with orgasm. Now I know quite definitely when I've had an orgasm. It isn't possible to confuse it with anything else. It begins with soft waves of pleasure which ebb away again until the excitement becomes really very high, and just as I think it can't go any further, I feel a spasm deep in my cunt a few times and then the tension ebbs away.'

'To me the heightening of the tension is a little like the feeling in your belly when the lift goes down very fast, but it's a very good feeling, at first mostly in my clitoris but then just about through my entire body. I notice that I involuntarily tense up my whole body just before I am at the climax.'

'I still find it a very unique feeling which is difficult to describe, only it's nothing like the weird images of waves or fireworks you sometimes see in films. It's a bit like the moment when I need to wee very badly, and then the moment when I really let go. Or like getting the sneezes when you look into the sun, but then a really good, big, super sneezing fit.'

For some women every orgasm feels the same, but many women experience them differently at different times.

'It's most important for me how I make an orgasm. I can regulate it very well if I do it with my fingers – then I let it surge up and ebb away again a little, so that it lasts a very long time before I do come, and it comes from very deep inside. If someone else makes an orgasm with me, I experience quite a different feeling, it has more connection with my whole body, but then it doesn't come from such a deep place, and the spasms aren't so strong.'

'I have my best orgasms when I am menstruating, then I really feel my uterus contract. It also helps stomach ache when I have menstrual cramps.'

'Sometimes it is disappointing, it's suddenly over, very quickly. And another time I can really stretch it out longer and longer and longer, and then, wow, as if you are picking up speed in an aeroplane and then suddenly it takes off.'

2. What it does

Every orgasm begins with stimulation of the clitoris. For every

94 woman the clitoris is the central point from which her orgasm

starts. But the best way to stimulate the clitoris differs from woman to woman. Some women have their best orgasms when the whole area around the clitoris is softly caressed. For some women the little tip is so sensitive that direct touch easily causes irritation or even pain, and they come most easily by moving the foreskin backwards and forwards over the clitoris. It is possible for some women to make an orgasm by moving something up and down in the vagina. Because the lips go with the movement, the same effect is achieved. But it isn't as common as we have been taught. And even if you *can* do it like that, the question remains, do you *want* to?

There is a lot of confusion around the way we get orgasms. For a long time we were told that women had two kinds of orgasm: a clitoral orgasm through stimulation of the 'outside', and a vaginal orgasm through stimulation 'from inside', by having a penis pushed into your vagina. That is untrue: all orgasms are clitoral. Some women can get an orgasm from what we usually call fucking, because their clitoris is in such a position that the pressure from the lower half of a man's body is enough, or because her lips are perhaps shaped in such a way that they get enough movement during fucking so that the stimulation is exactly right. But very few women experience this. In some investigations it is said that about fifty per cent of women orgasm from fucking. In *The Hite Report*, it is thirty per cent. Of all the women I know, of all the women I have asked, there were exactly *three*. The statistics given in the research projects are probably distorted because we have for so long believed that we *ought* to have vaginal orgasm. Because it is 'normal', and we don't want to say that we aren't normal or even that we have never even had an orgasm.

Inside the vagina is pretty insensitive: there are almost no nerve-endings there. Small operations on the sides of the vagina can be carried out without pain-killers. We know from our own experience that we can put a tampon in there without feeling it and you don't notice a cap either once it is in. That doesn't mean to say that some women don't get a really marvellous feeling from having a penis in their vagina. You certainly do feel the pressure, but much of the excitement from that way of making love seems to be emotional rather that something to do with getting an orgasm. Yet very few women put something into their vagina when they make love to themselves, and if they do, it is usually something in addition to stroking the clitoris. Although pornography likes to show pictures of 'lesbian women' going at each other with plastic penises, parsnips and candles, it seldom happens in real life. It is a male fantasy, an incapacity to imagine that women would want to do something different with each other than a kind of imitation 'intercourse'.

It's also not true that women take longer to come than men. When women make their own orgasms, they can do it just as quickly as men do – if they *want* to. (But why should you, if you wish to give yourself pleasure?) If we make love with someone **95**

else it takes longer, but that is precisely because we don't always make love to someone else in a way which is most pleasing to us. Anyway it isn't a competition, and it shouldn't matter how long it takes. It is only a problem if you are making love with someone else and you worry that they are thinking it is taking 'too long'. But it's important to know this because it puts an end to one of the reasons women are so often considered 'old-fashioned' on a sexual level.

3. How it happens

We don't know exactly what it is that makes an orgasm such a very nice intense feeling. It has something to do with blood-vessels which fill up because of a special kind of stimulus until the tension becomes so great that with a couple of contractions of the blood-vessels and the muscles, the blood flows away again. But that doesn't say much about our feelings about it. Technically, an orgasm is divided into the following phases:

● Excitement. The clitoris swells – sometimes only a little – and becomes more sensitive. Your vagina begins to 'sweat'. Your muscles, especially in your abdomen, begin to tense up. The inside lips of the vagina become thicker and darker in colour. The deepest part of your vagina becomes wider, while the part near the opening becomes narrower because of the swelling. Your heart beats faster, and your breathing too. Perhaps you 'blush' in a few places on your body and your nipples become hard.

● The approach to the orgasm, the 'plateau phase'. The area round the vagina and the clitoris swells up, even the part of the vagina closest to the opening. If you like having something in your vagina, that's the moment you are most sensitive there. Your breathing gets faster, your muscles tense up even more. Your clitoris retracts a little. If you don't know that, it can be confusing if it is suddenly 'lost'. If you are making love to someone, you may think you are less excited because your clitoris is less visible. In reality you are close to an orgasm. In the final approach, we tense our muscles 'rigid', and even perhaps hold our breath. Precisely because we have been told that women should moan and groan while coming, it can be distressing if you are extremely quiet and rigid just before you come. The transition from 'excitement' to 'take-off' isn't so clear. It's a little like the lift-off an aeroplane makes: you start, go faster and faster and suddenly with a jump you are off the ground. Most of the time the excitement doesn't progress in an even line, but ebbs away and returns again. That can be most pleasurable, but if you are still practising, you can get the feeling it is going away altogether. If you are really just about to have an orgasm, you reach the stage where you can't go back, if you were to stop, you'd have one anyway, but not as clearly – you'd 'lose' one.

● The orgasm, the release. When the tension is at its height, the muscles contract. For one or two seconds the muscles in your **97** cunt pull together, a few times, one time after another, dependent on how much tension you have built up. Sometimes you can feel it right in your uterus and in your anus. Sometimes throughout your whole body.

● Relaxation. After an orgasm it take half an hour for the swelling to subside, and for your muscles to relax again. You can also hold on to that tension and while you are still 'high' make another orgasm and another. Most women have the capacity to have more than one orgasm, close together: men have to wait much longer before they 'can' again. But just because you *can*, doesn't necessarily mean you want to. It would be ridiculous if we made our number of orgasms into a kind of competition in the same way as some men count how many times they can do it in one night. If you have already made the approach, but haven't had an orgasm, it can take longer before you are relaxed again, and that can be an unpleasant feeling. This often happens when you can't go on making love the way you like until you orgasm, when after 'foreplay' you suddenly have to switch to 'normal' fucking, which may perhaps break your excitement. If you make love to someone else, it is better to find out first for yourself what you like best.

4.   Learning to make an orgasm

For most women the strongest orgasms are those they make themselves. However, I have only described the physical part of making love. I don't deny that it often means a lot emotionally to experience it with someone else. We can do it best on our own because we can concentrate completely on ourselves, and that is the first important condition. What often holds women back is that they are so busy with what the other person is feeling that they don't think about what *they* want. You can't get an orgasm from someone else; whichever way you look at it, it is a happening focussed on yourself, in which you forget someone else's needs. For that reason it is especially important for women, who might anyway have difficulty with it, to practise on themselves first before finding out what is pleasurable with someone else.

Your clitoris likes a warm, smooth, slippery and light pressure best. It is quite easy to get the precise pressure and rhythm you need from your own fingers, and you can wet your fingers with spit or with moisture from your vagina. It is more difficult with someone else's fingers, unless you can tell them whether it's too hard or too soft, too slow or too fast. A tongue on your clitoris, or a soft sucking, is just about ideal and approaches what men feel if they move the penis in the vagina, which is also warm and moist and gives exactly the kind of soft pressure which is so pleasurable when it is slid in and out. Rubbing it against something soft is also good. If you have the luxury of a bath with a hand shower you can learn a beautiful way of reaching

98 orgasm, or of making a celebratory orgasm: let the bath run half full and lie in it with the warm jet from the hand shower gliding onto your clitoris under the water. A hundred soft tongues! The only problem is whether you will make it before the bath overflows if you don't have an efficient overflow. And hard luck when you've got a boiler that lets the water run cold just at the most exquisite moment! In America many women use a vibrator, but it isn't so popular here because it seems cold and technical. It's a little machine you connect to the light bulb, or which runs on batteries, and then gives off vibrations which you can't make with your hands. Some women who have had difficulty making orgasms have used a vibrator with great effect. You don't have to be scared that you will become addicted to the vibrator, or won't be able to get an orgasm without one. If you have come easily once, in whatever way, it's easier after that to learn other ways. Vibrators are usually shaped like penises, which is a little stupid, since they do almost nothing for the vagina. Besides, because it is something you hold against your clitoris, it doesn't matter what shape it has. Probably the manufacturers thought we would be looking for some kind of substitute penis. But an electric toothbrush or a massage set are just as effective. And some women manage to come if they stand against the washing machine. You can buy vibrators by mail order (see the advertisements in *Spare Rib*). You can also pay a visit to a sex shop with a couple of woman friends, if you don't feel like going on your own.

Some women have an emotional block against orgasm; they are scared to let go, and stop if they are on the edge of one. Sometimes this has to do with being scared of letting your emotions go, sometimes with suppression of anger or pain, which you aren't allowed to express either to yourself or to those around you. Some women cry during or after an orgasm because the release of tension releases other emotions as well. Some women are afraid that if they let themselves go they will be out of control, or ugly. Very occasionally a woman is afraid to have an orgasm because she might piss. This can happen, but if you practise first in the bath, or with a towel under you, you can learn to control your muscles so that you do come, but don't piss. Making an orgasm seems a bit like jumping into the unknown; you don't dare allow yourself to slide over the edge in case you don't have an easy landing (you always do). But if you don't want to lose your self-control and are blocked about it, you won't be able to let go.

Sometimes your first orgasm is disappointing, it's over so quickly. If you had expected fireworks, that little jump over the edge is perhaps not enough. But once you know what it's like, it is possible to develop it, for example by stopping for a moment when you are just about to orgasm, then continuing, then stopping again until you can't bear the tension any more.

So it's important to be able to concentrate on yourself even if you are making love to someone else. If you are making love to yourself, you need to have uninterrupted privacy, without the 99 feeling that someone could come in at any moment, or that the telephone is ringing. You need warmth, a place where you feel good, where you can make a 'fool' of yourself because you are at home.

In America, and in other countries too now, there are groups of 'pre-orgasmic' women who haven't been able to come *yet*, women who used to be called 'frigid'. Half the time spent in such groups is spent on learning to assert yourself, learning to value yourself, and the other half on exercises you can do at home. It's pleasant to talk with other women about your 'progress'; it removes some of the idiotic taboos about not talking about sex, and you can help each other if you don't know what to do next. It isn't always easy to find such a group – there are some contacts in the useful addresses at the end. You can also try it on your own by using a book. You can follow the directions yourself. In general terms being in a group goes something like this (although each group will have its own particular way of proceeding):

● Tell each other your sexual herstory. This is important because of the 'messages' you have picked up and which may still be stuck in your head: don't touch yourself there, that's dirty, nice girls don't do that, a mature woman doesn't need that. If you are doing it alone you can also keep a diary, in which you can write down memories which come to the surface, and hold on to what you feel during the exercises, bad thoughts as well as happy discoveries.

● Learn to spoil your body. Massage yourself with baby oil or something that smells good. Lie in the bath for a long time, or mess around under the shower.

● Learn to appreciate your body. Look at it in a long mirror when you are naked and tell yourself honestly what you don't like, but especially what you do. We are used to looking at ourselves in our most flattering positions, or else we get so fixated on our

well, now, this looks promising ...

hmm .. do I put it somewhere ??

short legs or tiny thumb-tack breasts that we never see the rest of our bodies.

● Look carefully at your cunt.

● Make a list of your best qualities and try to add to it (I look after myself well, I am warm, I am clever, I am strong).

● Learn to enjoy your body. Stroke your skin and find out where it feels the best. Continue the massage, between your legs now. Take at least fifteen minutes to massage the most sensitive part of your cunt. Try other ways, with soft objects, with water, with a vibrator.

● Choose your favourite fantasies. Perhaps you'll dare write them down. What parts of films excite you, do you remember books in which there were passages which did something to you?

● Eventually take three quarters of an hour to find out the best way of making love to yourself. You need to be able to relax and enjoy what you're feeling without trying to reach a goal as quickly as possible. But relaxing doesn't mean doing nothing with your body. When we are close to an orgasm, we tense our muscles, especially abdomen and leg muscles. It can help you a lot if you learn to tense your abdominal muscles, especially the muscles in your vagina. These exercises are simple. First, try to stop in the middle of a pee. The muscles you use are the same as those you tense when you make an orgasm. You can do your exercises on the train or watching TV without anyone noticing. Do it ten times, one after the other, tense and relax, a sort of daily knees bend, but with your cunt.

● If you are scared to let go, you can make exaggerated groaning noises, or other noises, or move up and down. No one is looking.

● Not everyone manages to make an orgasm on their first try. Sometimes it's really a question of a couple of weeks doing 'homework' for an hour a day. That is not so terrible; it is, after all,

or in here?

In my cunt?!

an hour's pleasure, even if you don't get an orgasm. In the groups, ninety-five per cent of the women find that they do. Often the biggest problem is finding enough time for yourself, especially if you live with other people, and it seems egotistical to shut yourself in the bedroom or in the bathroom for an hour a day. Still, one hour isn't much, if we think about how much time we give to others. And even if you don't get an orgasm, that little hour may become so valuable that you might not want to give it up.

'I don't have a bath in my house, but occasionally if I babysit for friends over the weekend, I take along the bath oil, put on good music, put out the bathroom light, and place a few candles on the edge of the bath. I pour a glass of wine and slide slowly into the hot water — and then make an orgasm. A good petting session can't compete with it!'

Further reading

If I haven't given enough steps in how to learn to come, there are more in Carmen Kerr's *Sex for Women* (import). It's well written and clearly from the woman's point of view, with extensive practical exercises. She is overly optimistic though about equal relationships with men, as if it's easy to find men like that! Although she starts with female-male patterns which she wants to change, she gives little insight into the origin of these roles, and therefore little analysis of how they could be changed. She seems to think it's just a question of misunderstandings which have to be talked through and then everything will be all right. Aimed primarily at heterosexuals, but at least she admits that.
For Yourself (the Fulfilment of Female Sexuality) (import), written by Lonnie Barbach, a therapist in California, is good too, though dryly written. Mainly about how to make an orgasm. Anne Hooper's *Body Electric* (Virago) charts the progress of six women in a pre-orgasmic women's group. A classic is Betty Dodson's *Liberating Masturbation* (import) — about 'becoming cunt-positive'. There's also *Becoming Orgasmic* by Heiman and Piccolo (import), which has a step by step programme. It's still aimed at fucking, albeit with exra attention to the clitoris — completely heterosexually-oriented.
Good Vibrations, a pamphlet by Joanni Blank (import), is a guide to using vibrators. You can also get back copies of *Spare Rib* with some good articles on masturbation and orgasm.

VI. Sexual fantasies

There is a difference between sexual fantasies, daydreams and dreams. You dream when you are asleep; you have no control over what you dream. Sometimes you dream you're making love to someone whom you've never considered in your waking life – and that's fun. Sometimes you have vague erotic dreams about people you don't know.

'Occasionally I have very erotic, exciting dreams. Strangely enough they are not usually very sexual, I mean I don't fuck in a dream like that. But somehow there's an excitement in a kiss or a touch which I hardly ever feel in ordinary life. When I have sex, there's always a part of my head which still observes what I'm doing: I feel cold, or I can hear the neighbours, or I get a cramp in my thigh. In a dream it's pure ecstacy. Once I had an orgasm in my sleep which woke me up. Unfortunately, I can't dream like that to order. Sometimes I try to steer my thoughts in a certain direction before I fall asleep, but it doesn't really work very well.'

Sometimes dreams tell you something about your feelings which you can't easily admit to yourself.

'I often dream about women. In my latest dream I went swimming with a young woman who used to be in the same class as me. She looked exactly the same as she used to, only somehow she was the same age as I am now. We swam under water, alongside each other, with the same movements. We didn't touch, but it was terribly sad and beautiful and erotic.'

'Just before my lover and I broke up, I suddenly began to dream about other men. It didn't make me feel guilty when I dreamed about men who didn't exist, but once I also dreamed about my lover's best friend. Once, when I'd been dreaming about how we made love passionately, he turned up. I was blushing because the images from the dream kept coming back when I saw him. I suddenly began to think, hasn't he got lovely body, I wonder whether he really looks as he did in my dream when he has no clothes on. I think I acted rather strangely. I did feel a bit guilty because of it.'

Daydreams are different, you evoke them, you have control over them. Thoughts about someone you love, and what you could do together. Thoughts about the last time you made love to someone. Imagining scenes in a film, with yourself in the star role. Our daydreams are often more exciting than the ready-made films on TV, because we can place ourselves in precisely the situations we want to be in, and we can do what we like with other people without imposing on them.

For many women, daydreams are a way of getting through a boring day. They are the only way to survive if you are sitting behind a punching machine or packing tins of soup. It is also a way of enduring the eternal repetitiveness of washing up, making beds, vacuuming and other chores which occupy your body, but hardly your mind. Daydreams are gratis. But if you spend the major part of your day in a haze, it probably means that there is little excitement or pleasure in your daily life, and you should think about other ways of bringing some colour into it. Sexual fantasies aren't the same as daydreams, even though daydreams can be erotic. Sexual fantasies are images that we use consciously as sexual stimuli. Most men and many women have images that excite them and which help make orgasms, for instance. We call up the images ourselves, but what can sometimes be confusing for us is that we seem to have so little control over the content of our sexual fantasies.

'When I masturbate, I always have sexual fantasies about men I don't know. I don't mind that too much, but I do feel bad when I'm making love to my husband and getting these same fantasies just before an orgasm. I have tried to stop them, but that makes it much more difficult to reach a climax. I have also tried to have fantasies about my husband, but that just doesn't work so well. I do feel a bit unfaithful, as if I don't really want to make love to him, but to the bloke in my head.'

'In my most effective fantasies I am overpowered by two men at once. I am ashamed of this, I don't really think it is right.'

About fifty per cent of women have regular sexual fantasies. The most common fantasy that married women have while making love is of an unknown, romantic lover or an earlier sexual experience with another person. Many women feel guilty about this and don't want to talk about it.

Another common fantasy is of being overpowered. A popular interpretation of that kind of fantasy is that women enjoy being dominated, and are by nature masochistic. Just when you are trying to explain to people that you don't enjoy being pushed around, it's unpleasant to catch yourself with such fantasies. We have not yet been able to explain why certain images in our heads are more sexually exciting than others. We do know a few facts though:

- Most women fantasise, so it is not abnormal.
- If you fantasise about being overpowered, it doesn't in the least mean that you will enjoy being raped in your daily life. It is important to understand that the best thing about fantasies is that you yourself are the one who is imagining what is going on, you can stop it, you can choose the protagonist, you can send him away if you want someone else. Even if your fantasies are about being overpowered, the difference between that and rape **105**

in the ordinary world is that you yourself are in control, you choose someone yourself.

In fantasies, what looks like overpowering has more to do with desire, while actual rape has more to do with aggression. Aggression is never fun.

'I once dreamed that a man, when he saw me, was overcome with desire and I couldn't stop him. But when a colleague of mine had too much to drink and tried to grab me, I was just disgusted.'

Perhaps there are elements of our oppression in many of our fantasies. Perhaps fewer women would dream of being dominated if it wasn't assumed that we ought to be underneath. A mixture of sex and aggression is also just about the only form of sexuality we have experienced; these are just about the only sexual images we see.

Women can become just as excited by sexual images as men, but most women react more ambiguously to them. This corresponds of course to the ambiguity in reality: we react positively by becoming excited by erotica, because we are erotic beings, but we react with disgust to the obvious domination of men over women which seems to be part of 'ordinary' sex. We have too many memories of situations where sex wasn't enjoyable, but oppressive.

During a research project where women and men listened to erotic tapes, it transpired that women tended to become excited in situations where they themselves took the initiative, where they could determine for themselves what they enjoyed. The same images worked for men too as a matter of fact, but even there you can see the gap between fantasy and reality. Because although men can fantasise that they are seduced, in reality

most of them shut off quickly if they don't control the situation – if *they* are no longer the ones who decide what will happen.

You don't have to pay for sexual fantasies. What is acted out in our heads for our own pleasure, is ours: we don't have to justify it. We certainly don't need to be ashamed of it.

The images which surface in our fantasies will certainly change as our sexual relationships change. But we still don't know what our sexuality would look like if we lived in a world where one half of the population didn't literally keep the other half under. 'Perhaps there will be absolutely no sex any more,' says one of my woman friends, 'because then we'll have so many other ways of fulfilling our needs!' 'Perhaps we will be able to make love to anyone we like', says another. A pleasant daydream, for the moment.

Further reading

You can read about the sexual fantasies of other women in a book by Nancy Friday, *My Secret Garden* (Quartet). Rather a commercial book but where else are fantasies really described? Nancy Friday is suspected of having included some fantasies written by men. She's also published a follow-up, *Forbidden Flowers*.

VII. Making love with another person

A good relationship with yourself is essential before you can begin to have a relationship with another person. But it feels different – the warm skin of another person, a hand caressing your back, a smell which is not your own.

Making love to someone else is often seen as something you do with your genitals and which ought to climax in an orgasm. Relief of tension through an orgasm can be a strong need, but the need to be cherished, to cuddle up with someone else, is just as strong. That person doesn't have to be the one with whom you are assumed to have signed a genital contract. We impoverish our lives by receiving from only the one relationship the cherishing we should actually experience from all the people around us. It can be delightful to be physical with small children, because they are so shameless in the things they do to give themselves pleasure. Association with a small child can be at least as erotic as a relationship with an adult. Sensual contact is also possible with animals. A cat who seduces you into caressing it not only gets pleasure, but gives it as well. For many women, breast feeding is an extremely erotic physical feeling. When giving birth, provided the pain is not too overwhelming, contractions can be a fantastic experience. Touch is important in our daily contact with the people around us. Someone who isn't touched for days on end can begin to hate her body and get depressed.

Not all touch is pleasant. When men touch women, the gesture often has a double meaning. Often power games are hidden underneath it. A man who teasingly grabs your neck may want to say at the same time, look what I could do with you if I wanted to. A hand on your knee is often an attempt to see how far he can go, or a possessive gesture meaning: this woman is mine. Many men have learned to see sex in terms of conquest or prestige, and have neglected their capacity to enjoy warm skin against warm skin. When heterosexual men touch each other, they do so as if they are afraid of showing tenderness: a punch in the back or a blow on the shoulder. It is only when someone has died, or when a goal is scored in a football match, that they put their arms around each other in public. When men touch women, it is so likely to have sexual implications that most women don't like it. Men deprive themselves, and we would also be deprived if we allowed ourselves to be touched only by men. Everyone knows how good it is if someone holds your hand when you're sad. But there's no reason to wait until you're unhappy.

'I am a strong person. I don't allow myself to be put down. I can't stand men who only fancy me when I'm feeling vulnerable, for **109**

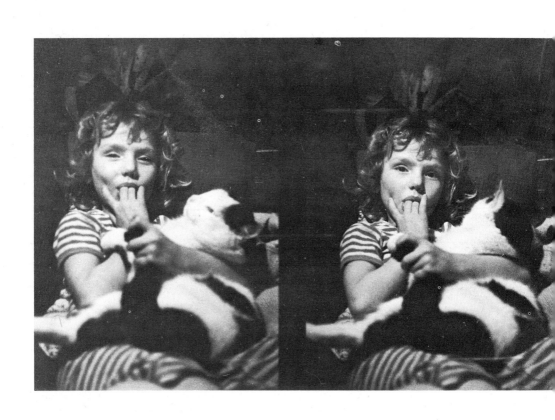

instance when I cry. If they don't like me just as much when I am strong, I don't need their help. It's not easy for me to ask for help, not even from women. In radical therapy I have learned how much I lose out because of this. Precisely when I need it most, I shut myself off the most and hardly allow myself to be touched. The group made me promise to see to it that I got at least four hugs a day. We practised that in the group. At first it was very artificial, but afterwards I noticed how much easier it is for me to hold someone's hand now, or to stand close to someone if I want to.'

Many women find physical contact unpleasant – too much intimacy makes them nervous. That may have something to do with the fact that in our dealings with men we have learned that touch doesn't mean tenderness, but a demand for something else, and we no longer trust someone who caresses us, but think: what do they want from me? In a women's group, it is quite possible slowly to unlearn that old feeling. *One* way is to massage each other. That doesn't have to run into a nude situation straightaway. It can feel marvellous if someone massages your neck muscles for five minutes, or your back while you're lying on your stomach. It can also be very pleasant to be in a situation where, for the first time, you don't immediately have the feeling you have to do something in return. Especially if, as a woman, you are accustomed to knowing that a caress on the back isn't meant to caress you, but to get something as quickly as possible. I have been present when a woman, realising how much warmth she had been deprived of, asked her women's group to stroke and massage her for ten minutes. One person massaged her feet, another her neck, a third stroked her back. She cried for at least a quarter of an hour when she realised how she always gave – to her children, to her husband – and how little she received.

Even when we are making love to someone else, it's important that we don't forget ourselves. That we make it clear what we want. That we don't let ourselves be pressurised because we ought to be 'normal' or fashionable. We can control the circumstances in which we make love to someone else. If you don't get pleasure from just a 'quickie', then you don't need to do it. We don't have to perform any acrobatics we don't enjoy, just because modern sex manuals are like cookery books with recipes for different ways of doing it: standing against the fridge for foreplay or starters, and hanging from the light bulb wearing black stockings for afters. It can be marvellous to make love outside with the sun on your skin, when you have just had a swim, but if you are too distracted by the possibility of a troop of boy scouts turning up, then the dunes aren't perhaps the ideal place. Certainly if you are underneath, then fucking on a cold floor is more fun for him than for you. Perhaps you like it best when you are lovely and warm under the blankets. Perhaps you concentrate better and develop your fantasies more easily in **111** soft lamplight or candlelight, rather than under a fluorescent light or strong morning sunlight.

It is also up to us to determine what kind of sexual relationships we want. It used to be oppressive that we had to be engaged to be married before we were allowed to take our clothes off. Now it can be just as oppressive to be called a prude if you find it more pleasant to get to know someone before you make love. After years of emphasis on the one relationship which had to last your whole life, it is now recognised that you might meet more than one person in your life with whom you might want to share sex, perhaps one after the other, perhaps at the same time. Monogamy, when it's elevated to a law, is difficult for most people to stick to. But the opposite – when it becomes the norm and is seen as the height of progressiveness to keep up sexual relations with many people at the same time – can be just as oppressive. Some of us have found that it is possible to love more than one person at a time, but we also know how much energy and how much tension that costs, and you need to have that to spare. In addition, more than one relationship at a time often causes pain, where it concerns people who don't all relate to each other from similar positions, and who aren't equal. For example, take the 'classic' model of a man in the middle, a 'permanent' wife on the one side and a 'free' woman on the other; a pattern which has long been exposed as an old form of oppression in progressive clothes. All too often, the women are played off against each other under the guise of 'anything goes', and neither of them gets what she wants, and both have to put up with behaviour they wouldn't stand for if they weren't so scared he would leave them for the other. A power game called 'divide and rule'. The 'open marriage' also looks progressive from the point of view of the marriage. For the third party, who is allowed to participate as long as it is fun, but must leave if it gets too heavy, things don't look so jolly.

Relationships with more than one woman at a time are also not always easy, or those with a woman and a man. There are no rules for what should be, what ought to be, what is progressive. We decide what we want. If we don't feel like swinging, we don't do it. We can choose where we want to put our energy, whether we want to share our sexuality with more than one person, or whether for the moment we'd rather make love to only one person, or to no one. There should be no rules other than those we make ourselves.

For the one woman, sex is best with someone with whom she has had a long trusting relationship. For another, the best thing is the ecstatic experience during a passionate love-affair. We all know how dependent sexual feelings are on other emotions. Someone else's skin feels different if you love her or him, from the skin of someone you don't care for; yet all skin is made of the same stuff, all skin is the same temperature. For that reason too, we can't measure 'sexual satisfaction' by how often we make

love to someone, or how many orgasms we get from it.

'Twice in my life I have been completely carried away when I was with someone. The first time was with a man who was to leave shortly afterwards – that made it even more dramatic. We made love as if it was the last time in our lives. I can't remember whether I had an orgasm, I was much too far gone to worry about something like that. I was much too excited, much too concentrated on him to be able to concentrate on myself. It was, all in all, one huge orgasm. The second time also began with lots of fireworks, but he didn't have to go away, and so it became slowly more peaceful and ordinary. Then I gradually began to want to come while we were making love – before that I hadn't really been bothered.'

'I hardly ever get an orgasm if I fuck with someone. The few times it did just happen were when I was terribly, madly in love with a young man. He gave me the feeling that I'd come just by him looking at me. And a few times when we were fucking, it happened of its own accord. Otherwise it is usually a huge bother if I want to come at the same time as someone else. It wasn't that we did anything special, it was more the emotions that were part of it.'

And sometimes sex has almost nothing to do with sex.

'The most erotic moment was when we sat opposite each other at the table. We didn't touch each other, she just looked at me and said: "I love you".'

VIII. Women and women

Women choose for other women for many reasons: emotional, sexual and even political reasons. Because you are emotionally close to another woman and because sex is only one step further. Or because you get the feeling from a woman that she likes you because of your strength and not just because of your vulnerability. Or because when you are with another woman you don't have to make yourself smaller than you are. Sometimes it's the old-fashioned love at first sight. Sometimes it's a friendship which slowly turns into something else. Sometimes in the beginning it's just the feeling: this woman fascinates me, I want to get to know her. Some women have known all their lives that they love women. For other women, like myself, loving women only became possible in the new context of the women's movement. I don't know if I would ever have made the discovery if I hadn't lived in a situation where I was relatively free, had my own income, my own work, a tolerant circle of friends, or if I hadn't lived during the past few years in an atmosphere in which I began to value women instead of looking down on them as I used to. And in which I was able to build up my own self-respect and self-confidence with the support of other women.

1. Choosing for a woman

It has become clear to me that making a choice for a woman doesn't just mean that I find a woman's body attractive. When I was still convinced that lesbians were 'the other', that *I* could never be like that, I still had a male idea of homo- and heterosexuality: it was about what kind of object you happened to find most satisfactory to make love with. And as I didn't have too much against men's bodies as such, I thought that I would never find women attractive as well. It was only when I began to see women as interesting people and also began to like myself a little, that it was possible to overcome the taboos, and the fear of not being normal. With hindsight it is now clear to me that I used to find men attractive because they helped me to do things I couldn't otherwise do, because they were a passport to a male world which, as a woman, you couldn't penetrate – the world of art or of politics, for example. Now that I don't use other people in order to get on, but have made my own life, my own work, and can't imagine that I would want someone else's life, I am no longer seeking someone who can offer me something which I can't achieve on my own. I'm not asking to be completed, made whole. I am attracted to equals, to people who are emotionally close to me, with whom I can share what is important to me. And they are, on the whole, women. So for me, being a lesbian is about more than sex. It's not just about a certain kind of body, it's **115**

also about self-respect, loving yourself, recognising how much women can give each other, how strong we can be together. It's about another kind of living, another kind of human relationship. Not all lesbians feel this to the same degree. Some women start to love women from a very early age. And there are a few women who choose women just like men do, for the sex, and have little love for their own kind. Like Elula Perrin, who in her latest book, with its inappropriate title, *Women who Choose for Women*, says that in the horizontal position she prefers women, but in the vertical, men. How much self-hatred that reveals! But does she notice that? It is a normal cultural phenomenon to despise women and certainly women themselves aren't free of it.

'I have never had a relationship with a woman. I used to get shivers down my spine at the very idea. I couldn't imagine it. But now I know my own body better and have begun to like myself more, I notice that now and then I think: wouldn't it be a fantastic feeling if I could put my hands on her breasts just like I do to myself? What would it be like to lie in the sun with her and let my hands travel over all that roundness?'

It appears from the Kinsey report that most people have experiences both with women and men. There are also women who marry three times and then fall in love with a woman, not because all their relationships with men have 'failed', but because that is what is closest to where they are at that moment.

'When I realised I loved her, it was very difficult for me to leave my marriage. I hurt my husband terribly and I didn't have anything in particular against him. I didn't know what I was doing to my children. But I still had the feeling that I had to get out. I didn't choose for her, I chose for myself.'

Being a lesbian is often assumed to be the same as being a man-hater. Many lesbians have had nasty experiences with men, but this is just as true for straight women. In fact, women who define themselves as heterosexual have more reason to hate men: lesbians expect little from men; they aren't dependent on men for most of their needs, and for that reason they have fewer unpleasant experiences. But choosing a woman is choosing a woman, not a choice against men, even though many arrogant men do experience it as such.
The rigid divisions which are drawn between the two groups of women, the 'normal' and the 'others', are used to play women off against each other. As long as we are afraid to be called 'lesbian' or 'dyke', we will do our best to prove how much we love men and what 'real' women we are. We will be afraid to let women come close to us, to take our friendship with other women seriously, to allow intimacy. We are letting ourselves be divided. We allow men the illusion that we need them. And

perhaps we believe it ourselves. And so the struggle of lesbians is important to all women, including those women who at this moment choose to be in a relationship with a man. If we can respect ourselves, we can look at other women as important people. People with whom we could have a real relationship. Then we only choose for a relationship with a man if we like him, and not because we *ought* to go with a man. *All* women should feel offended by the assumption that you are heterosexual until the opposite is proved. It says something about how women are perceived: we are clearly not independent enough to decide what we want, and women must, by definition, be a second choice – we'd have a man if we could.

A lot has been written about homosexuality. The crucial question is usually, how did it come about? Is it a congenital deviance, or a sort of 'third sex', is a lesbian a kind of failed man? Or is it learned, were our mothers too dominating, did we identify too much with our fathers, were we allowed to climb trees too long before we were told to wear dresses? Or is it an adolescent phase which 'normal' women grow out of, but in which we got stuck? We don't care a damn how it came about. How it's caused is only interesting if you want to be 'cured', or if we think we need an excuse – that we really can't help it and will people please tolerate us. No one thinks they need to explain how heterosexuality is caused. Do you start loving men because of bad experiences with women in your childhood, or because you were seduced by a man before you could develop your normal homosexuality? Or did you get like this because everyone told you that you would get broad shoulders and hair on your upper lip if you dared say you were in love with the games mistress? I think it is more interesting to ask ourselves why we suppress so much of our feeling for other women, why we are so afraid to show it.

It is a big step to come out as a lesbian. There is a lot of opposition to that in many of us. Prejudices surround the word, like Freudian theories that lesbians are stuck in a childish phase. In modern books, you still come across the idea that lesbianism is a neurotic disturbance, or too great a dependency on your mother. Lesbians, it is said, are looking for an alternative mother. Girls who have these 'tendencies' are going through a phase, they say, you can still force them to become 'normal'. Lesbians really want to be men, or have had bad sexual experiences with men. Whoever chooses to call herself a lesbian must first wade through a sea of prejudices, perhaps even fight her own doubts.

'I read a book which said that lesbians were unnatural because they wanted to find a mother in another woman. I have always disputed that. Until I realised what was actually being said. Naturally I look for someone who understands me, who is warm and who will be loving towards me. Women are better at that, we are trained in it. As a matter of fact, all men look for a woman who will care for them, who will be loving towards them, but that

isn't called childish, that's called maturity. Women can "mother" each other on an equal basis, while men can't easily look after another person. They want to be looked after properly themselves though. Naturally they get at us if we refuse to be their little mothers any longer. Their theories are there to keep us in our place.'

'For a long time I thought, I'm not a lesbian. I just happen to love this woman. If she didn't exist then I definitely wouldn't be like this. But that still didn't feel right. As if I didn't really want to belong. Once, when homosexuality was talked about in my women's group, I became very tense, and suddenly heard myself talking about "us" instead of about "homosexuals". Back home I realised what a step I had taken. I didn't want to hide it from myself any more, I didn't want to keep myself safe from the prejudices. I was relieved and also afraid.'

We are all brought up to be heterosexual. Perhaps there are now beginning to be a few parents who don't automatically assume that their children will bring a fiance home, but we did still grow up with the idea that sooner or later we will have a relationship with a man. We suppress feelings for women or hide them, out of fear of not being 'normal' or of not belonging. And that isn't just something in our heads: it *is* more difficult for women to live without a man. So that has also meant that almost all of us have learnt to suppress our sexuality. We learn that we will 'get' sex from the man with whom we will have a relationship. If we are reasonably satisfied, the idea that we might enjoy making love to another woman too doesn't occur to us. And if we aren't satisfied then we join the army of women who believe that sex is just something for men, that women don't get much pleasure from it. There are really many barriers against choosing for a woman. If, for example, you have children and no job of your own, it is terribly difficult to decide to leave your husband. The choice for a woman isn't just a little step if you know that the whole of society won't accept you any more, and you have little hope of another kind of life because you aren't used to supporting yourself. The fear of so many far-reaching changes in our lives, together with so much uncertainty, makes it difficult for women to acknowledge that our attachment to a particular woman can be more than friendship. We have been taught that women are weak and need protection, so we naturally don't find it easy to regard another woman as a possible partner. If we add to that all the propaganda – lesbians shown as not 'normal', as 'failed men', as creepy, aggressive, moustached, square dykes who wear leather jackets – then we can understand why only very strong women, or women who are really so much in love that they can no longer deny it, dare call themselves lesbian.

2. Isolation

We need to be wary of new fairy tales. It used to be the prince on the white horse, and that one is still alive and well. We haven't changed if we exchange the prince for the princess and expect that everything will be just beautiful. It is one thing to cope with people out there who say you are perverse or pathetic or that you are like 'that' because you didn't have a father or because he was too strict, or conclude pityingly that you couldn't catch a man. We are inclined to idealise our lesbian relationships precisely because of this pressure from outside. We can't endure it if someone regards our relationship as less than perfect, and we don't give up easily if it doesn't turn out to be the dream of our life. We have the feeling *we* have failed if the relationship fails.

'We were together for seven years. I think that the first three to four years were the best. After that I began to notice more and more that we didn't have so much in common. We went around together a lot because that was the accepted thing. Our friends saw us as a "couple". We would always be invited out together and indeed went together, even if one of us didn't feel like it. Slowly we landed up in a kind of marriage. Now and then I began to feel suffocated by it, but we never really talked about it. I think I was much too scared that I would find myself out in the cold, alone again and having to build up my own life. And just like in any marriage, we shared a flat, got rid of any duplication of books and records. You couldn't say whether the dog was hers or mine. Perhaps we would have carried on for years. We were very much wrapped up in each other. But she fell in love with another woman. For a while we tried to carry on, but I couldn't bear the tension and went to live somewhere else. With the dog. It was a very painful period. For a while I felt deserted by the whole world. And I also had that feeling of disaster, that I'll never find anyone again. Lesbians of my age aren't plentiful. I discovered how much we had isolated ourselves, how we had hidden ourselves in our nest.'

We have a strong inclination to protect ourselves from the outside world. A relationship for us is so important because it is at the same time a refuge. So we put a lot of pressure on a relationship. It has to be good. Sometimes it means that we make a relationship more important than it really is. In our infatuation, we immediately decide to live together and ignore the fact that we have very different life-styles. We neglect our other relationships, just as we are expected to do when we are married.
We adopt heterosexual norms, for example that a relationship which is over is a relationship which has failed. Instead of saying: 'It was terrific – for a year.'

'I have the feeling that we have just learned how to begin a relationship with a woman, but that we haven't yet learned how to end it without destroying each other.'

If you choose for other women, you don't get there by searching for the one and only woman. We need more women, women friends, women who appreciate us, with whom we belong. Lesbians need to come together for political reasons, to let the outside world see that we exist, like the first joyful lesbian demonstrations. But also because the pressure of one relationship is dreadfully heavy and the fear of loss becomes much too overpowering. We also need other women to complain to about quarrels and things we don't like, without immediately being confronted with those superior I-told-you-so faces. A group around you that you can trust can do more to help you in difficult times than a therapist or counsellor, who will probably have the same opinions as the rest of the world when it comes to relationships between women.

3. Making love

Sexuality between women is also not always such a breeze as we would like to believe. It certainly helps that as lesbians we are less stuck in prescribed roles, and that in principle we are much more equal to each other than a woman and a man.

'The best thing about making love to a woman for me is that it doesn't have such a predictable end. Not: this is foreplay, and now comes the real thing, now I have to have an orgasm (which never succeeded), and then it's over. With my girlfriend there was no beginning and no end when we made love. Without deciding about it, we went from talking into caressing and kissing. Sometimes she had an orgasm, or I did, but that was never the end, never, right, that's that done. It was just one of the things that could happen along the way.'

'It was only with a woman that I discovered how sensual ordinary touching is. The way she stroked my back or the inside of my thigh. I had never thought I could get so turned on from just being stroked.'

The first condition to being able to make love well with someone else is to know your own body, your own needs and to be able to make them clear to someone else. But not all women like the same things.

'I can get an orgasm from very light stroking over my clitoris. If I have been very excited from making love, I need very little touching, and even that is almost too much. It wasn't the same for my first girlfriend: she didn't come so easily. She said orgasm wasn't important to her, but I still felt awful, it seemed so **123**

unequal. I wanted to share it with her. Then one time she said very shyly that perhaps it would be good if she was licked. I was a bit shocked at that because I had never done it. I needed to get used to it.'

It is not true either that we can automatically overcome all the taboos just because we love a woman. If all your life you have been told that your cunt is dirty and stinks, then it can cost a lot of effort to be liberated in your erotic experiences, without shame and disgust.

'At first I was a bit scared of all that wetness. It was all right with my hands, but it took time for me to kiss her there. She had much less trouble with it. She was already more experienced than I was. She said she enjoyed kissing me there, but in the beginning I could hardly believe it. And then it was a long time before I came, I couldn't give myself so easily, because I couldn't imagine it was a nice thing for her to do. After we had bathed together, I tried it with her. It was strange, but not at all revolting. And it didn't smell as I had thought. Very clean actually. And I found it really fantastic to experience her orgasm with her. Later I tried it with another woman. I didn't enjoy that so much, but I wasn't very close to her.'

We can make love with our entire bodies. We can explore a body with our lips, we can discover smells with our noses, we can find hollows and folds with our fingertips in which we have not yet been. We can make an orgasm together. With fingers, with a mouth. We can try to come at the same time, but we can also lie back and let ourselves be given pleasure, and then later reverse the roles.
A tongue on your clitoris can be a fantastic feeling, and rhythmical licking or sucking is sometimes enough to make two or three orgasms. You can stroke the clitoris softly with one finger or stroke around it, or rub it softly between thumb and forefinger. Every woman has her own rhythm. One woman may be so sensitive that direct touch on her clitoris doesn't arouse desire, but hurts, and she would rather that the area round the clitoris is stroked. Another woman finds she only wants direct stimulation. Another woman likes feeling pressure in her vagina when she comes, or not at that point, but before. A finger in the vagina is a finger, not a penis. Some women don't like penetration, although in the past they've had satisfying relationships with men. Other women, who would never think of making love with a penis, enjoy a girlfriend's hand.
We can soap each other under the shower and dry each other, for pleasure or because we prefer to make love to clean bodies which have just been bathed.
There is an endless range of possibilities. We don't have to make it a 'performance', we don't have to save it for in bed. We
can make love just to make love, with or without orgasms.

How to make love to a woman if you're a woman

by Jennie Orvino

Think of yourself
and what you like
    then do that.
Ask her
what she wants
    then please her.

Imagine the most delicate
caress you have ever known
    and give it to her
      everywhere, slowly.

Speak her name
into the openings
of her body
    and listen
      to her answer.

Remember
the fierceness and power
of all our great grandmothers
    who rode horses
    and plowed fields
    and bore children
    in anguish.

and share that with her.

Love her in daylight.
Treasure what you learn.

4. Lesbian mothers

Many women already had children before they began a relationship with a woman. Occasionally, courageous women, who know they are lesbian, choose to have a child. Lesbian mothers are doubly oppressed. There are cases where the husband has been awarded custody at the divorce. In one such case the mother was described as unfit to bring the children up properly, though she had been doing so for years. She wasn't even called 'lesbian', but 'unstable', which turned out to mean nothing more than that she had stayed over for a few nights with a woman friend, leaving her husband to look after the children. We aren't saying that the children should automatically be given

to the mother. When men understand that fatherhood means more than shooting seed and providing money, then it might sometimes be a good solution for the father to take responsibility for the children after the divorce. We must, however, fight against the argument that a relationship with another woman, or with feminism, are grounds for the mother to be called 'unfit'.

Motherhood makes us doubly vulnerable. I know a lesbian feminist who says that she feels much more oppressed as a mother than as a lesbian or as a woman. You yourself can choose how far you will go, how much you wish to say about yourself, how many battles you will fight and how many you will avoid. But it is difficult to make those choices for your children.

'My daughter accepts that I am divorced. Gradually there are more children in her class with divorced parents than with parents who are still together. She has also never found our relationship a problem. She always used to ask: "Is she coming too, is she coming on holiday with us?" In the mornings she climbed happily into bed with us when she woke up. Then the slogan "Lesbians Ignite" appeared on all the walls. A few children in her class reacted badly to that, and the teacher let it pass. An unpopular girl was called a lesbian. When my daughter understood that my girlfriend and I were lesbian, she got upset. "I'm the only one with a lesbian mother", she said. Unfortunately I don't know any other lesbian mothers in her school. And the teachers won't come out easily because it could cost them their job. So she is stuck with the feeling that she is the only one with a mother like me. She has to defend something which she herself didn't choose.'

Children with lesbian mothers don't always have an easy time. They live in a society where everything revolves around women and men – the books they read, the day off school when teacher gets married. At home they watch TV where everything reinforces the family and heterosexual love. Even heterosexual feminist mothers have difficulty finding enough space to offer their children a greater freedom of choice, when there is so much propaganda for 'normal' relationships. For lesbian mothers it is even more difficult, because everything that goes wrong is automatically blamed on her being a lesbian, and the children will also find it difficult not to blame her for the problems they encounter outside the home.

'I had the feeling that everything was my fault – when my little boy couldn't concentrate at school, when my daughter wanted to experiment for a while with her freedom and was disobedient. Everything seemed to happen just because I am not a normal mother. I did know that children of "normal" mothers had just as many problems, but they seemed to be less picked on. I get the feeling that I have to prove all the time that I am a super-good mother.'

There are women who wonder whether they can inflict this on their children, who try to suppress their own needs until the children are old enough. The question is if that can be successfully done, and whether it helps. And whether you are able to give enough warmth, if you yourself are chronically starved for it. There is also the question of who benefits if all lesbians hide in the closet; in that way nothing changes, and it is still just as difficult for every lesbian who comes after us, and for her children. We don't want to feed our children lies. The trouble is that if we first have to prove that we are 'normal' mothers, it can take a long time before we can honestly admit that perhaps we shouldn't be trying at all to bring up our children to be 'normal'. We don't want our children to participate unthinkingly in heterosexual family life, so that our sons will become breadwinners without questioning that, and our daughters simply suppress their own talents and independence for the sake of their family. We want our children to grow up with more life-choices in mind. So it's important that we let them see that women can love each other, and not be ashamed.

5. Coming out

The more people show publicly that they are homosexual, the easier it is for those that follow. For a while some of us thought you shouldn't broadcast the fact. Until we understood how we are permanently surrounded in our daily lives by heterosexual propaganda. That it is important to let it be seen that we exist in order to make others realise how unquestioningly they define what is 'normal'. Coming out is not always easy for everyone. It's certainly less difficult if you are living independently, have no children and have a more or less safe career.

'I found it very scary to tell my mother that I was having a relationship with a woman. First I said carefully that I now lived with a woman friend who meant a lot to me. And I also always told her that we went on holiday together. Once she saw a TV programme about lesbians and then she asked straight out if I was a lesbian too. I swallowed hard and then I said: "Yes." Then she said: "You know, at junior high school, I had a girl friend, and when I think about her I get such an odd feeling. Perhaps that was lesbian too. But you musn't think I don't love your father, you know"!'

'It wasn't difficult for me to call myself a lesbian. I had already had the real hard knocks when I came out as a feminist. Everyone assumed all feminists were lesbians. I only had to fight that battle once.'

In some jobs it is difficult or practically impossible to come out. As long as there are still people who think that you can be
128 seduced into being a lesbian, teachers will have difficulty coming

out as lesbians. In America, attempts are being made to make it illegal for homosexual people to teach because they could seduce the children and make them homosexual too. The seduction theory was disproved long ago, but the prejudices remain. That men, statistically, abuse girls far more often, and that that can have dreadful consequences, has never been given as a reason to keep them from entering certain professions. In some other countries the situation isn't so bad. Yet there have been cases of teachers being sacked. Many women would choose not to risk their jobs by dancing too openly with their girlfriends at the school party.

In other jobs you are expected to prove your heterosexuality by walking around all the time like a doll, by pretending to enjoy nasty compliments, by not following your reflexes and kicking a man on the shin if he feels inside your blouse with his hand. As a matter of fact it isn't pleasant for heterosexual women either, but the aggressive jokes you would have to let pass if, in such a situation, you were to say you were a lesbian, wouldn't improve the atmosphere at work. Even men who don't say anything against homosexuals (some of their best friends are homosexuals, take John, such a nice fellow, you'd never think he was one of them), often become aggressive when faced with the idea that you don't need them, that you aren't available. A man with a vulnerable ego, who constantly needs female approval to feel like a man, can take it as a personal insult if you openly prefer women, even if you would never have fancied him anyway, and he probably wouldn't have fancied you. Some women, after they have come out publicly as lesbians, experience significantly more arguments with men and notice that many women have become afraid of them.

We can't demand of each other that we all come out publicly in the same way. But we can support each other so as to make it possible for more women to do so. It is important that we do come out. Because we've had enough of showing our true faces only in our free time. Because by doing so, we make it easier for other women to come out of the closet.

Further reading

There are quite a few positive lesbian books, magazines and newsletters now in Britain and the USA. Take a look in the Sisterwrite catalogue, or your local alternative bookshop or women's centre. Among the best is *Loving Women* by the Nomadic Sisters − 'a sex manual by, for and about women'. Through subtle drawings and some text, it shows lesbianism as a loving, sharing, sensual experience. It shows 'how to do it' without looking overly technical.

Kass Teeters' book *Women's Sexuality: Myth and Reality* (import) is also useful − it's not specifically for or about lesbians, but its view of sexuality is very woman-centred and warm. *Our*

Right to Love (a *Lesbian Resource Book*) edited by Ginny Vida (import), is a very comprehensive 'guide' for lesbians, though the organisational sections aren't so relevant here, as it was produced, like all too many of these books, in the USA.

The Lesbian Primer by Liz Diamond (import) is a witty, well-illustrated introduction to lesbianism. Excellent on attitudes, but it's a great pity it doesn't have more on sex, as such. Very accessible to young women, who won't unfortunately find much positive feedback about lesbianism in the two best books about sexuality for young people that are generally available in Britain – *Make it Happy* by Jane Cousins (Penguin) and *Boy Girl Man Woman* by BH Claesson (Penguin). There's also a youth liberation pamphlet called *Growing Up Gay*, written by American High School students (import).

Rocking the Cradle: Lesbian Mothers by Jacky Forster and Gillian Hanscombe (Peter Owen, soon to be a Sheba paperback) interviews lesbian mothers in Britain and explains all about AID – Artificial Insemination by Donor.

Sappho was a Right-on Woman, by Sidney Abbot and Barbara Love (import) remains a key lesbian book. A collection of articles, it looks at lesbians in society both 'before' and 'after' the gay and feminist movements began.

We're Here by Angela Stewart-Parks and Jules Cassidy (Quartet) is a series of interviews with lesbians in Britain. And finally, *Rubyfruit Jungle* by Rita Mae Brown (Corgi) – a racey novel about growing up gay – and *Cactus*, a novel by Anna Wilson (Onlywomen Press), speak worlds about what it means to be lesbian in a sexist, heterosexist society.

'The gentlemen visitors had to be out by eleven o'clock, but my girlfriend could stay the whole weekend'

**Interview 2
Ariane Amsberg**

— *Have you ever talked to your mother about sex?*
— Yes, in great detail. Not before, but when I told her I was getting a divorce, I also told her that there was a woman I like a lot and that I was going to live with her. I was a bit vague about it at first, as the divorce was already a big shock to them. They had been so troubled about my marriage – I didn't fit into the housewife role at all. He studied at home and I did an apprenticeship. I would leave the house at half eight and come back around eight at night. So I thought he ought to do the housework. I never washed up, for example. We didn't have a vacuum cleaner either, just a broom and a brush and pan. The only thing I did was the shopping on Saturdays. My mother did our laundry, in that way she could still keep an eye on us. Well, it was all very difficult, and just when she had at last got used to it, I came to tell her we were getting a divorce.
— *How old were you when you got married?*
— Nineteen, we were just mates. We didn't live in the same town and my parents had already expressly forbidden us to sleep together. We still did it secretly though, and when they found out, my father had us on the carpet and said to my boyfriend: 'Well, now you must take the responsibility for your actions and get married.'
— *You weren't pregnant or anything?*
— No, just because I was no longer a virgin.
— *And did you want to get married?*
— Yes, we thought it was a great idea. We really took it as a joke, sort of, yes, let's do it! Then we'd get them off our backs. We'd been going out together for two years already.
— *What kind of sexual instruction did you get from your parents?*
— I never spoke about it with my father. My mother dealt with it very progressively, so that when we were four we already knew where babies came from, but we knew nothing about making love and erotic experiences. From school, and from an older brother, I knew there was something exciting about fucking, but there was a veil of mystery around it, sort of oooh oooh.
— *Did you ever look at your cunt when you were little?*
— Not at my own cunt, but we used to have a 'cunt show' with girlfriends. Let me look at yours and you can look at mine. Once I did it with a whole group of children at my house. We weren't allowed to play in my room because it had just been tidied up, and so the five of us went to stand behind the curtains, in a circle, **131**

and I stood and held my cunt open to let them see. It was something like, who dares? Oh, and I used to play 'doctor, doctor' endlessly when I was about eight years old. If I visited cousins or friends, we lay in bed with each other and then we had to decide who was the doctor and who was the patient, and then the patient rang up: 'I am sick, can you ex-a-mine me?' That was the key word. The doctor first looked at arms and legs, but of course it was really about tits and cunts which had to be carefully examined. And I clearly remember the doctor saying with a face full of commiseration: 'Madam, I have to remove something', and then with your hand you pretend to cut something from tits or cunt, sometimes the whole cunt had to go, strange, isn't it?

— *Did you orgasm then?*

— Oh no, I just remember the tension and the excitement about lying there and letting things be done to you. I also know that my little brother and a cousin began to fuck together, and that they lay naked on top of each other, my cousin on top, and said: 'It's good, isn't it, do you like it?' 'Yes, I like it.' They didn't do anything more than that. When I was five, I went to play with a little girl and all the other children said: 'Don't play with her, she does dirty things.' That sounded interesting to me. I had just been given a doctor's suitcase and took it with me. She took off all my clothes and covered me with a blanket, it was very exciting, especially when her mother came into the room and we had to hide my clothes quickly under the blanket so she wouldn't notice.

— *Did you actually have the feeling that what you were doing was naughty or bad?*

— No, it was just nice and thrilling, and not so much that we couldn't just get on and enjoy it. But I didn't talk about it at home. My mother knew very well that I played these kinds of games, but she clearly suppressed it. I had a kind of dual feeling about it. I would have preferred it if it had been possible to speak about it, so you could say that it was nice and thrilling. The morality was: 'It's very natural.' Being naked, that was very natural too, although of course no one really thought so. They pretended it was natural. The bathroom was open territory, but when I turned thirteen, a lock appeared on the door, and I wasn't allowed to see my father in the nude any more, I could still see my mother, but not really. I wanted very much to enter my parents' bedroom, but had a clear feeling that it wasn't allowed.

— *Have you ever seen them fuck?*

— Yes, but then I was a bit older, about fifteen. It gave me a dreadful shock, I thought it was really foul, and I disapproved dreadfully — you don't do things like that. God, that's an old memory . . .

— *What did you see?*

— The three of us were on holiday, I slept with my mother in a double bed, and my father had a single bed. It was the middle of the night. I was asleep, or was thought to be asleep and they lay next to me under the covers, my father on top, panting a bit. I turned my back on them and went to sleep again. When I was little, my father sometimes stroked my mother's breasts under her pyjama top, when we were all together in the big bed on Sunday mornings.

– *How did your mother react?*

– Well, she pretended nothing was happening. I think I would find it difficult too, to get into it if there were children around. I would feel a bit uncomfortable.

– *I take it from what you say that you've never made love to more than one person.*

– As a matter of fact, I have. A whole group of us women often get together on a weekend, just to cuddle each other, just to huddle together and cuddle. Not to make love and such things, just lovely caresses. And I once made love and had orgasms with three people. That was when I was married, together with my husband and another woman. Then the two of them fucked, and I held them both with a feeling like, 'Go ahead, so I don't have to.' I enjoyed it, but afterwards I did get jealous about it, thinking, my god . . .

– *How did that woman come into your marriage?*

– For a year we had a very intense, closed relationship, but after that we both decided that I should be more independent. My husband himself bought the first books published by women's liberationists. I had to learn how to fill in a giro, had to do things on my own, go out more with other people. He would do it too, and in our contact with other people we were no longer supposed to say: 'So far and no further and we stop at lovemaking.' We decided it should be possible and we then began to experiment with it. We both had other relationships, lived completely independently, had our own income and kept to no single official marriage rule. That was why we divorced after four years, but still lived together for two years after that. There were still lots of nice things to do together – cycling, listening to music, being good friends. We still made love to each other too.

– *Did you enjoy that?*

– No. I can clearly remember the pressure of, I must do my best to enjoy it. I even went to therapy about it.

– *What wasn't good about it?*

– The most concrete complaint was that I couldn't orgasm with him.

– *How did you know that you couldn't?*

– Because it was easy to give myself an orgasm. I had been able to from when I was twelve. I used to do it at night in bed by moving the pillows between my legs. Later I did it with my hand, but no way could I make it clear to my husband what I needed. It was always a very tense situation in which I said: 'You must be more gentle', and then he said: 'I am gentle.' Instead of saying: 'Oh stop the damn thing', I just felt terribly guilty because I didn't enjoy it, because that was so sad and horrible for him. He was also desperate because I couldn't come at all. We once went to a therapist, a woman, and she said: 'Now, now, you'll learn, you **133** put your finger on the clitoris and move it very carefully with a loose wrist.' But that didn't help either.

— *You didn't really expect that you would come from fucking?*

— Oh no, but I didn't like fucking either, it was always a disaster. I can get quite wet but not that quickly — but we'd start anyway, and it was always painful. The way in which it happened was awful too, like, that thing has to go in, go on, push. It never came about from being comfortable or safe, but always with this tense feeling of, now, let's have another try.

— *Did you never try to stimulate yourself in your husband's presence?*

— No, I never thought of that. I did it on my own, and he knew about it. That was first class.

— *How many times did you do it in a week?*

— I don't know exactly, it varied, sometimes not for weeks, then three times a day. It's still like that now. I used to see making love to myself as something that you do because you are melancholy or alone, but now I make a party of it — I shower beforehand, light candles, have a delicious meal with myself first, put on beautiful music and make everything the way I really like it or find exciting.

— *Do you have different ways of masturbating?*

— Not really. I like my hand best and occasionally I enjoy putting something into my vagina, a pencil or a vegetable, or a plastic bottle. I enjoy that very much and walk round at the chemists to see what has a nice shape.

— *So can you orgasm without touching your clitoris?*

— Oh no, I just like the feeling. Especially sliding it in and then out again, that excites me a lot.

— *Do you do that when you make love to a woman as well?*

— No, then we only do it with our fingers.

— *When was the first time you made love to a woman?*

— I had my first woman friend when I had been married for two years. I had a good time with her, just spontaneous lovemaking, and I used to come with her too.

— *Did you find it difficult to touch a woman's body the first time?*

— Oh no! Not for one moment! It went very easily. We had gone out together quite a lot and walked together. I didn't know she was a lesbian, she hadn't told me. And at one point we were in her room, and we looked at each other, and then suddenly it dawned on me that I was terribly in love. I saw it and felt it suddenly, the beautiful big blue eyes — and we fell into each other's arms. I still remember it, we kissed each other thoroughly and then lay together on the bed and got totally wrapped up in each other, very lovingly and beautifully. It was also very sexual. The first time we kept our clothes on, and another day when we lay naked on the bed, I went on a voyage of discovery. I loved it, it was terrific. And I still remember that when I felt her cunt, I was surprised it was so soft and warm and wet.

— *You say that you did come with her.*

134 — Yes. The first time it happened because I felt her leg between my legs. I call it riding, the same as what I used to do with the pillow.

– *Did you tell your husband you had a girlfriend?*

– Yes. He thought it was all right.

– *Wasn't he jealous?*

– Oh yes, he wasn't jealous of men, but he was of her. It scared him. But the relationship broke up after six weeks. Apparently I couldn't take the lesbianism. I was capable of loving a woman, but she lived very openly as a lesbian, and once she took me to a women's bar. The women who go there are pretty hard and quite stereotyped; they have absolutely nothing to do with feminism. For example, there were butch women and dolly girls – the one with a collar and tie, the other with a little dress, and the one kissed the other in the corner, and all that narrow sexist behaviour. My girlfriend also became someone completely different from my nice girlfriend who usually wore tight jeans and a plastic jacket. She was wearing a beautiful suede suit with a long skirt and high lace up boots, and she suddenly carried herself like a woman of the world. It seems as if the social side really scared me off. As soon as I thought of the word 'lesbian', I began to ask myself whether I was doing the right thing, whether I shouldn't conform to certain demands. I only did what I enjoyed, I didn't know the rules of the game. Later on I noticed when I had girlfriends who weren't feminists, that lesbians behave just like hetero people. For example the slogan: 'She's good in bed', or the rule of: 'I must give the other person an orgasm', instead of an orgasm being something you give yourself. The times when I made love to women who tried that, I thought, hello, you can try what you like, but I won't do it. Then I say: 'No, please stop.'

– *What is it they're trying to do then?*

– To excite me and make me come, without me feeling cosy or comfortable. Real goal-oriented lovemaking, because that's the code – first you kiss, then stroke, and then you have to have an orgasm, while I think first you make sure everyone is comfortable and giggle a bit or eat sandwiches or just lie together or whatever, discover each other's bodies, see how they look. This week I stayed over with a friend, it was wonderful. We stood together for a long time in front of the mirror and looked at each other. When I stand I have a big bulge in my back, here, and we spent ages looking to see how it was with her and with me, and then we looked who had the roundest belly, lovely, standing with our bellies against each other. She had all these lines running downwards from her neck, and I didn't have them, I had small lines, here. Oh, it was such fun. Very warm. It is such a secure feeling. And what I really like is to lie in the morning completely naked against each other. Look, caress shoulders or backs, you can always do that, but I like it best to lie flat against each other. Oh, I love that. At this moment I have a great need for it, to feel my whole body touched, snug and busy with each other's bodies.

— *Do you make love with that woman as well?*
— No, never. I make love to myself, I don't need that so much.
— *After your first girlfriend, did you only make love to women?*
— Oh no. After that I didn't make love to women for years. Only with my husband and two more men. I did ask myself regularly whether I wasn't a lesbian, though. And I continued to judge that by the fact that I could have an orgasm with her and not with men. I never came across anyone who I could identify with. I only knew characters in books, who mostly turned out badly, a sort of Radclyffe Hall association of *Wells of Loneliness*. And I had a reasonably happy life, and you don't exchange that for something so difficult. It was only after I joined a consciousness raising group and found recognition, that I could grow. In this group, making love to a woman was regarded as a discovery, something you could find out for yourself, something pleasurable. In the meantime I often fell in love with women, but didn't do anything about it, and during our women-only study week, I was actually in love with each and all of them, all week, until on the Thursday night my eyes fell on a rather quiet woman, with very big blue eyes, and then I thought, no, I'm not in love with everyone, I'm in love with her. Something came over me like, now or never, something must happen now, I'll do something, wham. I stood next to her at the bar, my arm against her arm, I thought this was very daring, and I thought, I can't think of anything better, but when her glass is empty, I'll say: 'Let me get you a drink', and then we'll have made a start. And I tried to see whether her glass was empty, and then she ordered her own beer, and I just managed to say: 'That's on me.' She looked at me and laughed and said: 'Thank you.' After that I didn't move from her side. I just always sat next to her. One time we all lay in a circle on the ground, talking, and I thought, oh, I want to be next to her, I want to be next to her, I don't care, I'll just do it — and then I walked round and lay next to her. I stroked her hair a bit, she liked that, and then she began to stroke me too. Then I began to kiss her, she liked that too, and then we began to get into it. But she didn't like that, in such a big group, so we went to the passage and we had hardly taken three steps when we fell into each other's arms and stood for a long time looking into each other's eyes and kissing and caressing. Gradually everyone went off to bed and, thinking it all splendid, gave us a hug in passing, wishing us 'Goodnight . . .' I thought, something has to happen now, so I said: 'I want to sleep with you.' I thought I did very well, just saying what I wanted. Well, she wanted it too, and we pulled our mattresses together, and she took off all her clothes and went to bed. That was a shock for me, like, oh god, I've got to do the same. But we caressed and cuddled a bit, and it was lovely, I don't know how sexual it was, a bit perhaps. We were very much in love and enjoying being physical. The lovemaking was a bit awkward, but we sorted it out fine, it was all great fun.

136 — *How did you express your love?*

— By taking her into my arms and looking at her and showing her with my eyes the feeling I had inside me, showing her with my hands, my body. Very direct contact. When I got home again, I thought, now this is just another, additional relationship, but after only two days I began to understand why I was never happy with my husband and I wanted things to change, and I thought, I can still try to change thousands of things, but there will always be *one* thing that is missing. I just don't like it. So I made a number of decisions very fast, and within three weeks I had left and moved to a room of my own. That was four years ago, when I was twenty-five. It seems as if those four years have been my whole life. My relationship with her lasted a year.

After two months she called if off because she couldn't stand me being so mad and crazy about her, but then I collapsed completely and cried for three days. I thought, this can't happen, and went to her, and then we were together for another year, although with ups and downs. She wanted to be more independent.

— *Could you make love together satisfactorily?*

— Yes. I was certainly satisfied with the relationship as far as sex was concerned, it was wonderful. She was scared to experiment, and so it always went the same way. We would lie next to each other, half on our sides, and then she stroked my clitoris with her hand and at the same time I stroked hers.

— *And did you come in this way?*

— I did, but she didn't. She found it impossible to, even on her own.

— *Did you mind that?*

— No, maybe I was sorry for *her*, because it was so apparently a problem for her. She was ashamed of it, but on the other hand we also had something like, let's do what we enjoy. She had a lot of hang-ups, because I wanted to look and lick as well, but she didn't want to. When that relationship was over, I was, for the first time in my life, completely alone and without a permanent relationship. I had a madly difficult time, but when I had finally overcome all the fear, I began to enjoy being alone very much. I went out alone, along to Lesbian Line parties. I'd make myself look beautiful and then go out. I tried everything, no bad things, you know, but just a feeling of this is me, I'm beautiful and strong, and I can do what I like. If I meet someone tonight who is fun and exciting, then I'll say so. So whenever I saw a nice woman, I went up to her and said: 'I want to talk to you.' And if it was someone very special, I also said: 'I want to sleep with you . . .'

— *Was that just sleeping, or also sexual?*

— I really don't like the rules which say: 'If you sleep with each other, you must also make love.' I like to follow my own feelings and then see what happens. I've had very pleasant experiences from doing that. Sometimes it does get very sexual and exciting, and other times we cuddle cosily together and caress each other until we get drowsy and fall asleep. The next morning we'd have breakfast all comfortable and snug.

– *Have you ever been refused?*

– Not often. I think I can judge whether I have a chance or not.

– *When you make love to a woman, what do you do first, look or touch?*

– No, I haven't been very keen on looking, but I am beginning to be. I learned that from another woman friend, who does do that. She said 'Now I want to have a look first, let me see!' And then she'd extensively examine my cunt.

– *How did you like that?*

– I still have this feeling of, well . . . ugh . . . you could say that slightly more politely or subtly, but she just came right out with it and experimented and found out how I fit together. Mine is behind a curtain, as we call it, and that was unusual to her. It was lovely, she put her fingers behind the hood, *on* the clitoris, and moved it just a little bit. I came straight away. She actually helped me over a threshold, because I like that now too: yes, why not, looking and being curious as to how it looks exactly. It's just lovely, just kind of nosing around.

– *Do you feel aroused if someone looks at your cunt?*

– Oh no. When I do it, it's just out of curiosity too – and I often don't find it all that beautiful.

– *Do you think your own cunt is beautiful?*

– What shall I say . . . OK I guess, but a bit messy with all those folds. I like drawings of cunts, but real cunts, no, I don't easily find them beautiful. Nice though, nice to feel and to smell and to suck. The first time I didn't think it tasted so good, a little salty, and when I'd got over that, I also found a lot of pleasure in what I could do. My last girlfriend loved it, she could surrender herself completely and for a long time. She also found it easy to control her orgasm and hold back. I can't actually put it off, with me it goes in a very friendly and comfortable way – I become excited, go quite quickly to the top and come, and that's nice and always different, and then I sigh, hmmm, and then it's over, and I don't want to be touched there any more. Very simple, but not so that my whole body opens up.

– *How long did your relationship last?*

– Over two years, it's just finished and I am very sad about it.

– *Did she like licking you?*

– Yes, but at first I didn't like it so much, a bit embarrassing. I felt something like, yes, that is my territory, you shouldn't just go there and lick . . . But you must open yourself up, and give yourself, don't you think? I'm getting better at it all the time now.

– *Did you both have a really good wash before you got started? Did you feel you had to wash before you could let her do it?*

– She didn't give a damn whether I had washed myself or not, but I did mind with her. If I said: 'Hmm, you don't smell so good, have a wash first please', she'd either say: 'Oh well, don't bother then', or she'd run off to wash herself.

– *How did you reconcile your different needs?*

138 – She'd make love to herself then, and I'd just hold her a bit. She often felt like making love to herself. Or she did it alone. And if I felt like it, I began to pet her, I loved that, cuddling up against her, giving her kisses, stroking soft places, we had a very easy-going time together.

— *Did it ever happen that she would come but then didn't want to continue making love so that you could have an orgasm too?*

— Certainly not with her, or I would have said: 'Now me too, now me!' We could say everything to each other, ask about everything. No, it's more that we had problems with the equality syndrome. It hardly ever happened that we didn't both come in turn, because of this sort of norm: 'Both should be able to get an orgasm.'

— *Yes, that is more a burden than a pleasure. Did you like looking at her when you made love?*

— Looking is very important to me, I enjoy it very much. If I stroke, I look where I am stroking. If I kiss, I look where I am kissing. In the beginning I didn't dare look very carefully. She had a very big clitoris and very firm outer lips from which the rest protruded a bit, and I thought it a bit crude. I was also scared this cunt would rule me, perhaps I'd even disappear inside it. I always had the feeling she became much more passionate than I did. At least I have the idea of myself that I'm not passionate enough. I do become passionate though, through someone else's excitement — for example, when they make sounds or panting in my ear, and if I hear breathing. I always fantasise about lust, about being so passionate that you can't stop coming and being lustful again and coming again . . .

— *Do you fantasise that with women?*

— Yes, but recently I've fantasised again about men. I do that because we've just broken up, and if I make love to myself, I immediately think about my girlfriend of course, and then I lie awake crying. If I fantasise about men it's easier.

— *You didn't live together?*

— No, but we slept with each other four or five nights a week, and also spent the weekends together. I fell in love with her while I was still with another girlfriend. Then I had two relationships at the same time, but the other girlfriend couldn't cope with that at all and split. Then I went to Femø, the holiday island, and had a girlfriend there . . .

— *Another one?*

— Yes, a holiday romance. I spent four very intense days with her. We slept on the beach, talked, danced and made love, I just loved it. Now, that hurt my girlfriend terribly, and caused her a lot of pain. When I saw how dreadful and difficult it was for her, we decided we should have no more relationships with other people. We kept to that for a year and a half, although I did once break our arrangement and made love to another woman.

— *Were you in love with that woman?*

— No. I was never in love with her. I am still very good friends with her, and we still make love to each other.

139

– *Did you tell your girlfriend?*

– Yes. I had to tell her, out of a kind of honesty. I couldn't keep it quiet.

– *If it wasn't important for you and you knew your girlfriend didn't want you to and couldn't cope with it, why did you do it then?*

– Well, why do you make love to someone? Because you go out with them and you feel close. Very simple.

– *Why do you laugh?*

– Because it seems so crazy to me: everything is allowed, you can have woman friends, you can cuddle, sleep together, but as soon as you make love, it becomes a problem. You draw the line at being erotic. I do so as well, I can't bear it either when a girlfriend of mine makes love to anyone else. I find it extremely disgusting.

– *If you know you can't stop yourself, why do you agree that it should be like that?*

– My ideas about that have been changing recently, because of all the pain I've been through. I would give up all my ideas about freedom, immediately, and would want her to do so as well, if only I could have a relationship with her again.

– *How did she react to that one-off affair?*

– At first she was angry and sad, but she calmed down when she saw I didn't love that woman, and we renewed the promise. But that got me into trouble with the other woman, who wouldn't accept it. She didn't see the sense in it, all that fuss about exclusive relationships. She has herself as centre. She has three open relationships all at the same time, all equally important and she still also makes love to anyone she likes. She can do that, and if I had the choice I'd try to as well, when I'm a bit less mournful. I have become much too afraid of pain, and yet I really do want to find one love with whom I can be completely one. What I clearly miss is a very intense and inward-looking relationship which opens out after a while. Because after a while I did want the freedom and said: 'I won't wait until you can bear it, I want it now.' I felt stifled. I couldn't really grow.

– *What was it that you didn't get from her?*

– Fun. An evening just stroking each other, looking at each other's bodies, tracing the lines on our bodies, being happy with each other's knees, or the hollows under our arms – that kind of fun. As soon as she began to caress me, she got so passionate, and then we would make love very happily, but afterwards there was no more cuddling.

– *Do you expect to get everything you need from one person?*

– Well, secretly I do, of course, although I know it isn't possible. She really showed me that she loved me a great deal – she made that cupboard for me, she made my bed, the table, but I still want the fun as well. It's just a cupboard, I can't do anything with it. I did try to accept what there was, and not always think about what else I wanted. But I don't want to fence myself in, and

later on my girlfriend also agreed and said: 'It isn't right not to do something because the other doesn't want you to. You must decide for yourself what you want to do.' And then she fell in love with somebody else herself, very soon after that. At first I more or less encouraged her, saying: 'Look at that, isn't it great she's doing her own thing.' But afterwards I got terribly jealous, especially because she was very much in love and made love very passionately.

— *How do you know?*

— She told me.

— *God, what misery! Did you want to hear about it?*

— Yes and no. On the one hand I wanted to know everything down to the gory details. On the other hand, of course, I didn't want to hear at all.

— *I recognise that. I also want to know, but when I hear it, I just go to pieces. And then I just can't forget the images. I keep seeing them in front of me like on a film. You too?*

— Yes, I began a kind of competition in lovemaking, like, I'll show you. I can do it like that too.

— *Did you try harder than before?*

— I began to make love more often. But it wasn't at all pleasant, more like, look at this, that's one nil, that's two nil. I kept on asking her: 'Have you done this with her too, do you like her body better, is she more passionate than I . . .?'

— *I always become terrible if I'm jealous.*

— Me too. Then I get hideously angry. And scared, crazily scared. I was also scared she would give to the other woman everything she hadn't given to me. I let my anger have free rein, and in my fantasies I want to do everything: go to them and separate them, or start screaming at them, or bang their heads together against the wall, or lie between them saying: 'Piss off you two', or make love to the other one.

— *Yes, that's a good one, to make your girlfriend jealous. Did you know the other woman?*

— I've spoken to her once and my girlfriend was terrified because she was scared I'd tell the woman all kinds of things she was ashamed of. But I didn't think of it, why should I?

— *Oh, revenge.*

— Oh yes. Yes, it could be that, but I'm a bit too polite for that.

— *I wouldn't dare either, but I do fantasise that I take terrible revenge. I curse my partner and the other one, an accident, something really horrible – quarrels and sickness and death.*

— Yes, I do that too. Let them suffer for it.

— *And what do you do in reality? Do you make a dreadful scene?*

— Yes, terrible, screaming and hitting the couch: 'Goddammit, you dirty whore . . .', it comes right out of my toes!

— *How did she react to your rage?*

— She could easily imagine how I felt and said: 'Let it all hang out, I hope you live through it, grow out of it and that we can go on together again.' She comforted me too.

– *Up till now a relationship with a woman hasn't been easier for you than a relationship with a man?*

– No. I also always fought for tenderness with them. I believe that relationships with women are much more painful than with men, for me at any rate, because it's all so close and so recognisable. But making love was much better with women. With her I wasn't troubled by that peculiar sense of duty and felt less inhibited or forced.

– *What do you miss most, now that it is over?*

– The familiar feeling of having someone close to me, someone who is there to look forward to, to live for, to ring up afterwards, to say goodnight to, or good morning, and with whom you spend Christmas. I really could not bear it any more that she had someone else and there was steadily less for me. At the end she slept with me only twice a week. When she saw me crying and hurt she was completely open and said that she loved me very much and that she liked me and she would never let me go because I was much too important to her. But the day after she said that, she turned everything around. She really loved me out of guilt, and naturally that drove me crazy. I saw that nothing made sense any more, and in a flash I listened to myself, until I could say: 'No, it doesn't work any more, this must end.' We could only have carried on with each other if she had made it very secure for me and stopped seeing the other woman, but she didn't want that. She didn't want to make any concessions, but she didn't want to lose me either. I should try, she said, I should take what was still good, which was still a lot, she wanted to remain friends with me always.

– *Is the pain of break-up easier to endure than the pain of carrying on?*

– I can't compare it, but I know that carrying on was very bad for me. What I would like to achieve is a kind of loving . . . yes, without possessing the other.

– *Not loving out of need, but out of self-knowledge, knowing who you are and where you are vulnerable, so that you can keep your self-respect, independently of what someone else thinks of you or feels for you. I'd love to reach that, but I'm very far from it. It's not possession, although naturally, you are dependent on each other, if you lay yourself open, if you allow yourself to be vulnerable – you can't love without expecting pain.*

– I think that secretly I still want to look if there isn't a way to achieve it after all!

– *Did you ever think of having children?*

– Oh yes, I have fantasised that we both had a child. To be pregnant together seemed to me such an amazing idea, the bellies against each other . . . I am very conscious that you need to create quite a few favourable conditions, otherwise you shouldn't begin it.

142 – *How did you imagine becoming pregnant? Through artificial* *insemination, or by going to bed with a man?*

— Well, I personally always think about insemination. Perhaps you can ask a friendly man to give sperm, and then spoon it in together with a girlfriend. I often look at men in that light, you know.

— *Do you think a man would do it? A child of his walking around in this world?*

— I've no idea. If you know what you want and ask openly and honestly, why not? The best thing, it seems to me, would be a man who would like to have some connection with the child, without you bringing it up together – a kind of nice uncle to whom it goes now and then for the weekend.

— *How did your parents actually react to your relationships with women?*

— That developed very gradually. I always talked to my mother who then discussed it with my father. She asked me about everything, for example, whether women really could have satisfactory sexual relations with each other. Then I explained to her why it could indeed be very good, that you could make orgasms by yourself, so you can also make orgasms together, because making love isn't just fucking. But I think for her that's exactly the point: she had never enjoyed it. I explained to her that you have a right to your own sexuality. Women are mostly not expected to have their own sexuality, we're only supposed to have it in combination with a man, while fucking. So they ask us: 'What could a woman possibly do alone, or with another woman?' People always think like that. And that is a serious denial of my sexuality as an individual and so also of sexuality among women. In the house where I rented my first room, the rule was that gentlemen visitors had to be out by eleven o'clock, but my girlfriend could stay the whole weekend. That is an absurd piece of denial, and we made use of it gratefully, but it is the purest form of oppression: total denial. It just doesn't exist. If I don't say out loud: 'I am a lesbian', or 'I love women', then I'm not regarded as one, but am automatically categorised as 'normal', heterosexual and it is assumed that I do something with a man. If I walk hand in hand with a woman, people shout after us, things like: 'Aren't you getting enough', or 'Dirty lessies!'

— *Do women do that too?*

— No, women don't shout after us, but teenage boys and men do. Men look at you too. I am stared at as if I came from another planet. That gives you the feeling you are something different, and that's what I am in this society. I'm like an outlaw, and that's why I want the difference to be visible, and why I want support for the pain. I hardly ever walk hand in hand, because I want to avoid nasty situations – I know women who have been beaten to bits, or who've been given a black eye. The anxiety is always with me – where can I be myself? . . . I can't risk going *too* far, but I do work very hard to be myself in all aspects of my life – my family, my neighbours, my street, my work, and that's a whole lot of **143** people. My mother is really learning to accept it. She has even asked herself if she has the same feelings for women, and last time she asked me if there were women who were lesbian without knowing it. I said that it was quite possible because you get so little opportunity to discover this for yourself, because you never see it around you to identify with, and so you hardly ever come across it. Now that she has me as an example, she is analysing herself. The funny thing is that I now give *her* instruction about how lovemaking feels, and the whole bit that I never got from her. She also has got rid of her guilt feelings to a large extent, because I say: 'What? Guilt feelings about dad, because you never enjoyed it? It's a bloody scandal that you never had any pleasure all your life long! That's what it's for!' You know, she had never looked at it that way. I can still see us standing together in the passage. She told me her own story, and why she thought she had never enjoyed it. When she was thirteen, she was raped by the headmaster of the school, many times. It's horrific. Making love was for her a sad business. Oh god, I can remember so well the sound of my mother in her slippers walking to the bathroom. She had made love and was going to wash herself in the bathroom. And I remember the sound of the slif slof along the passageway, and then the taps running, and then slif slof back, I don't know of a more tragic sound.

IX. In between women and men: bisexuality

Most of the time we assume that we are heterosexual. That one can also be homosexual is something that has to be discovered. And some of us notice that we are attracted both to women and to men. A surprise. And sometimes confusing. We are probably born bisexual, and only later do we land up in a set pattern. For some of us the pattern never becomes fixed, and it depends on the circumstances and a person to whom we feel attracted, not on her or his sex.

'When, after many boyfriends, I had a sexual relationship with a woman, I thought, this is it, so I'm a lesbian. I didn't mind, I was already in the women's movement and noticed that I was gradually growing close to women. So I thought that it was logical that my sexual feelings would follow. After all, if you put so much energy into relationships with women, it's so much better not having to step abruptly out of that to have sex with someone of the other kind. But perhaps precisely because I was no longer so preoccupied with men, I had a very relaxed relationship with a man who belonged to a political group I was in. We could talk about everything. He agreed with a lot of feminist ideas that mattered to me too. We could also talk very easily about relationships and so on, and then I discovered that I fancied him when we met somewhere at a party. That was a surprise, because I had made up my mind that one was either lesbian or straight. I found it confusing, but also liberating: the perspective of a future, in which I had the chance to get involved both with lovely women who were in transition and with the few really nice men who were also busy changing.'

'For fifteen years I've been having a very peaceful relationship with a man. We've got three children. During the past year I've

also had a very special relationship with a woman. When at one time she was having a lot of anxiety over a difficult relationship, we began to see more of each other. She stayed the night with me. I slept at her place. We made love. It was very tender, very precious to me. The strange thing is that the man with whom I live didn't feel threatened by it, and that's saying something about the strength of our relationship. We continued seeing each other, the woman and I, but it became increasingly difficult. She was on her own. I had a husband and three children with whom I was happy. Even so, that wasn't the main difficulty – it was the different needs. Eventually we broke up. It did rather hurt me, and for months we couldn't bear to see each other. She has had other relationships with women since. I'm glad about it, as if a part of me is going on. I know now that I can love both a woman and a man. But my relationship with my husband is important to me, I have no reason to break it off.'

Sometimes it's difficult to say to onseself: 'I am a bisexual.' One doesn't always have a relationship with a woman and a man at the same time, and when we are very much in love we tend to think that this is going to be really it. Often we didn't even know that such things were possible.
You don't always have an easy time, being a bisexual woman. Sometimes it's very confusing, and almost by definition you don't know where you belong. You get strange looks from the straight world: why want another woman, if you could also have a man? Some men think it is marvellous and exciting, but in a rather unpleasant way. The idea behind it is often that you are still available for him, that a relationship with another woman represents no real competition. It's also typically male for sexist men to get turned on by fantasising over images of women making love to one another – as long as they can still get in between, literally. We don't want that kind of 'approval', and many bisexual women certainly don't want to be approved of merely because they haven't yet identified themselves with 'the other camp', and so have left the male ego still intact. For this reason, many bisexual women call themselves lesbian. On the other hand, lesbian groups are suspicious of women who haven't 'yet' cut all ties with men. There are enough reasons for that suspicion. A number of lesbians have real bruises from women who didn't want to choose.

'She was married, this woman who fell in love with me. At first I didn't dare because I had had quite enough nasty experiences with married women who thought it fun to flirt with me, experimenting without running any risks. I was beginning to feel rather used. But she was very serious and also understood how difficult it was for me. The tug-of-war lasted for a year and a half, her husband on one side, me on the other. At first it didn't seem so difficult; he didn't feel particularly threatened. I think he hardly took it seriously, he would have minded a lot more if 147

she'd had a boyfriend. But when she started not only staying the night with me every now and then, but also wanting to go on holiday with me, he became very aggressive and threatened to leave. That seemed to me an excellent solution, but she was very upset. In the end I broke off the relationship because I couldn't stand the nightly scenes any longer – the guy who phoned in the middle of the night or stood crying on my doorstep. I still don't know whether she stayed with him in the end because she was married to him and didn't have the guts to take the step, or because she was really fond of the guy.'

It does sometimes happen that women hide behind the label 'bisexual' in order not to have to come out as a lesbian, for fear that they will definitely have to leave their old world. After all, you do have to give up a measure of approval. But it also possible to see bisexuality as a positive choice, an advance towards a future in which we won't have to choose a label, because a choice for the one or for the other won't carry so much weight any more.

'Now and then I do get a feeling of being caught between the devil and the deep blue sea. I call myself a lesbian because I love women. But there are women in lesbian groups who think that I have no right to do so because I do have the odd relationship with a man. Then again, if I don't say I am a lesbian, it looks as if I want to hide it, or that I am letting the other women down. In my view it would be dishonest to deny the one or the other. If I choose, I'll be denying a part of myself. Perhaps it is too idealistic to think it possible to choose for women and at the same time not to deny what I have with some men. I'd better shut up.'

X. Women and men

Women and men experience sexuality very differently. You just have to look at the way advertising uses images of easy-to-get sex to entice men into buying things, while women are fed images of true happiness and eternal romance. Or look at the books people read: magazines for men are full of nudes – female nudes of course. Magazines for women focus on relationships, emotions, love. The ways in which women and men experience the world are wide apart. Perhaps that wouldn't be such a problem if we didn't live in a society where the bond between women and men is meant to be the most important of all. We are expected to spend most of our lives with a man. This relationship is supposed to be so important that we'll give up our woman friends, mothers and workmates for it. We ourselves usually seem to assume that all our needs, and especially our sexual needs, will be satisfied by this one relationship. Usually we aren't very conscious of this, but we are brought up with the idea that women and men are different, but in some miraculous way complementary – if only we can find Mr Right. If Mr Right turns out to be Wrong, we say it can't have been true love, it should have been someone else. Or we blame ourselves.

Once women start talking honestly to each other, it becomes clear again and again that the misunderstandings between women and men aren't just chance, aren't just individual 'problems' and can't just be put down to the wrong choice of partner. Women's experiences with men are so similar that it becomes obvious that we're talking about specific patterns.

'If John comes home late from a meeting, he just flops down on the bed, drinks a couple of beers one after the other and talks excitedly about everything that happened. He feels very happy so he wants to make love. I often get the feeling he hardly sees me, that it doesn't much matter how I'm feeling and that he could just as well fuck with some other woman.'

'My boyfriend says he doesn't mind if I don't feel like making love, but he has lots of little ways of letting me know how hard done by he feels. Picks fights over nothing. Sulks behind his paper, leaves his clothes lying around for me to pick up. That's when I start feeling guilty. I try to be extra nice to him, cook something special or pour him a drink. But that looks like an invitation, so in the end we make love anyway.'

'If we're having a row, I can't go to bed with him. I have to feel we're in touch with one another before I can feel turned on. But for him it's just the other way round. He wants to go to bed with me to make up. We just can't agree on that. I say I want to talk **149**

things over first before making love with him. He says it doesn't help to talk, says he feels closer to me if we make love first.'

'Really I think it's true for most men, only one sort of relationship is possible with them: a sexual relationship. Between sex and nothing there's nothing.'

'Once in a while he has an affair. He says it doesn't affect our relationship, and that it would be good if I had an affair occasionally too . . . But I never feel like it, I don't like casual sex. And I don't believe he should take it so lightly. I think he says it because he's not worried – he doesn't think I'd really do it. And why fuck with someone else just to prove a point . . .'

Though men aren't all the same, any more than women are, sexuality does have a different place in men's lives than it has in women's. For women, sexuality tends to be a means to an end, a good way to be with someone, a way to communicate. For men, it's more likely to be an end in itself. If you were to exaggerate a bit, turn it into a caricature, you could say that women are interested in men and as a result of that are interested in sex, while men are interested in sex and as a result of that, in women. We tend to assume it's natural for women and men to be like this; the animal world is often used as 'proof' that naturally men are hunters out to conquer their prey, and naturally women are mothers, much more into caring. There are enough variations in the animal world to prove almost any point, but *one* thing is clear: it's quite unheard of in the animal world for females to mate against their will. Rape is a typically human phenomenon.

1.   The problem of heterosexuality

I wonder if I should get a job??

From the moment we are born, women are given a different vision of the future from men. We are expected to become mothers, to find our life's fulfilment in marriage. We are supposed to give up gladly any ambitions for a career when we meet the prince on his white horse. Men are expected to marry and have children, but they will have to work hard at a career in order to support wife and children. From an early age we are taught to cultivate the qualities which will fit our future image: boys are encouraged to be clever, because later they will have to compete for the best places in the labour market. Girls, on the other hand, are encouraged to sacrifice their own interests and needs, because later on they will have to look after other people. By the time we are grown up, the patterns are fixed. We don't experience them as patterns which have been imposed on us, but as a natural part of our characters. And we don't need to be told any more that as women we shouldn't be ambitious. We actually feel guilty if our work starts taking on more importance than a relationship. We worry about being 'unfeminine' if we are assertive. Women are taught to nurture, men to be breadwinners. **151**

This happens to all of us, even if we don't marry and don't have children. Even in an 'open' relationship, you can usually see that the woman takes more responsibility for the emotional side, that she is blamed if things aren't going well, and that it is she who takes the intitiative in doing something about it.

'If he behaves badly, then it's me who appoaches him and makes sure that we talk about it. But if he is annoyed about something, then it's still me who goes to him to draw him out of his shell so that we can work it out. Sometimes it takes hours before he'll admit there's something wrong. If I don't ask, he'll walk around the house in a sulk for days with a steely face. I can't bear it, I can't sleep because of it. He can, it seems. It's easier for him to put it aside. So it seems as if it's almost always my problems we're having to sort out.'

Our conditioning makes it difficult for us to change these patterns. But they're also firmly rooted in society. The choices we are faced with make it very difficult for us to change the conditions of our lives. We may choose to put our energy into a relationship, with a partner or with children. In our society that almost automatically means that we become housewives. Not only will we take care of the emotional side of the relationship, but we are also lumbered with washing our beloved's socks and taking the lion's share of caring for any children we may end up having. Being a woman you can also put your energy into building a career. You can get trained in some job and try to build an independent life, despite all the prejudices against 'career women'. Then you will come up against a society where many jobs are closed to women. And even within a profession, you still remain a housewife. As children we've all dreamed of becoming pilots, just like our little brothers, but by puberty most of us have settled for a more realistic wish – we want to be a stewardess.

Unlike most men, if you are a woman with a career, you have no woman behind you to look after you. Having children is almost out of the question. Like many women nowadays you can try to combine the two worlds of career and family. This means a double burden, with guilt feelings all round. Sometimes it's possible to divide the work so that your husband or lover takes on a part of the domestic responsibility. You're most likely to be able to do that if you're both in part-time jobs which pay enough to live on, and there aren't too many of those around. And you still have to find a man who is willing to share. However much men proclaim that they don't understand why women make such a fuss about housework which is really such a nice job, it still takes about as much energy to get men to do housework as it does to do it yourself. We're still waiting for the first action groups of men organising for the right to be a house 'wife' – they aren't that keen. Even 'progressive' union leaders who're concerned about 'labour' don't think it strange to leave 'domestic labour' to

women. The only men who really understand what it's like to be totally responsible for children and housekeeping are those who've been forced to do it, if their wife has been ill for a while, for instance, or divorced fathers.

'Luckily we both have the kind of elite jobs where you can work part-time and still manage on the money. And we deliberately didn't have children until we were both established in our jobs, because it's so difficult to get ahead at work once you have children. We each do the same amount of childcare and housework, or at least we try to. But it's still not really easy, you know. I feel fine about my work. But he's aware that his old friends, who don't work part-time and who have wives at home to do the housework for them, are getting promoted and leaving him behind. It bothers him, though he wouldn't really want to compete. And then, I often go out with women friends and do all kinds of things outside the home, while he does less. So sometimes there is quite an atmosphere in the house. Of course it's me who takes the initiative in talking about it. It turns out that he feels that I make him take more responsibility for the children and that I go out too easily without taking him into consideration. But when we really look at how much time he spends with the children and how much I do, it's about the same. Just as I'm getting the feeling that everything is now equal, he starts thinking too much is being demanded of him. Recently he's got very interested in a younger woman at work. Our agreement is that we both have our own friends. But I'm uneasy at the moment. I get the feeling she's much more attractive than me and he doesn't have to argue with her about who'll fetch the children from school and whose fault it is that the cats haven't been fed. She thinks he's fantastic and admires him because of his work. Now and then I wonder whether he really wants me as an equal, or whether he'd rather have an old-fashioned girl like her, who makes him feel like a big man.'

Men don't have an easy time either. It's a heavy responsibility for a woman to make sure that everyone around her is healthy, satisfied and happy, without entirely forgetting about her own needs, but men also feel they have a big responsibility to bring home enough money so that everyone can live well. This means they're under a lot of pressure to succeed. Most jobs really aren't very pleasant – would most men stay in their jobs if they didn't have to for the money? Would they work so hard if they didn't have to? Women and men have both been pressed into moulds. But it is still true that being a man has certain social advantages that men don't want to give up. If we break the moulds, men have more to lose than women. Men get power from the fact that they earn the money, or at least earn more money than we do. And men can take out their frustrations on women.

It's because their life patterns are so different that women and men experience sexuality so differently. A woman's task is to look after her man, and that doesn't just apply to married **153**

women. It crops up in very many different guises, and is just as true for single women. 'Caring' doesn't just cover material things like meals, a comfortable house, clean clothes – it also means looking after emotional needs. Housewives are often built-in social workers. We often don't experience that as work; we just think he's upset about something, he doesn't feel well. We feel responsible and try to do something about it. It would be nice to think that this sense of responsibility was mutual, but it rarely is. We are trained to notice that he doesn't look well before he actually says that he feels lousy. Because of our conditioning, we're more prone to feel guilty. On the whole we feel more responsible for his needs than he does for ours.

One of those 'needs' is sex. That isn't written down on the marriage certificate, but we all know it. Without sex, a marriage isn't a 'true' marriage, and a relationship is 'only' a friendship. In the past, men used to act on the belief that sex was their right, and a woman used to believe it was a part of her duties. It isn't quite that bad any more, although research has shown that married women get very little pleasure from sex, while considering it normal that they should be fucked. Men still see sex as a reward for good behaviour, a way to relax, something to do in their time off. For many women, sex is on the same level as the other caring work we do to keep the relationship going: cooking a nice meal, showing understanding for his tiredness, and fucking because *he* needs it so much.

Sex isn't just something technical or romantic that happens under the sheets far removed from the rest of our relationships. It has everything to do with how the rest of our life looks. So it isn't only women and men who experience sex differently, but also people in different social positions, in different social classes. Women of all classes are worse off than men in terms of getting sexual pleasure. But all investigations show that people with less education, both women and men, seem to be worse off than those with more education. We used to have hardly any explanation for that, except for a vague idea that perhaps more 'educated' people were better informed. I don't think it has much to do with information. If you look at the woman-man relationship right across the classes, it's clear that he's expected to have power over her, to be superior to her, and that she is responsible for his needs. It's also clear that the more men are humiliated outside the home, the more they take it out on their wives, or at least expect them to provide compensation. Men with jobs that offer them a friendly surrounding and comradeship – jobs in which they aren't ordered around – might have less frustration to take out on their wives. But those jobs are scarce under the current economic system. It's possible that it's those men who derive the least self-confidence from what they do who are the ones who have the most 'need' to prove in their relationships with women that they are 'real men'. And a 'real' man in this society is someone who doesn't do women's work, who doesn't get 'sentimental', and who knows how to score sexually. From

naturally our female nature is unnatural !!

HOORAY

investigations we also know that sexual pleasure for women depends a lot on experiencing an equal relationship. On the feeling of sharing the same problems.

In relations where women are supposed to listen to men's problems, but men think it unmanly to be bothered with the details of a woman's life, there is little of the togetherness that makes for a good sexual relationship.

'We didn't mind much at first when he lost his job. "At last we've got time for all the things we didn't get round to", he said. But I noticed that it did trouble him and he felt a failure. For example, he used to make up excuses for not fetching the children from school. When I talked about it, it turned out that he felt uncomfortable waiting for the children amongst all the women. "The only men who stand there are unemployed", he said. "I don't want to belong with them." And I noticed that he got terribly randy and wanted to fuck all the time. It was as if he wanted to prove that he could still do something.'

As long as men take out on women the misery they experience in the world, and as long as sex is seen as another way of getting prestige, sexual relations between women and men will be problematic. And as long as men use women to jack up their manhood, they will of course prefer relationships with women where their superiority is built-in. It's no longer fashionable in most circles to say out loud that you would prefer a submissive woman, but it is still the case that men tend to choose women who are younger, smaller and 'inferior', and in pornography the objects are getting younger and younger. But fewer women now find the old-fashioned 'strong man' image attractive. Women are looking for men who don't think they're inferior or call them 'shrew' if they object to being trodden on. The 'market' for men who can only fuck when women are 'under' them is shrinking as fewer women accept being 'underneath'. This makes men aggressive, especially towards 'those women's libbers' who stir up 'ordinary' women.

Even men who think they aren't particularly guilty of taking advantage of women's oppression, still follow a pattern where they like *talking* to intelligent women, but are still a bit afraid of them and would rather fuck women who look up to them. Independent women may command respect, but can't necessarily expect love. So it often happens that women make themselves 'smaller' so that the man they like will find them sexually attractive. They don't give their own opinions too quickly for instance, but ask interestedly about his. Or try to seem just intelligent enough for him to have a 'good audience', but not more intelligent than that. They pretend helplessness with opening doors or getting into cars, although they're quite capable when they're alone. That might work for a while, because many men do fall for it, but it has its own revenge. In the end many women don't find it at all pleasant to repress themselves, make themselves seem stupid, and carry on acting 'the little wife' or being daddy's little girl long after they are grown up.

There are men who are making efforts to unlearn their old conditioning, just as women are trying. They are trying to see women as people. But sexual patterns are deeply ingrained and not so easy to change. It's hard when the whole social strucure is continually reinforcing the idea that men should be bosses, and that a man must be a doormat if he doesn't equate sex with power.

A woman can rule out most men as potential lovers if she can't stand being found attractive only by making herself 'smaller'. So it's all the more vital that we stop making our erotic needs dependent on the prince on the white horse.

Further reading

You will find out more about the power relations between women and men in political feminist books than in the average book about sex. *Dialectic of Sex* by Shulamith Firestone (Women's Press), a very influential feminist text, makes an analysis of those power relations, attacking the family and women's biological role as mother. Ingrid Bengis' *Combat in the Erogenous Zone* (Wildwood House) also set a lot of women thinking about 'the social barriers, the personal barriers, the desires and frustrations . . . that turn relations between men and women into a war zone'.

Books like *Of Woman Born* by Adrienne Rich (Virago) and *Gyn/Ecology* by Mary Daly (Women's Press) try to trace the history of women's oppression in patriarchy. Sheila Rowbotham's *Woman's Consciousness, Man's World* (Penguin) shows quite personally how it feels to be a woman in a man's world, placing that politically. We can also learn a lot about sex and power from Marge Piercy's novel *Small Changes* (Women's Press) and Marilyn French's *The Women's Room* (Sphere).

XI. Rape, and what it has to do with 'normal' sex

Almost every woman comes into contact with rape and battering at some point in her life. One in every two hundred women is thought to be raped every year in the Netherlands, or has to ward off an attempted rape. Those are the statistics only for that form of sexual violence usually defined as rape. There are many more situations where sex is forced on us, which don't fall under the legal definition of rape.

Battering is also much more widespread than we would like to believe. Wherever a Women's Aid refuge is set up, women and children stream in, and it is full up within a very short time. If you think how difficult it is for women to leave home, then it's clear that what we see is only the tip of the iceberg. At casualty departments in hospitals, it is an accepted fact that women who come to have a split lip sewn up or with a broken rib haven't just fallen down the stairs, but there is little publicity about this. Women who 'just' have a black eye would rather hide at home until it has worn off than go to the doctor.

We are all involved. Even if it is just because we hear the woman next door screaming and don't know what to do. Even if it is because we behave differently at night on the street if we are with a man than we would do if we were walking alone.

...and at night I keep a hammer in my back pocket as well

The popular image of rapists is that they are abnormal men, men who are disturbed. Another idea which goes with that one is that women who are raped have asked for it, or even get pleasure from it. When there is battering in a marriage, it is often taken for granted that the wife must have made him do it: perhaps she nagged him so much that he lost his self-control. Because of these ideas we see rape and battering as private problems which other people have – until they happen to us. Then we are made to feel guilty that we were so naive as to put ourselves in a situation where we might be raped. Or else the feeling of failure, that we weren't able to maintain a good relationship so he wouldn't feel this urge to smash everything, makes us so ashamed that we can't easily talk about it. If we have a car accident we feel free to tell everyone about it, but if we are raped, it isn't so easy.

We must make our experiences public and refuse to be ashamed any longer if we are attacked or humiliated. We have to work through our experiences and analyse them, because then it becomes clear that rape is not so unusual or exceptional. There are many different kinds of rape, from pestering you to fuck and telling you that you shouldn't be so prudish, to forcing you with a knife at your throat. Rape is just the extreme consequence of generally accepted ideas about sexuality – the consequence of the power relations between women and men. **159**

Battering too is the extreme form of a relationship in which the woman is made powerless because she is denied the means to live an independent life, and in which the man thinks that with his wage he has bought the right to his wife's body.

1. The facts

- Rapists are seldom 'abnormal'. Research on rapists has shown that they are not more disturbed than 'normal' men. Only a small group of rapists, who repeatedly attack strange women, have been shown to be on average more aggressive than other men, and to have repressed that aggression for a long time.
- Rapists are not by any means scary men who drag you down dark alleys. In half the cases of rape, the rapist is an old friend, a neighbour, your husband or father. A rape doesn't always take place outside; a great many rapes happen at home, or in an environment where you feel familiar and safe.
- Rapists aren't primarily men who are sexually frustrated. Our female conditioning makes us sympathetic to men who are supposed not to 'get enough'. It makes us care about men who are having a hard time. But we have to realise that rape has little to do with sexual needs.

Rape has much more to do with the need for revenge – to humiliate someone, to get rid of pent-up aggression – than with sex. Many rapes involve beating, knifing, choking, spitting or urinating on the woman – this has little to do with a man trying to get an orgasm. It is a way of passing on oppression. If a man is frustrated, he can regain his sense of 'manhood' by beating up his wife in the kitchen.

If *sexual* frustration were the cause of rape, then women, not men, would be the rapists.

- Rape does not happen because a man is suddenly overcome by uncontrollable urges. Many rapes are planned beforehand, to punish all women, or a particular one. Some rapists say they wanted to go out and 'grab the first woman I see'. Rape situations are often the kind where the man sets a 'trap', offers a lift, asks himself in for a cup of coffee and acts on the assumption that a woman asks for it if she unsuspectingly agrees.
- Women *don't* ask to be raped. It is *not* true that if a woman doesn't want it, she can resist a rapist. Sometimes a woman is paralysed by fear; sometimes she is astounded because it is someone she trusted; sometimes she is threatened with weapons. Often rape inolves more than one man. Occasionally a woman succeeds in evading rape by screaming and fighting, but when you scream and fight you risk being murdered. For this reason many women don't defend themselves.
- Women who are raped are *not* women who asked for it by behaving in a provocative manner, or by flirting. Age makes practically no difference, nor does what you look like. It can happen to women of sixty who thought they were safe, and

popped out to walk the dog, just as easily as to a woman with a

woolly cap pulled over her ears and a shapeless coat, who ta[...] a walk through the woods. It can happen to you in your own [...] The most you can say is that you have less *chance* of being raped if you never walk in the streets without a man, never walk in woods or by the sea, have three locks on your door and never open it unless your husband is at home. If you never accept a lift or go out with a man, even if he is a friend or a colleague at work. And if you never actually live with a man, because he might do it too. It would be just as idiotic to say to every raped woman that she asked for it, as it would be to accuse every man who goes out with a wallet of asking to be mugged or robbed. It would be equally absurd to expect women to lock themselves in forever to avoid rape. You lock up criminals, not victims.

● Rape is *not* sex, as it is often assumed to be. Sex is nice, isn't it, the line goes, so why do women make such a fuss? There are men who say: 'I should be so lucky as to be raped.' Few men have any notion of how humiliating it is to have someone use your body against your will as if it were an object. Until it happens to *their* wife or daughter, but that often has more to do with bruised male pride than with sympathy for her. His 'possessions' are being used; he has failed because he hasn't been able to protect 'his' wife. The idea that rape is sex makes the courts and other people look into the sexual experience of the woman who has been raped. To rape a married woman is considered worse than raping an independent woman who lives alone and has lots of lovers. A prostitute can, by the accepted definition, hardly be raped. So the fact that it is a question of the right to determine what happens to your own body is obscured – a question of choosing for ourselves with whom and when we wish to experience something. That is just as true for an inexperienced girl of fourteen as it is for a prostitute with ten clients a day.

Women often find themselves in a position where they aren't free to leave or to say no. Because of the myths that rapists are always raving psychopaths and that the women actually did want it ('they always say no, even when they mean yes'), many men have a beautiful excuse. Many men would be astonished if you were to call the way they force sex on women, rape.

'I left my husband after a lot of pain, when I found out that he had another girlfriend. At that time I had a terrific need for support. Among other people who gave it to me was a friend who visited a lot. At the time I had a great need for warmth, but not for sex. He seemed to understand that, and said: "It's as if you're still in mourning." Then he said: "But surely that doesn't mean you can't allow yourself any happiness?" And I fell for it too, when I realised that by happiness he meant that we should fuck. Only afterwards did I realise that he was talking about his happiness, not mine. It destroyed the friendship, that he couldn't respond to my needs at that moment.'

Because of our misconceptions about rape, we don't recognise **161** ns in which there is no obvious physical violence, as ou define rape as a form of forced sexuality, then rape is nmon. It occurs when girls are abused by fathers or rs; when a woman is forced to have sex by her own ., even though that isn't called rape by the law which assumes that by signing the marriage contract you have signed over to your husband all rights over your own body; if at work you are pressurised into sleeping with your boss and you give in for fear of losing your job; if a friend attacks you and you give in because you don't want to scream in case your landlady throws you out of your room.

2. Power relationships

As long as rape is seen as being dragged into the bushes by a psychopath, no one need ask why men rape. Most women can't understand how anyone could get pleasure in sex with someone who doesn't want it. I know no woman who could imagine that she would enjoy it, and to me it looks extremely unattractive. So we may conclude that men are 'different' people from us, monsters from Mars with strange passions they can't control.
But if we look at the division of labour between women and men, and the part that sexuality plays in that, things become clearer. Men act on the premise that they have the right to sex. If they are married, they've 'paid' for it. And sex means women. If you don't get it free, you take it. This is made even easier by a male culture where virility is equated with being able to conquer a woman. Advertising and porn continually reinforce this image. Women are portrayed as objects, as commodities which can be bought, as leisure occupations, like cars and drink. So it's not so strange that some men conclude that if you can buy sex, a woman, you can also take it. With that goes something else. Oppressd groups have a tendency to take out their oppression on groups 'beneath' them. Everyone knows the story of the boss who scolds his employee, who then shouts at his wife, who then boxes her child on the ear, who then pinches the cat. In our society, it is normal for a man to have to prove all the time that he is a man. For men in pleasant jobs, where they get enough respect for the work they do, and enough respect for themselves as persons, there might not be such a need to prove that they are 'real men'. But there are a lot of men who take their virility so seriously that almost everything is an attack on their male ego – even a woman who forgets an appointment, a woman who earns more than he does, or who doesn't obey him when he forbids her to go out to work, colleagues at work who laugh at him, or perhaps when he was young he was teased because he was small and thin, or his voice hadn't broken when all the other boys already had hair on their chins. Many men feel that their status as a 'real' man is directly related to their sexual performance.
Incest is clearly not so much about sex as about power. Fathers who regularly abuse their daughters are just ordinary

authoritarian men acting from the premise that they are the boss in the house. They are just exaggerating what we have all learned to accept as normal: that the man is the head of the family, that he brings home the money, and that, in exchange, he is looked after. It is much the same as the daughters doing the housework when the mother can't. These fathers assume they can satisfy their sexual needs with their daughters if their wives are sick, or if they are, in the man's eyes, unattractive. Girls who are raped by their fathers are in an even more powerless position than adult married women. They are still under the guardianship of their parents and can't leave without their permission. They are often terribly isolated. It's these same authoritarian men who forbid the women in 'their' family to make contacts outside the home. And anyway, almost no one believes a girl if she has the courage to tell anyone that her father abuses her. In America, one quarter of all women are thought to be sexually abused before they are eighteen years old, and mostly by someone they know. So rape is nothing out of the ordinary. It has everything to do with the prevailing power relations between women and men. In a rapist's own words:

'I wanted her to take everything off by herself, making her feel ashamed and abused. I grabbed her by the throat, and started shaking her, feeling powerful and not wanting to stop. I said something to her like: "Listen you bitch, you start stripping now or I'll kill you. Who do you think you are?" I felt so strong, and maybe I would have killed her.
'I had distinct feelings of satisfaction at her reactions to being made to walk naked in the street and to carrying out the sex acts, all obviously embarrassing and humiliating for her. That was a primary concern of mine. The rape was secondary. In fact, it took me some time and a lot of trying to maintain an erection and reach a climax.'
From Understanding Sexual Attacks, *by West, Roy & Nichols.*
See bibliography.

We can understand that in this society men are always pushing each other to prove that they are men. The less powerful they feel, the more likely this is to be coupled with violence. But there is no reason at all why we should accept that this aggression is taken out on us.

3. What rape does to us

Rape has many consequences for us. Women who have lived through it find it a very difficult experience to come to terms with. It can leave a revulsion for everything to do with men or sex for a very long time.

'I was in an expresso bar with a woman friend. Then a man came to sit next to us, who told us he was from some political **163**

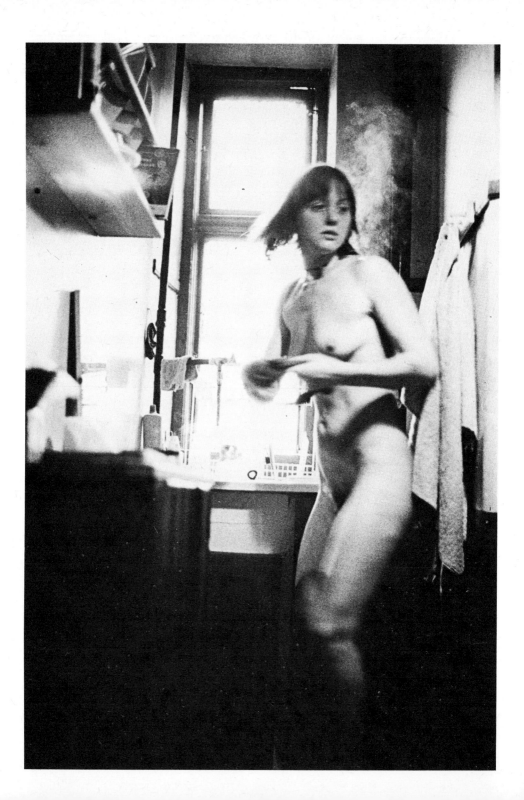

group I used to be in. Because I was with a woman friend, I found it easy to talk to him. If I had been alone, I might have cut him short more quickly. I had a long talk with him about why he was in the city, about what he was doing now politically and so on. I really felt good about it. When he asked me if I could visit him the next day with my woman friend, my first thought was, why not? Then she said she couldn't make it, and he said: "Why not come on your own?" I had a flash of, you shouldn't do that, but it seemed so childish and suspicious, especially after all the talk about the things we agreed on. I didn't want him to think I didn't trust him, or that I was prudish and childish, not daring to be alone with a man.

'As soon as I got there, he locked the door and grabbed me. It was immediately clear that I had been very stupid. I thought, if I'm not careful, he'll shut me up for days on end, or he'll do something worse because I can recognise and report him, because I know where he lives. So I let him do what he wanted. He thought I enjoyed it. He pressed me to come back another time. He probably thought that by visiting him on my own I knew beforehand what would happen. I never reported it. I thought, I don't have the ghost of a chance. No one will believe that I didn't want to. For weeks I felt terribly dirty, and often cried hysterically. Partly because I felt so terribly betrayed because he had done that to me when I'd let him see that I trusted him. Of course now I'm more careful, I don't even dare to go and visit men I considered to be friends before.'

Rape has consequences for all women.
It makes us feel unsafe in this world.

'I am on the street around midnight. I hear footsteps behind me. I realise there is no one else about, I start walking faster. I notice that I will have to pass an area with lots of dark doorways. My throat is dry, my heart starts beating faster, I feel in my coat pocket for my key ring, I look to see if there are any lighted windows. As I turn the corner, I no longer hear the footsteps, I breathe again.'

This is an average daily fear so normal that we hardly notice it. If we took stock of all that anxiety, we would be able to see for ourselves that every time we walk alone in the streets at night, we react with fear if we hear footsteps behind us or see a group of men approaching us. This is how it affects us all: it makes us feel like unwelcome guests in our own world. We don't dare to take a walk alone at night, or go on holiday alone, and we accept this as normal. Many women aren't even aware of how much they are used to living in a hostile world, because they avoid all the situations which could obviously be dangerous without even thinking about it. We don't go to the cinema without a man; we don't go out alone after dark. And then it's even more shocking if **165** you're raped in your own bed by a man you know. Sexual attacks are shattering, because they can make you feel that you aren't safe anywhere. So we become much more suspicious than we would like to be. We lose our spontaneity, and with reason. If you aren't suspicious, and you trust a man who offers you a lift, or asks you to go for a cup of coffee, you've 'asked' for it if he grabs you. If you are so suspicious that you never go out without a man, never allow him to bring you home by car, never let a man friend who visits you at night into your home, then you are in their eyes, and probably also in your own, 'neurotic'. This double message means we can never get it right, and that we almost always feel guilty whatever happens. If you are raped, a common reaction is one of terrible confusion and self-disgust.

As long as the power relations between women and men are as they are, rape will continue, and women will be forced to have sex against their will. It's relations themselves that must change. It should not be possible for a woman to let herself be battered because she doesn't have the means to leave. Or for a woman to fuck against her will because otherwise her husband will divorce her and she'll be left with three children and have to live off social security. But while this is still so, we must keep on struggling around rape. We need to begin by making our experiences public. We mustn't accept the definition that rape is a private problem, an exception. There are now groups working against sexual violence, and more and more women are gradually daring to say in public that they have been raped. This is a great support to other women. It makes rape visible as more than an individual problem; it shows it is a problem of power relations. In the Netherlands, by our repeated pressure, we have gradually managed to get better treatment by the police and in the courts than we got some years ago. In a recent case against a group of Hell's Angels who gang-raped and abused a girl, 'a woman's right to self-determination' was used for the first time as an argument in court, rather than the old 'assault on public decency'. Unfortunately this gain was cancelled shortly afterwards when they were let off on appeal. And we question what would have happened if it had been a gentleman in a suit in the dock, instead of a group of young men whom everybody already regards with disgust. Shortly afterwards, a man who raped three mentally retarded girls was acquitted. The girls hadn't defended themselves, it was said, and what's more the man's wife was ill . . . However, we still feel we have gained by taking public action.

It is slowly beginning to sink into people's minds that it isn't relevant whether or not a woman who is raped had had sexual experience, or whether she had put herself in a 'dangerous situation'. Women should have the right to determine what happens to their own bodies, in all situations. Men who don't understand that, obviously regard themselves and each other as
166 some sort of animal incapable of thinking, driven only by

'instincts' – as though it were normal human behaviour to smash the baker's shop window when you are feeling peckish.

It is important for us that we become more self-confident. We need to follow our intuition if we have the sense that a certain gentleman doesn't mean a cup of coffee when he says a cup of coffee, even if he will call us a bitch if we say so.

It's difficult to say what to do if you are attacked. The police never used to believe an accusation of rape unless you arrived at the police station bleeding, with bruises and torn clothes. In the Netherlands, most of the police now know that many women choose not to defend their bodies when they are in a situation where they feel totally powerless, in case anything worse happens. Some women have managed to get away with a very bad fright by shouting at the tops of their lungs and hitting back. Shouting 'Help' doesn't help much, because if a woman is attacked by a man, other people regard it as a private business. If you call 'Fire!' you might get a response. A good kick in his groin can incapacitate him for quite a while, though most women are afraid of doing that.

So it always depends on the situation. There are no definite ways to escape or avoid rape. Some women have said they got off by acting as if they enjoyed it, then running when his attention was distracted. There are apparently men who believe their own myths so completely that they really think you will enjoy being raped. Some men are genuinely surprised when a woman reports them to the police.

It is difficult to decide whether you should report to the police or not. You may feel that having to repeat the same story four times is like yet another rape – especially as police officers are often very unsympathetic. But for other women it can be very important that the police have more evidence to catch someone. They also hope it will make it clearer how often rape actually occurs – especially if action groups take care that police and courts don't hide these facts from the public.

Further reading

The best book I know about rape is Susan Brownmiller's *Against Our Will* (Penguin). It sees rape as 'a conscious process of intimidation by which all men keep all women in a state of fear'. Horrifyingly informative.

Susan Griffin's *Rape: the Power of Consciousness* (import) consists largely of reflections on the effect of a rape-culture on women's consciousness. *Against Rape* by Andrea Medea and Kathleen Thompson (import) calls itself a 'survival manual for women'. It too is American, so some of the information isn't relevant, but I found it forceful and thought-provoking – if perhaps over-optimistic about the possibility of physically fighting back.

You can't really learn self-defence from a book – you need to **167** practise, long and hard, with other people. But there are handbooks that might give ideas and inspiration – *Defend Yourself!*, for instance, by Bromilyn Smith (Pelham).

On incest I recommend *Kiss Daddy Goodnight* by Louise Armstrong, a speak-out-style American book (import). On battered women, there's a good book called *Violence against Wives* by R and R Dobash (Open Books) – detailed research material with personal accounts too. Del Martin's *Battered Wives* (import) made a big impact in America. And of course there are many Women's Aid Federation publications (see useful addresses) – cheap pamphlets giving information on refuges, injunctions, housing and the law.

XII. Porn, and its consequences for us

1. Sex as war

It's rare now to find so-called 'innocent' porn. Simple naked bodies are becoming too commonplace. The fashion is for an escalating mixture of violence and sex. Pictures abound of gang rapes, battering, bondage. Torture as a sexual variation, films where women climax from rape, or where sex with a young girl is shown as something joyful, are everywhere. (Just look at *Pretty Baby*, a romantic mystification of the life of young prostitutes.)

If you buy a cheap porn magazine somewhere, secondhand for a few pence from an ordinary local shop, you will see at once how close sex and violence are.

'He wanted to grab her head, so as to bury his cannon barrel right behind her whirling tongue. His battering ram was like a pile-driver. With each upward jab, his weapon slid deeper into her hole. "Oh god! It hurts!" she moaned. But her words were in vain. He thought only of her cunt and his desire to drill inside her. He quickly withdrew and slid again inside for another shot. His prick fired another sea of sperm.'

'Leo wanted to scream. He wanted to shoot, to attack her, to throw her struggling body on to the floor and drill through it with his merciless prick.'

' "Auugh! Hmmm!" she cried, when Matt's prick penetrated her pussy. His prick was like a spear, which lusted after the hidden warmth of hot meat.'

'Leo's hand slid under Lisa's dress and his fingers penetrated like a bullet deep into her cunt. His face was a grimace, his hands balled into fists, and he stormed her hips with heavy angry thuds.'

'Stroud used his long socks to bind her. She was now completely at his mercy. "Oh, yes . . . that's how I like it. As helpless as a bull which needs to be branded. Auuggh!" '

It isn't accidental that the words which describe sexuality are mostly taken from the vocabulary of war: shoot, weapon, storm, drill. A woman's body is like enemy territory which has to be conquered. It's no coincidence either that you often find porn next to cheap war comics in shops: they are written for the same male public. Porn was once banned because it was considered immoral. Then it was sold under the counter. The people who read it knew that what they were doing wasn't publicly accceptable. Now pornography is becoming commonplace. What was sold in secret is now used as a way of selling the *Sun* – or just look at the calendar in your local garage. A great many people think of porn as an innocent pastime for men. Those who object to porn are often the same people who think everything to **169** do with sex is dirty, and also deny women the right to choose on abortion, contraception and what happens to their bodies generally. Why are women called prudish when they say publicly that they find porn offensive? It seems you're only allowed to object to pictures of domination if, at the same time, you prove that you are mad keen on men in every other way. When women protest about porn, 'progressive' men argue freedom of expression. But I don't think those same men would use that argument if it were about anti-semitic literature, or if there were special shops where the kinky could see films and books in which black people were systematically beaten with whips, or where animals were tortured. Pictures of black people as stupid slaves, that isn't right, that's racism. But women are fair game. Showing a woman as a stupid piece of meat, just a cunt with two tits above it, is just being a healthy man with an appetite for sex. Porn is said to relax a healthy man – if they didn't have porn magazines and films as safety valves, they might become really dangerous. Investigations into the effects of porn have not been able to prove that it is a direct cause of sexual violence. That fits with what we know about rape. Aggression against women is not caused by women. Not everyone who looks at war pictures gets the urge to go out and kill. Aggression is caused by all kinds of frustrations.

But porn certainly does play a part in the way that aggression is calculatedly turned towards women and disguised as sex. Porn doesn't cause aggression, but it points to a possible target: a woman.

2. Women as objects of consumption

Porn shows women as things, as objects to be used. Without a will of their own, and available. Pornography suggests that women love all kinds of sex, that pain and desire are the same for us, that we don't mind who fucks us. It also gives men the idea that sex is for the taking, that they have the right to use a woman's body. And this encourages the aggression against women that they already feel.

The kind of women you see on the covers of *Playboy* are actually very rare. Few women have the kind of body that you see in pin-ups. And if women didn't have such a hard time earning good money, and if posing in the nude didn't seem an easy way of making a lot, few women would choose to do it. Women who are used to sell lousy products clearly aren't respected much by the manufacturers either. These men say they aren't doing anybody any harm, but they don't bother to hide their own contempt for these women.

A young, sexy, willing bird is a status symbol like a fast car, but the young, sexy, willing birds are as hard to come by as an E-type Jag. If women are always being presented to men as things, then it really is just one step further for them to grab one, if they can't get hold of her free or cheap.

This continual projection of women as things affects the way women think too. Even if, like most women, we try to cut off the 'hundred insults a day', the message does get through to us. When the by-line on page three reads: 'You can look at this lovely piece, but you'll still have to put up with what's at home', then it's pretty clear that we, with our ordinary bodies and with more in our heads than the thought of being continually available to men, are being presented as second choice. We become unsure of ourselves when we are constantly faced with images of 'femininity' which we couldn't possibly match, even if we wanted to. Only afterwards do we get angry. It's time we got a lot angrier.

As long as men think they like women because they like using women, and don't recognise their own hatred of women in this, as long as they make no distinction between sex and sexism, they will be extremely unerotic and unattractive sexual partners for us.

Further reading

There's been very little published in this country about pornography – outside of Women's Liberation newsletters – so a new American book will be invaluable. *Take Back the Night (Women on Pornography)*, edited by Laura Lederer, is a collection of articles, with an afterword by Adrienne Rich (import).

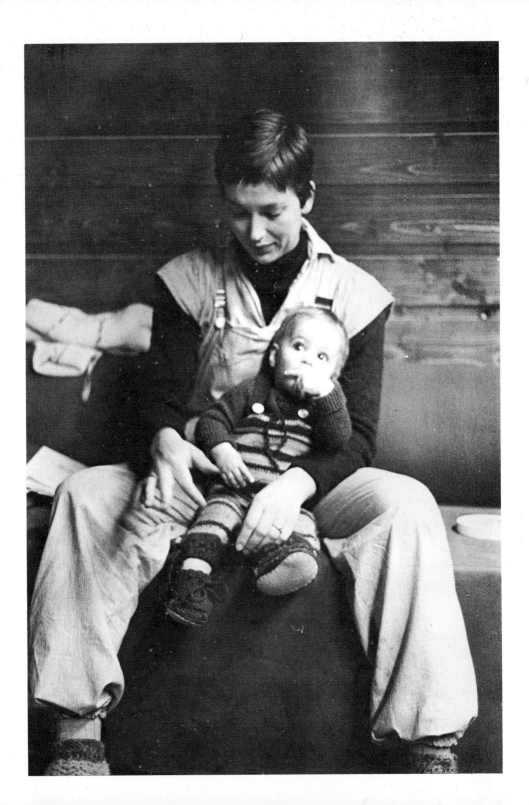

XIII. The right not to have sex

1. Anxiety about not fucking

Sex is the basis of most relationships between women and men. When the sex is over, there is often precious little left. Many women fuck against their will. They find it hard to say no, or even to admit to themselves that they don't want it, because it's the only way to keep the relationship going. Because they feel they should. Because it is the only way to keep the man's interest. Because they don't want to be prudish. Because otherwise he'll go to someone else. Because they don't know how to enjoy themselves with a man any other way. Because it's the only way to reach him emotionally. Because they might hurt him if they said no. Because otherwise he'd sulk for hours. Because they don't know how to have a warm relationship with a man any other way. Because if they've been out with him and had a good time, it just happens, or because they need to cuddle up to someone.

We should never have to make love if we don't feel like it, ever. Yet it is very difficult to say no. There are different reasons for women in different situations, but perhaps it'll help to look at some commonplace situations.

● It isn't considered normal not to want sex, or to have a fluctuating desire for sex: to want it once and then not again for weeks. In reality, so many women have little or no pleasure in routine sex that it seems absurd to call it 'normal' to want sex three times a week, which is supposedly the average in the Netherlands. Sometimes men don't feel like it when their wives do, but that isn't usually considered a problem. Men always have a good reason to refuse: if they don't feel like it, they 'can't'. A woman always 'can', that is to say it's possible for a man to fuck her without her feeling the slightest bit of pleasure. The irony is that a man could easily satisfy his wife without having an erection himself. As we already know, a penis isn't always the best and certainly not the only source of pleasure for a woman. But I think many men would be absolutely outraged if they were expected to satisfy their wives without having an erection and getting an orgasm themselves. Yet this is what happens daily to millions of women. *The myth that the penis is the only organ that can give pleasure makes it easier for men to say that they'll fuck if they want to and can't fuck if they don't want to, because their penis isn't up to it.* I don't think many women would enjoy making love with a man who didn't feel like it, but by changing things around it becomes clear how unequal the actual situation is.

● Women easily get the idea that they are failures, and that they aren't real women if they don't feel like sex. No one would think it odd if you didn't feel like going to the movies or diving off the top diving board three times a week. But not wanting to fuck **173**

regularly is 'abnormal' and a 'problem'. It's mainly a problem because it's expected of you. Being kind to a man is your job as a woman. If your husband isn't satisfied, you're a 'bad' wife. If your sense of identity is dependent on being kind to others, your self-confidence can be badly shaken if you don't give enough sexually. One of the myths about male sexuality is that we cause his erection. Because we lie next to him in bed with our warm body, because he has seen our breasts, or just because a woman is near him. Men tell us that they suffer if they can't fuck us. But it's not our fault if they want to fuck and we don't. It's their problem, not ours. There's no point in us feeling guilty or heartless if we leave a man to cope with his 'problem' on his own.

'I told my boyfriend I didn't feel like fucking any more and that I didn't know when I would want to again. I tried to reassure myself and him by saying I was sure I would want to do it again, sometime. He asked if I would still sleep over, just for the company, and I wanted to do that, because I still liked him a lot and I enjoyed eating and talking with him. But each time I did, it was so difficult. He lay there sighing and tossing and poking me in the back with that thing. I hardly dared touch him any more, because at once he'd be lying with this great big pole asking if I really didn't feel like it at all? It stopped me getting to sleep. I'd lie right on the edge of the bed. Then I said that I wouldn't spend the night there any longer if that went on. He said he didn't mind and asked me to stay, but all the time he let me know that he did mind a lot. And I became terribly tense because he kept on trying, instead of leaving it to me.'

• We are often scared we will lose someone, and that doesn't help us be more independent sexually. When the sex isn't exciting, often the whole relationship falls apart. It's difficult enough if you're in a relationship where you are emotionally dependent on each other. If you are economically dependent on each other too, it can be catastrophic. Every woman knows it's considered 'normal' for a marriage to be dissolved if the man doesn't get his sex. One in four marriages ends in divorce. And many more divorced women live on welfare than on alimony. Divorce has slowly become common, but no less frightening for that. Many women aren't always conscious of the underlying threat of ending up alone, a threat which is even greater if we have given up our job to be a good housewife and mother. Many women would rather repress that fear, but it shows in our behaviour. We are afraid of being a bad wife. And a good wife ought to enjoy making love to her husband.

2. Forced fucking and power games

We don't always see how we are put under pressure. Not all men are unsubtle. Not all men come out with it and say it's their right. **175**

But few men don't secretly feel injured. In her book *Sex for Women*, Carmen Kerr lists the kinds of arguments men use to talk us 'round'.

● 'If you don't go to bed with me you don't love me.' That's a terrifying remark because it says both that you're a hard, cold bitch, and that he should look for a more loving person. The misunderstanding, of course, is that love doesn't have to be proved by sex all the time, and he has a curious idea of love if he wants to force someone against her will.

● 'You are a frigid prude.' In the aftermath of the 'sexual revolution', that's a hard thing to hear. It's important to realise that sexual emancipation means just as much the freedom *not* to fuck as the freedom to fuck. And with that freedom goes the right to decide for yourself with whom and when. Saying you're neurotic about sex is seldom meant in a friendly way in order to help. It's a challenge to you to prove how liberated you are. The word 'frustrated' is a handy accusation too, often and especially used in connection with feminist women. The fact that it *is* frustrating to be pressurised, and that you are likely to be *more* rather than less frustrated if you fuck when you don't want to, is conveniently ignored. We have to realise that other people can't judge what we need. And if we *are* 'frustrated', what business is it of theirs?

● 'Why not, why not now, just give me one reason why not?' A war of nerves. The idea is that you'll give up and give in because you want to go to sleep and be rid of the nagging. There need never be a 'reason' why not. Just that you don't feel like it. Just the same as the only reason why you should do it is because you *do* feel like it.

● 'But I have done so much for you.' Taken you to dinner, for example. And there are still men who think they've bought you with a few drinks and a meal. Sometimes it isn't said like that – but it's clear from their attitude. Sex is not a reward for services rendered, and if he doesn't take you out to dinner for the meal, but for a fuck, he should have said so before, so that you could work out if you wanted to. A more subtle and modern version is the lovely man who works hard to do his share of the housework, and then wants his reward for that. But we shouldn't have to say thank you for what should be normal. And certainly not with sex.

● 'You didn't feel like it so I went to . . . ' Clearly a power game. And insulting to you and to her. As if you were easily interchangeable. As if it didn't matter whom he fucked, so long as she had a cunt.

● 'You do want to really.' And keeps on niggling at you until you are screaming with irritation. And perhaps you do give in so that he can say: 'You see, you did enjoy it, I can see that.' Insulting because he assumes that he knows what you want better than you do. And difficult to get angry at, because his lack of understanding is hidden behind his 'longing' for you. And often you can feel his aggression just under the surface, and you are scared of the explosion. However it turns out: a power game.

So it's not always easy not to fuck if you don't feel like it. It goes against our feeling of wanting to be nice to people, wanting to be approved. It is terrifying not to be normal, or to lose someone. We must become conscious of our fears so that we can see if they are rational. Will he really go to someone else? And is it worth trying to stop him?

It is also obvious that men need to do some thinking about it all. It's not an unnecessary luxury for men to analyse, just as we do, what their sexual needs really are. It would be a much happier situation if men would realise that they don't always have to fuck if they have an erection or if they want to have an orgasm. You don't *need* anybody else to be able to come. The solution is literally in their own hands!

If a man takes it for granted that he will always get satisfaction from a woman's body, even if the woman in question isn't too keen, it means he is seeing that woman as an object to be used. *Men who believe it is childish or unmanly to make love to themselves, unless there is no woman 'at hand', should realise that that is exactly what they are doing when they fuck a woman against her will. They masturbate, but it just so happens there's a cunt there.*

Men, just like women, probably have a need for warmth, understanding, tenderness. Many men have learnt to see it as childish, and so deny it to themselves. Most boys suppress loving emotions because they don't want to be 'like a girl'. The emotions considered suitable for men are aggression and lust. Probably many men would feel less need to fuck if they explored other emotions.

Being able to say no is for us a condition of being able to say yes. Unwilling sex is always unpleasant, even when the unwillingness is hidden. Presumably it is also unpleasant for men if they get the feeling that women are hiding behind headaches, or if they

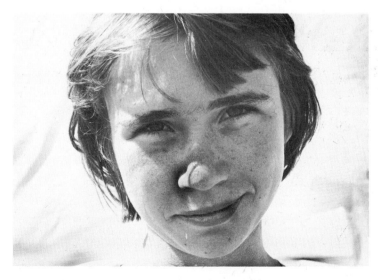

notice that women are just pretending to enjoy fucking. But the only alternative to making excuses is to be able to say no. And you need to be in a situation where saying no is not so threatening that it's easier just to pretend.

It is clear that we can't be more free in our sexual behaviour than we are in the rest of our lives. We have to be able to feel more free in all our behaviour, less scared of being considered unpleasant or unfeminine. Consciousness raising groups can help, as can radical therapy or assertion training. But it is clear too that we aren't really free unless we are able to stand alone. Even if you're married and aren't planning to divorce, knowing that you can earn your own living makes you stronger and more able to look after yourself. To be really free in our sexuality, to have really equal relationships with men, we would need to feel independent in the rest of our lives too.

'With my present lover I made sure it was completely different right from the start'

**Interview 3
Ariane Amsberg**

– *You are twenty-nine now. How has your sexuality and the way you feel about sex changed since you first started having sexual experiences?*

– They've changed completely. In the first place, I have orgasms now, and I never did before. With my first husband, I always acted like a filmstar, with terribly deep sighs and theatrical screams. I saw images from a film in front of me, and I copied them – how you swoon backwards, how you let your hand fall softly when he kisses you, how you vibrate to each touch. I was absolutely out of touch with what I felt, I was just following what was happening to him – when he started panting more loudly or softly – I managed to make sure there was never a dull moment! I was always told I was terribly good in bed. Silly, isn't it . . . I don't do anything like that now.

– *. . . you aren't good in bed any more, you mean?!*

– Oh yes, yes, but now I'm *real*. That filmstar bit lasted seven years. I did that with my first husband. I was married to him for three years, but I'd known him for four years before that. He was the first man I went to bed with. With my second important relationship, the man I've lived with now for six years, I made sure it was completely different right from the start – I was much more shy. I was terribly nervous, and got soaking wet with sweat, because with him I began to concentrate on myself. With him I came close to the feeling I have when I satisfy myself, but that really scared me because I thought: if I come when he's there, then I won't know what to do and I can't bear that!

– *When did you have your first orgasm by yourself?*

– When I was still a young child. Mostly by rubbing against a chair or a table. I have a photo where I'm sitting on the edge of a chair, and I know that I was doing it at that very moment. I was about six or seven. When I was twelve I did it quite consciously. I knew then that what I was doing was sex, and that it had to do with men and marriages and so on.

– *Did you know it was an orgasm?*

– No, I didn't know it was called that. When I was fourteen, and had my first period, my parents began to talk about how you had children, but I found that so embarrassing that I quickly said I knew all about it already. They never talked about orgasms or good feelings.

– *What did you think was so embarrassing about it?*

– It seemed so dirty, the idea that people could mess around in there. They shouldn't want to do that kind of thing!

– *Were you brought up religious?*

– Yes, Catholic.

– *Did you ever confess that you masturbated?*

– No. I felt intuitively that it wasn't their business. After all, I didn't say how often I needed a shit, did I? When I was ten, we moved, and because the school wasn't a Catholic one, I had to go to the priest once a week for catechism. There were about five children, and he used to take us on his lap in turn. That was fine, something like: 'Come and sit comfortably on my lap, little girl.' He touched my little breasts to see if they had grown, and said: 'So, you are becoming a big little woman, aren't you', and then he put his hand between my legs to pull me towards him, but let it stay there. I didn't like that and wanted him to take his hand away, but he was the most important Father, even more important than my own father, so I couldn't ask him. After he had done it for three weeks running, I didn't want to go back. I told them about it at home, and my father told the priest I wasn't coming any more.

– *Did you have any other unpleasant experiences as a child?*

– When I was about seven or eight a man used to come to our street on Saturday afternoons and give us sweets. We knew of course that we weren't allowed to take sweets from strangers, so a group of us children would bury them in the sand. But the third week one child had followed the man and told us that he'd bought a bag of sweets from the baker opposite just before coming to us, that he hadn't put poison in them afterwards, so it was safe to eat them. Mostly we'd sit and chat with the man near the garages. He was clearly building up a social contact with us. Most of the children got bored after a while, but I didn't. I stayed a long time with two or three others. Then he began to talk to us about sex, asking if we did things with our bodies, if we knew what a man looked like, if we wanted to see it. At that point the other children ran away and called: 'No, we're scared!' But he still took it out of his trousers, and then I saw something fleshy and limp. He said: 'Look there it is, do you like it?' 'Oh yes, put it away now.' And the man was satisfied and covered it up again. He liked me very much, he said. He'd come again next week and perhaps he'd let me have another look. 'Will you have sweets again?' 'Yes, of course.' I let him come three more times, but I was beginning to get bored – I'd seen it now. What's more, he was beginning to ask if I'd hold the thing, but I said: 'No', I wasn't going to touch it. He also asked me if I'd walk with him a little, but I said no. I wanted to stay put, then I could always call my friends if I needed to. At the same time I felt that I couldn't just ignore the guy when he waved at us again – I felt sorry for him. And so I went over to him on my own again – after all, he didn't *do* anything, did he?

– *What sort of age was he?*

– I think about thirty. Then he began to tell me how he made his bed into a trampoline – I can't remember the story exactly – he stripped his bed, took off all his clothes, opened the curtains, and then jumped so happily, free as a bird, up and down on his bed, **180** and then the people in the house opposite had to laugh about it.

He asked if I would go with him to his room the next week, then we could trampoline in the nude together, like two birds! I didn't have the nerve to say no any more, so I said: 'Yes, perhaps I'll do it.' He said something like: 'You just come along with me, it isn't at all scary, nothing will happen and then we'll have fun and trampoline, and that's great . . . .' It was said with such determination that I, as a child, could no longer resist it, and I became very frightened. Frightened that he wouldn't listen to my 'no' any more, that my voice wouldn't count any more. Also there's a taboo on saying no to adults, you don't go on saying no for hours on end to grown-ups. Then I told them at home. My parents got a dreadful fright and made phone calls. A little later a plainclothes policeman came. I had to tell him everything exactly – when I'd seen that man, and what he was wearing, and when he would come again. I still remember that I found it all very unpleasant. I was told to wait for him again the next Saturday, and if he showed 'it' again, I was to shout very loud: 'YEEES', and then two men parked across the road would come and grab him. And that's how it happened. Those people came running over to us – and this is the worst bit, I can still see it in my mind's eye – the man was dragged between them across the street into a car, and he looked back and shook his fist at me and shouted: 'What a mean trick!' and he cried. That was horrible. If I think about it now, I get so angry about it still! They shouldn't have used me for that, I was far too young.
– *What do you remember as the worst thing about that incident?*
– The guy shaking his fist at me, saying it was my fault, I had betrayed him. That image stays in my head. I just didn't want the man to come back – all I wanted was to make sure he didn't talk to me any more. I just didn't want to see him any more, but they took over with their grown-up fuss.
– *Did you play sex games with each other as children?*
– Yes, I paid a penny to see willies – I had no brothers you see – and I lay kissing with girlfriends in the grass, and thought that was very exciting. When I was thirteen, I played 'boy-and-girl' with a girlfriend – 'he' would come and fetch me, and we'd kiss each other. Later on I had boyfriends. I must have gone through about fifty of them, all kissers. When I was fifteen, I had my first petting session with a man at a party, and he had to be my boyfriend for six months before he was allowed to go to bed with me – it was a kind of contract. When the time was up, I was sorry I hadn't bargained for a year! The first time there wasn't any fondling or anything – it was more like an operation. His mother had the key to a woman friend's house, and he nicked it. Afterwards we did it in cars, in the hallway of the flat, in a gas meter cupboard under the cobwebs, always standing up, or in my father's bed if he was away. I thought I'd get an orgasm just from the penis moving in and out, like I got when I rubbed my fingers between my lips, but nothing happened. I started to think I was frigid, because I'd read about that in a book. It said that if **181**

girls masturbated too often, the vagina lost its sensitivity, and then you wouldn't get orgasms any more when you lived with a man.

– *And did you believe that?*

– Absolutely. After all, it was a sex education book, and what was in it had to be true. So, I thought, there you are, that's it. And whenever he went to the loo for a quick pee, having just made love to me, I would bring myself to orgasm as quick as lightning. Then when he came back, I'd say: 'Wasn't it great, the way we did it?' I didn't even know the clitoris existed. I heard about it for the first time from my present boyfriend. He said: 'Don't you know you've got a tiny knob which is actually a woman's willie, but a very very small one?' Together we pulled away the little skin, and for the first time I saw that tiny purple knob. I was twenty-three then.

– *How did he learn about it?*

– From *Sextant*, the sexual liberation magazine, and later on in detail at college from a lecturer who, according to my boyfriend, was a real womaniser. The same man also showed him films of women and men masturbating.

– *Your friend didn't expect you to come from his penis then?*

– Heavens no! He knew the clitoris was very important to make women come. And with him I thought: I'll tell him straight away how I like it. He also asked me what I enjoyed when making love.

– *You never told your ex-husband such things?*

– Not until a week before we got married. I'd been going to bed with him for over three years, but I had never come with him. He'd wriggle a bit with his fingers in my vagina, or grab my whole cunt – he liked doing that – but he never stayed on that one place. All the time I used to fake that I came, so I thought I ought to tell him that before we got married. So, one time, after we had made love, when he asked me as usual whether I had come, I said: 'No, as a matter of fact I never had an orgasm before either.' For a long time there was dead silence. But then he wanted to know all about what he should be doing. He began to rub my clitoris like mad, but of course it didn't work that way. For many reasons I didn't really want to get married, but we had a child together who was already two and a half, and I was a 'single parent' as they call it nowadays. During our marriage, he'd try with his fingers about one time in five, but he did it in such an unpleasant way, as if to say: 'You should get something out of it too, but it's not really part of it.' It made me feel like a kind of physically handicapped person. He wanted to hear about results, would ask if it was better this time – he clearly wasn't doing it because he enjoyed it. He did it rather crudely, clumsy with his finger, whereas I would touch it much more subtly or press it very gently. I did manage to get an orgasm a few times but then it was a really painful one, one of those high peaks which lose their effect almost immediately. It was so much trouble and was so unpleasant that I began to pretend again, so that I could just get it over with. I went back to playing the filmstar, panting, moving my body wildly, groaning, the kind of thing you always read about in cheap love stories. I groaned much more when I faked it than when I really came – I forgot to pretend then, but he never noticed the difference. Of course he did know that I didn't come any more when we made love, but then I'd say to him: 'Don't worry about it, I don't need it.' Quite often I'd do it to myself in the afternoons, or at night before falling asleep, because he worked evenings. I didn't blame him either for my not having a satisfactory sexual lfe. I took care of that myself. At night he would give me another going over, hold me all over, kiss me all over, then roll off again.

– *How often did he do that?*
– Five days out of the seven.
– *How did you feel about that?*
– Well, I got a kick out of it – it showed that I was desirable, or that's what I thought at the time: he enjoys my body so much that he needs it all the time to get his satisfaction, I must be beautiful. But I didn't experience myself as beautiful at all.
– *Really? You have an amazing body.*
– I don't feel happy with it all. My legs are too thin; I have stretch marks on my hips and my bottom; I've got quite a rounded child's tummy from all the sweets I eat, and my breasts are too flabby.
– *Did you breastfeed your child?*
– Yes, for six months. I had two breast infections which made them stand up under my chin like two blue cannon balls, and that stretched them very badly ... Before that I had very lovely breasts, honestly, and I was very proud of them. Yes, and what else is wrong ... my face – my teeth stick out and my ears flap.
– *What does our boyfriend think of your body?*
– Terrific, amazing, just very beautiful, but it doesn't convince me, I have to feel it myself. But it's getting better – I like my hands and my feet now, I've started with the extremities! And I don't think my face is as terrible as I used to think. And what is the real victory is that I can now appreciate even my peculiar fishy body odour. So I'm optimistic about liking everything of mine one day. I'm working on it, I can tell you.
– *What contraceptive do you use?*
– The pill. I used to use nothing, and so I got pregnant easily – that's why I had the child. But afterwards I started taking the pill, and I still do. I used the IUD for six months, but menstruation was dreadfully painful and bloody – it just poured out. And it was also terribly painful when I came. My uterus started to react when an orgasm was coming, and then I got such terrible cramps that in the end I didn't have an orgasm.
– *Why do you use the pill and not the cap or condoms?*
– Because I'm terrified of having another child, and I feel safest on the pill. That unwanted pregnancy changed my whole life. I didn't want any children, oh god no, those tiresome screaming things. They always want attention, and you just have to put up with them because you're a woman ... I had never planned for **183**

my life to be like this, I had other ideas entirely – it disrupted everything.

– *Was there a chance of abortion?*

– No. I tried to do it myself, but I didn't manage. I started by swallowing quinine pills, together with aspirins. I drank them with coca cola because that has quinine in too. After that I drank alcohol, which made me sick, but I thought it would make me bleed – that's what we both thought, my boyfriend and I. He was eighteen, and I was sixteen. I took hot and cold baths in turn, going from a boiling hot bath with a bright red bum into ice cold water in a very big basin, and then back again. I jumped off a high wardrobe until my ankles were sore. I sat on the pillion of a motor bike on very bumpy roads, but nothing happened. Then he put the pointed end of a paint brush into my vagina and tried to penetrate the cervix – we had heard it would come loose from that. Sometimes he hit the sides of the vagina and that was very painful. He did that for a couple of days – we were really desperate. Then we went to friends of his parents, who knew an address in the city where they would give us pills if we paid fifty guilders (about twelve pounds). I had to take them three times a day with a small glass of brandy. They made me dreadfully ill.

– *How did the two of you get the money?*

– He stole some of it from his mother's purse and borrowed some from a friend. After the first ten pills, I had a sanitary towel full of blood. I was delighted, but after that one towel it stopped again. I was already three months pregnant. We had to pay seventy-five guilders (about eighteen pounds) for the second dose of pills, but we couldn't get any more because in the meantime the man who supplied the pills had died. We didn't know what to do then. I was very fat by that time, and had morning sickness every day. We lived with my father when we were children, my mother had divorced him, and when she visited us one Saturday afternoon she said to me: 'You know what you are, don't you, you're pregnant. Tell your father.' So I did, and then I was terrified that it would be born deformed because of all the things I had done.

– *What did your father say about you being pregnant?*

– Not a word of sympathy. I was forced straight into adulthood. I was just seventeen. I was forced to be totally self-supporting as he decided that he didn't have to pay another penny for me – the boy had to do that. He had just left school and had his first job.

– *Did your father know your boyfriend before this happened?*

– Yes. He also knew quite well that I went to bed with him, but he never asked if I knew what to do so as not to get pregnant. He probably thought that I'd found out for myself. And so I became the housewife of the family. I was paid 150 guilders (about thirty-six pounds) a month and, my father said, board and lodging.

– *Weren't you allowed to continue at school?*

– No, I'd already been expelled because I was pregnant. Well, we were going to get married, My boyfriend needed permission from his father because he was under twenty-one, and when I was seven and a half months pregnant he said to me one afternoon: 'I'm leaving and I won't marry you because I don't love you any more.' 'Well then in that case I'll see you to the door', I replied. I cried and telephoned my father at his work and said: 'He's left and he's never coming back, and I'm all alone now.'

– *Did you have the child on your own?*

– Yes, it was terrible. I went to the midwife who had assisted my mother too, a big woman with a motorbike and a kind of leather helmet with ear flaps on her head, very rough, but loving. She examined me with a wooden trumpet and said everything was fine. I still thought then that you could feel if there was something wrong. I felt very safe with the woman, she was just like a big mother. But no one bothered about the psychological side of it. When I was eight months, I had to go to the hospital to be examined and to see how the child was positioned. A sister put me in a gynaecological chair, in the middle of a big room, and I was examined by a little man with glasses, who put his hand inside. I found that very unpleasant. No one said anything at all, and then they just walked away and left me lying there. I thought: I've been lying here so long, there must be something wrong, and got more and more scared. Suddenly the door opened and in came eight young people, girls and boys of my own age or a little older, and each of them began to knock on my stomach and put their hands inside, without asking or anything at all. I began to feel more and more awful. I lay there with a red face and just thought, oh god let it be over soon. When they had all had a turn, I was allowed to go.

– *Where did this happen?*

– In Scheveningen. A teaching hospital or something.

– *How was the birth?*

– I was delivered in a clinic, it was the cheapest there was. I had to pay for it myself, my father took it off the 150 guilders – I was bad, so I had to pay. During the birth, my father and the midwife sat at the foot of the bed talking and joking together. That was horrible, I wanted them to take notice of me. But the birth itself was fine: I had to bear down twice and suddenly there was a child. I wanted a boy because I thought perhaps the father would come back for a boy – he might be impressed by that. But when it was out, my father said: 'Aaah! A girl!' I got a terrible fright. 'Oh no', he said, and then the child was held up and I saw it was a boy. Luckily he was all right, no deformities. My son's father had telephoned at last the day before, to ask how things were going, and my father had picked up the phone and said: 'Yes, she is busy having your child right now', and then banged down the phone – he didn't even ask whether I wanted to talk to him. My father decided things like that for me, because suddenly I wasn't an adult any more. I had an awful time at the clinic. They called me 'Miss', always gave me my child last, and never said a kind word to me all the time I was there. No one ever asked me how I was feeling. There were three of us – one woman was nice, but the other one turned up her nose at me and thought I was a whore. It was always: 'Goodmorning Mrs Brown, Goodmorning Mrs White, Miss, your child.' At night there was always an hour and a half's visiting time for the fathers, but I wasn't allowed any visitors because my child *had* no father. That made me cry, and then my father kicked up a fuss, and after that I was allowed to have my mother or my sister or my best girlfriend. No one else because that disturbed the other women and their husbands. On the seventh day I did get a basket of fruit from the child's father, and he visited one afternoon with a winter coat for the baby – a white fur coat, when the child was born in June! Still, I was very happy with that, but he didn't come again.

– *Was there anyone who was kind to you in that time?*

– No one. I loved my son very much, as he was the only little piece of the earth which was mine, which I liked, and which also stretched out a little pair of hands to me. He was the only person with whom I could exchange hugs and cuddles. No one could take that away from me again. There wasn't much else which was pleasant. In the afternoons I went to visit women friends who had had the same thing happen to them. When the child was seven months old, I was walking him in a pram which I had bought myself when the father came up to me. He asked if I'd take the child home and then come out for a drive with him in the car he'd just bought. He said he wanted to come back because he really did love me and I was nice and thin again now – he'd had a horror of the big tummy. And so I started a relationship with the child's father, as if he was just an ordinary friend. But my father wouldn't let him come in the house, because he hadn't married me. I'd let him come in when my father wasn't there.

– *What did you do together?*

– Made love. I'd cook a meal and he'd eat it.

– *How did you feel about that?*

– I was alive again, with someone coming every day to go to bed with me. My father came home unexpectedly one afternoon. Suddenly I heard in the passage: 'Open the door, open the door at once!' My friend leaped out of the bed and put his clothes on in a flash, and I just screamed: 'Dad, just act normally! Dad, go away! I'm coming down in a minute! . . . ' but he kicked down the door and screamed: 'What's going on, you dirty scum, in my house! The boy ought to provide you with food and clothes, but all he ever does is fuck you!' When the child was two and a half, my friend finally said he'd marry me. So we bought a little house with my father's savings. After three years I ran away with the man with whom I'm living now. All that time I suspected my husband of being unfaithful to me. He always came home very late at night. He worked in bars and nightclubs. I often used to ask if he fucked other women, but: 'Oh no, oh no, how can you even think such a thing!' And then I'd get a new dress, and new shoes, and a gold chain and bangles and bunches of flowers,

and a fur coat. Oh, he was so nice to me, but something didn't fit.

I knew for sure that he went with other women. Once I got crabs off him. He started itching, a week later I had it too and wanted to go to the doctor. But no, that wasn't necessary, it came from the old house, out of the woodwork. We sprayed everywhere with DDT and I had to shake out my knickers a couple of times a day, because my whole crotch was full of little grey creatures with lots of legs. After I left him I asked him *once* more whether he hadn't always had it off with other women, and at last he admitted it. I'm so glad he was honest then, bcause I'd always had the feeling that it was wrong of me to think such bad things when he was really so nice to me. He did love me, he was terribly upset when I left.

– *Does your son know you didn't want to have him?*

– I haven't discussed the whole business with him properly, but he does know. He's uneasy, because sometimes he says: 'You didn't want me!' He's terribly interested in the abortion law and asks me about all the abortion demos I go on. He definitely does have bad feelings about it. But I've always told him: 'When you were born, I didn't want to get rid of you.' Perhaps, out of guilt, I've spoiled him too much. I feel guilty that I didn't want him, that he must have had a hard time without a father in the beginning, and that I deprived him of a father later on. Perhaps that has set him back a bit at the beginning of his puberty. He is eleven now. He tells me off: 'I want you to mend that for me tonight! I need buttons on it!' The other day, during a TV programme about discrimination against children, he kept calling out: 'Yes, you always do that! You see, you see, just like you!' That was just too much for me, I burst out crying, and the pain!! I'm telling you, a child can hurt you . . . dammit, just as much as a lover or a husband. I've talked about it with him, and said I think I'm quite a good parent to him.

– *Does he get on with your present lover?*

– Oh yes, terribly well. They hug each other and roll around on the ground together. My friend is very gentle with him, which is good because he gets to see the emotional side of a man. When we started living together, he was five. At first they left each other alone, and slowly a relationship has developed between them. They wear the same clothes, like the same music, my son asks him about his homework, and anything else he wants to know. My lover looks after the boy just as much as I do. He even goes to parents' evenings on his own if I can't go.

– *How did you meet this man?*

– He was the son of a woman my mother is friendly with. I often went there for tea or to have a meal because I was alone a lot. My ex-husband left at three in the afternoon. We got to like each other more and more, and later on he and his friends started coming to my house to listen to music. We were around the same age – he was just two years younger. One night he came alone, and after twenty minutes the tension was unbearable. Suddenly we both stood up, and we just held each other for half an hour. We felt so much for each other. A few days later I went **187** over to his place, we just crept into bed together. Neither of us could come, we just lay naked against each other, shivering, we couldn't help it, it was too much. He began to cry terribly and said that he'd never felt anything like it for anyone. A few days later he came round to my house and said: 'Either you and your son come and live me, or I'll never see you again, because I can't bear it.' He only stayed a quarter of an hour. I thought and thought and after a couple of days I rang him up and said: 'I'm coming. I'll tell my husband tonight and I'll come to you with the child straight afterwards.' My husband was alternately furious and sad – he cried, fell on his knees, promised to behave quite differently, said he *would* talk to me, he knew he had done everything wrong, I mustn't leave, he loved me so much – but I didn't care any more, I had my own happiness, although I did feel an intense sympathy for him. I put my clothes and my son's clothes into black plastic rubbish bags, and his toys too, nothing else. I felt a chair against my head, a lamp fell to pieces behind me, and when I left I got a blow in my face. And he shouted: 'Go away then, dirty whore!' I felt so bad that I was leaving that I left him everything. The house, that belonged to me, with everything in it. I didn't ask him for alimony either, just money for the child, because I thought, if I can't manage, at least I'll have something to feed the child with. Now I think that was very stupid, you know, because he has just sold the house for three times what I paid for it, and I wouldn't mind having all that money to play with!

– *Did you behave completely differently with your present boyfriend right from the start?*

– Yes, I started in a completely different way at once, but we're still changing, every day. It will last all our lives – every day we learn something more about ourselves and about each other. All the time we keep each other informed about our discoveries. It goes gradually, and we'll never finish. I also began to make love quite differently. We asked each other what we each liked, and I just told him how I wanted it. We started very carefully, step by step with each other.

– *I'm always scared that if I say what I like, I won't like it any more, and my excitement will suddenly disappear.*

– Oh yes, I know that fear well. You think: Oh god, do I have to give that many instructions! But I don't need to any more now. He always takes it very well and says: 'All right my darling, carry on. I love you so much when you enjoy it, don't say any more . . .' And then I carry on and get into it. One of the most wonderful changes is that we can be tender with each other, and we really enjoy caressing each other. I never knew that, ever. If I caressed my husband, it never stopped there – it always started the kind of tension before the big moment. And now I can do it for hours, very softly, and slowly. We hold each other peacefully, feel a leg on a leg, an arm on an arm. If he plays with my toes, I get completely carried away. If he caresses me very softly on my hair, I get such a rare feeling, like being in the mountains, you know. I never knew such feelings existed.

188

– Do you regularly make love without fucking?

– Yes, often. Sometimes I come, and he too, in my hand, just from stroking – I seldom suck him off. We often make love without orgasm, and we never go to sleep without touching each other. If we can't do that, then it's because we've had an argument, because something is wrong.

– Are you entirely satisfied with how you make love?

– No, I still want to get rid of a couple of inhibitions. You see, I can't imagine that it's nice to lick my cunt, it's so slimy and wet, and if he does it, very softly, I think: It's dirty, stop it. Then he really has to tell me twenty times that he enjoys it, and it's so nice that he loves it there and: 'Look how sweet the lips are, I think it's all so beautiful, the little hairs, and that tiny little clitoris, it's swelling a bit, everything is becoming so soft and warm, and it smells so lovely, and it makes me so excited.' Then he looks at me too and says that he loves doing it, but then I turn my head away and cry: 'Don't look at me, go away!' Because then he can see on my face that I'm enjoying it, and I shouldn't. I still find it so embarrassing. I love it when he strokes my knee and kisses it, so why not my cunt? I like my own smell on my fingers, but when he comes up, and his lips are all wet, then I cry out: 'No, don't kiss me now!' I'm going to practise licking my fingers. I've never done that. Recently when I was feeling a bit drunk, I went a bit further. I lay on top of him with my head at his penis and my whole cunt against his face, and I came like that, for the first time in that position. Afterwards we fell asleep like that, on top of each other. The next day he said: 'That was very lovely, what we did yesterday' – but he isn't allowed to talk about it, because I'll say: 'Shut up about it, that was much too difficult, and I won't do it again for a long time.'

– Did he come too?

– Yes. I don't take him completely in my mouth, I used to do that – you had to take the penis into your mouth and suck it up and down, but then I'd get this retching feeling in my throat, as if I were about to choke. So now I just lick it, and hold him in my hand and give it little kisses.

– Where does he leave his sperm?

– I don't take it in my mouth. I used to do that, before, with my husband, but it made me feel quite sick. I also don't think it's necessary. So now I let it spurt into the air, or against my shoulder, or into my hands, I don't mind any of that. It falls somewhere and slowly dries up.

– Has your friend ever tasted it?

– Yes, just recently he had a lick for the first time, he thought it tasted a bit funny. What else is there that I wanted to achieve . . .Oh yes, I want to learn to be able to make love at any time of the day, without always being scared that someone will call round. If he suggests it, I always set myself against it, for a while, and then he ends up saying: 'All right, if you really don't want to then of course we won't.' Every now and then we do it and I enjoy it a lot with a lovely orgasm, snooze afterwards, **189** hmm. So I don't understand why I'm so against it.

— I find it difficult during the day too, with children whining on the other side of the door, or if the children are due home from school.

— If my son comes home, we just say we're making love. We might be lying naked under a sleeping bag, with our hair all over the place and holding each other while he talks to us. Sometimes he jumps on to the bed for fun.

— Have you told him about sex?

— Little by little. We've always answered every question he's asked straight away. I've also said it's nice if you touch your willie while you're washing it. Later on I told him it's nice for me too, that I also have a very tiny knob where the good feelings are, and that the hole is to have children.

— Do you lose your excitement when your son comes in?

— Not any more. We did in the beginning, it used to sag the moment someone just walked in the passage. Other people live in the house too, but now if someone is busy in the kitchen, I keep my excitement and reach my climax unperturbed. I've just managed to do that during the past year. My orgasms are becoming steadily bigger, fuller, it's so nice that I can't keep it to myself any more, I really call out 'Yeeees!', and then my friend says: 'Sshhh, stop screaming', but I just carry on. I never did that before. I let myself go completely now when I come, it's just as if you see fireworks, and you call out: 'Oh!' I can bear it now too if he looks at my face when I come – I find that a bit exciting. And in the past year we have also been coming together. If I'm nearly there, I say: 'Yes, I'm nearly there', and then I keep it back and wait for him and then we can both come at the same moment. I love the way we can both go completely crazy at the same time, such an explosion for two people. I really love it.

— Can you manage that if you're fucking too?

— Yes. Then I usually lie on my stomach, and he goes in from the back. Then he can touch my clitoris with his hand under my stomach.

— Do you need fantasies to be able to come?

— Usually I do. I always fantasise about something that's not allowed. I'm lying half naked sleeping in the sun when a man passes by whom I don't know. He can't keep off me because I'm lying there so beautiful, and he begins to stroke me very softly, very tenderly and lovingly. I let him do what he likes. I pretend I don't notice, and he doesn't notice that I'm becoming excited and then I come very secretly, and he goes away again. Sometimes I build on a situation which I have experienced during the day. If for example I've bought flowers, I might fantasise that the man in the shop was very pleasant and said: 'Oh, come to the back room and I'll wrap up something special for you.' Then we make love very quickly standing up, while lots of people are waiting in the shop, and afterwards I go out as if **190** nothing has happened. In my fantasies that is very exciting.

— Do you feel guilty fantasising about someone else rather than the man you're making love with?

— I used to be ashamed because I thought it was proof that I didn't love him. But that's past now. I've even told a couple of fantasies to my boyfriend. I still have difficulties about that though.

— Do you understand why so many people feel guilty about it?

— I think because sex simply isn't allowed. People don't talk about it, they deny it, it doesn't exist and so it's as good as not allowed. I also always fantasise a forbidden situation like sex at the back of a shop when no one is looking, sex with me coming in secret. My friend fantasises that he makes love to very young girls whom he carefully teaches how to enjoy it, a kind of initiation. I can imagine that, we've talked about it and we've come to understand that you fantasise a *situation*, not the people who act in it, because they have no face. The situation is what makes it exciting, because it isn't allowed.

— Do you have more or less the same needs?

— I have slightly more. Perhaps I'm in my peak years. He gives up because of tiredness more quickly than I do.

— How do you get over that difference in your needs?

— We just don't do it. It isn't such a terrible thing.

— If you need to fart while you are making love, what do you do then? I always jump out of bed, run out of the room and fart in the passage. Often I don't get there in time.

— No, we just do it. We just say: 'Oh I have to fart.' 'Well go ahead then.' And if it stinks we shout; 'Gee, what a stink you made, terrible!' Then we flap out the bed, we often have to laugh a lot. It's just part of our bodies, the waste products from our bodies have an awful smell. You know what I did once? Held his penis when he pissed, then you feel the piss stream through it, it's really nice.

— I get the feeling that you get on really well together. Why do you think it's so good between you?

— A complete openness. We really do tell each other everything – what we feel, what we think, what we think the other one isn't thinking . . . We have no secrets from one another. Even if we go out with someone else, we tell each other everything we've done. We risk letting the other one see every aspect of ourselves – what hurts, what we're afraid of. And the best thing is, we can both be like children. When it had just snowed, he opened the curtains in the morning and called; 'Snooooow!' We ran out into the wood without breakfast with the toboggan and rolled in the snow. We are like comrades, on all fronts – we can cry together, and we can talk to each other like adults too.

— Do you feel in any way oppressed?

— Well, sometimes he is a bit like a teacher, and we have arguments about that. Then he'll try to explain it to me, but I just put my fingers in my ears, because I don't want to hear all that. **191**

– *He doesn't run away from a situation?*
– Oh no, never. We swear at each other and hit each other and things. Then we really hate each other.

– *Do you actually hit each other?*
– Sometimes I thump him, and he thumps me back, or holds me tight. It's really a power struggle. Then we say terrible things to each other, just to hurt: 'You're just like your mother, it's all no good and we'd better break up.' At such moments I feel like dying I can tell you – it feels as if it's the end of our relationship. Then we're stuck, we can't say anything else and go to bed furious. When we touch each other accidentally, we give out a cry of disgust. I'm the only one who can break through the impasse. He daren't put out his hand any more because he's scared stiff that I'll hit it – which I always do by the way. He used to stand behind me, put his arms round me and say: 'Darling, let's talk', but I always spat back: 'Leave me alone, go away!' Even though I really wanted him to keep on holding me. So now I always begin by suggesting we sit at the table and talk it out. And one by one we pull out the murderous darts we have shot at each other: 'You said you hate me because I'm like my mother. Is that true?' 'No, but I knew you would hate to be like your mother and that's why I said it.' So that's one out. And I say to him: 'I know it hurts you a lot if I say that you're just as egotistical as your father, but I don't mean it.' Another dart out. And when we have pulled them all out, we lie crying in each other's arms and say: 'It's all going much better than it seems; we mustn't have such dreadful rows!' Then we feel fine again and have an enormous love-making celebration and walk outside in the street, hand in hand, singing. We also make promises to each other. For example, I can't bear criticism, and he is scared to hurt me, and often holds back as a result. At New Year's Eve we talked about it and decided he would use a code word, 'New Year', before he says what he is feeling. We also have a beautiful gesture for something that is so painful that at the moment you can't speak about it at all. We act as though there's a dagger in our breast and the other person can immediately react with: 'God, god, how terrible, have I hurt you there so much, I'm so sorry', and hold you.

– *Do you also make love with other people?*
– Yes, I've met a lot of very nice men through my friend – I can talk with them easily, and have sexual feelings for them too. We've said to one another that there are a lot of people we like and find interesting, and if they give us signs that they want to make love, we'd like to be able to do so. We didn't act on it at that time because we were scared we'd lose each other. But we have so many good feelings for each other, and we're so convinced that we belong together and can't lose each other, that we can now confidently look outwards and explore. Our relationship is number one and we're still working on it – outside that, we only
192 do it for fun.

– *Who started this?*
– I did. I did it just for an ego trip. When I do it, I'm just a body, I let myself be admired like a doll. I walk into the room and they call out: 'Oh how beautiful!' And I take it all in, it's a laugh. I get so excited when I'm being desired, but I don't really let myself go with the young men. I don't come.
– *Don't they want to know why?*
– No, men don't ask that. They never ask me if I've used contraception either, they aren't bothered about it.
– *How many times have you done it?*
– With about five men, I think. All of them only once, except the first – with him it lasted six months. That was an amazing test of our relationship. I told my friend: 'If you want me to stop, you must say so and I'll stop at once.'
– *Did he have difficulty touching your body afterwards?*
– Yes, straight afterwards he did. He found it hard to touch my cunt because the other guy had been in there, but I helped him and said: 'Come on darling, it's really not important, it's just something nice I did, I don't think about it at all when we're making love together', and then he can get over it. Of course he's had other women too, but not so many, three or four I think, but I'm more jealous than he is. I hate it! The worst is that the women all have orgasms. I want to hear all about it, but at the same time I want to throw up. There were some women who burst into tears and said they'd never experienced that with a man.
– *Don't they want to go to bed with him again afterwards?*
– Yes, I'm afraid of that. Afraid they'll fall in love with him because he makes love so well! Luckily he always makes it very clear that it's just for *one* night. And I'm terribly jealous about it, goddammit – the men I meet who don't know anything, who are all clumsy or rough, and I don't dare tell them either; they'll have to find out from their girlfriends.
– *What a pity.*
– Oh, do you think I should? Yes, perhaps I should, then their real girlfriends would benefit.
– *How long is it before you can kiss your boyfriend again after he has made love with another woman?*
– He showers afterwards and cleans his teeth, then it's gone and I have to reclaim his body. I have to regain the territory and make love quickly, hold him tight, kiss him, get him to go inside me, come, and then it's all wiped out. We do that the night after, it's quicker than it used to be, but we have to talk about it first.
– *What risks do you run in doing these things the way you want to do them?*
– At the moment I don't run any risks with my friend because he wants to live like this too. We try to be as equal as possible, and he doesn't oppress me. We share the housework, and his tolerance of dirt is lower than mine, but then I only have to walk on a dirty kitchen floor, I don't have to eat off it, do I? I make no concessions in my relationship with him. I tell him clearly what I

want and why I feel that what I've been doing so far in our relationship has been constructive. And if after a couple of years he says: 'I've had enough and I'm off now', then it just means he's not right for me any longer, he can't take it, and I'll have to carry on by myself. That would be the greatest risk. But at the moment he supports me in everything I want to achieve. I am also beginning to stick my neck out more by being more open with people, by telling other people more about myself, and he helps me through that by talking to me about it. I notice that gradually I'm standing more on my own two feet; we lose friends who don't like our honesty. Men in my area have difficulty with emancipated women. The world is just a big doll's house: the women aren't allowed to do anything at all; they're at home in their houses; all the men are at work, and everyone visits each other in cars, and no one really does what they feel like. And there's me walking amongst them, wanting to do what I like, and all the people say: 'You're crazy thinking you can do what you like, it's not on.' So we don't have much social life. The greatest opposition comes from people who can't say: 'I'm doing what I want.' Of ourse I do have guilt feelings now and then and ask myself if I shouldn't spend more time with my child, or whether I should do the housework more thoroughly – these are the old role models which still loom up inside me, dark and thundery. I always say straightaway that I'm feeling bad about it, and I ask my little family if they miss me, if they want me to cook supper, but they both cry out: 'Go away! If we want to eat something, we'll cook it ourselves!' And my son adds: 'You wanted to be a feminist, so you'll have to let us look after ourselves.' That's the strength behind me, my friend and my son. I'm not alone in it anyway – we do it together.

XIV. Towards new relationships with men

1. Social equality

Because sexual experiences between women and men are connected to power relations, sexuality won't easily change unless those relationships change too. If women and men aren't equal outside the home, it's difficult for them to have an equal relationship inside it. To achieve equality we need to have the same opportunity to get jobs; we need to be paid the same wages, and the housework needs to be shared. All this will only be possible if there is better provision for sharing responsibility for children. To make that happen, a lot of other things will have to change. It won't happen overnight either, but *one* way of feeling more independent is to start working on it.

'When we had two children one after the other, I gave up my studies for a while. When they went to nursery school I couldn't see the point in studying any more. I began to feel suffocated at home. We had a lot of arguments. He got more and more interested in his new job. I didn't have much to really absorb me. When I helped set up a refuge with a couple of mothers from the nursery, everything changed. It became a huge organisation. In the evenings we started a women's group, and I helped to set up courses in the neighbourhood centre. I became a voluntary worker and am now trying to get better paid work. I feel so much better now and more self-confident, not just because of the money, but also because I do something well, something which has meaning for me and which is just as important as what he does. It also influences the way we relate to each other. When I stayed at home all the time I didn't feel like doing anything, not even making love, when he came home full of stories about his work. Now we both have something to say, and it's good when we're together.'

It isn't always possible to rescue a relationship when the balance of power shifts. When you become independent, *his* dependence comes to the surface, and it is difficult for men to admit that. Almost all women who are changing the balance of power in their relationships have the same problems, even if the change takes place carefully, even if your husband has said a hundred times that he thinks it's fine if you attend that course while he looks after the children, or that perhaps you should do more with your life because you are suffocating. Sometimes relationships get better after a few good crises, and sometimes they break up. Men have much less training in talking openly about their emotions,

certainly in comparison with women who have been in consciousness raising groups, or who have the support of other
women, and this doesn't make it any easier to make changes.
Whatever happens it's hard work.

2. Saying what you want

In relationships between women you often have the feeling that
you still have to invent the wheel: there are few examples, we
have to find out everything ourselves. In relationships between
women and men, there are so many rigid patterns that we have
to unlearn an awful lot before we can start to build something
new. Betty Dodson, in her book *Liberating Masturbation*,
describes two different patterns which recur in sexual relations
between women and men. One is where the man is responsible
for the development of the whole romantic fuck party. He must
have an erection, just by looking at her body; he ought to hold the
erection while he 'gives' her an orgasm, without having any idea
at all about what she enjoys. And of course, while she is waiting
so passively nothing much happens to her, and so as not to
disappoint him, she says that an orgasm isn't all that important to
her, that their love for each other matters much more. A more
modern version is where the woman is responsible for his
erection. She doesn't want to be prudish, so she does what he
likes best. She does oral sex to get him a hard on. He takes over
in the position which suits him best. She helps him and throws
herself into a whole act of sighs and moans and groans to excite
him even more. He comes and she fakes it. Two recognisable
patterns, and neither of them is what we want. We don't want to
wait passively until he gives us an orgasm, as if it were a present
– not to mention the fact that it doesn't usually work like that
anyway. And we don't want to be the sexy type either, who does
her best to help him to his sexual pleasure and allows him the
illusion that he is an amazing lover, if all we get from it is *him*
feeling fantastic. What do *we* want?
We do dream about it, but many of the dreams are influenced by
what we have been taught to expect. For example, that sexuality
ought to be something spontaneous and that it kills the romance
if we talk about it. For example, that a good lover can guess what
we like best. But how is he supposed to know if we don't make it
clear to him? Perhaps he has read books about it, but there's
often a lot of nonsense in books and anyway, there are no
general rules which apply to all women.

*'He really did his best. He knew the clitoris was important to
women and he could find out where it was. He'd read that a
woman needs extended foreplay to become aroused. Every
time he could see I'd nearly reached orgasm, he'd stop using
his hands and just start fucking. That was incredibly frustrating
because then nothing else happened to me. Instead of asking if
he could carry on using his hands a bit longer, I preferred to ask* **197**

him to stop using his hands altogether, so at least I didn't get right close to an orgasm and then have it cut off. Only later did I dare tell him that I liked it best if we first made love the way I needed to be able to come, and then how he liked it best.'

We need to ditch all the indoctrination about what is called 'normal' and how we ought to do it. It's nonsense to call the way most men enjoy making love 'sexual intercourse' and the way women like best 'variations'. There are hundreds of different ways that a woman's body and a man's body can do lovely things together, with hands, mouths, skin and hair, and the sliding of the penis into the vagina is only one of them.

'Usually we just make love normally. That is to say, ordinary fucking. What I like best is when he licks me. Occasionally when we are very much in the mood, he does it, but I've never dared ask because I think he doesn't like doing it. Definitely not when he's already had an orgasm. Then I have the feeling I'd really be asking him a favour. Well, then it stops being a pleasure, doesn't it?'

It isn't easy to risk saying what we want out loud. We don't have the language to say it in our own words. It's awkward if we have to be too 'technical', if we have to say, 'a little more to the right', or 'not so hard'. And it seems to conflict with our emotions too, if we think in terms of demanding our 'rights'. It goes against much of our conditioning to rate our own pleasure just as highly as someone else's needs. When we go after our own pleasure, we often feel guilty, we feel too demanding, or hard and unpleasant. It's important that we break through that guilt. In the end if we sacrifice ourselves to someone else, it turns into bitterness or vindictive feelings.

Another reason we don't find it so easy to be honest about what we want is that a man doesn't always react well, or we feel intuitively that we're hurting him if we suggest another way: we're implying that he isn't the ideal lover, that it could be better. Many men become bitter, aggressive or sulky if their sexual power is challenged. That's one reason why women often say they've learned everything they know about sex from their husbands, even if it's their second marriage, or if they've had other lovers before marriage. Even the sentence: 'You're the first person with whom it has been so good', will have been heard by a lot of men. It can be emotionally true – if you make love with someone you are terribly in love with it often seems like the first and best time. But it also has something to do with the ideas we have about how vulnerable the male ego is when it comes to bed; we want him to feel good, even if it's at our own cost . . .

3. Do what you like ...

A lot of women would like to take the initiative, if they only dared.

'I always fantasised that it was me who seduced him first. That I would slowly seduce him, would take him with me to bed. But it never came to that, because as soon as he noticed that I felt like it, he would take over as quickly as possible. Once I told him I'd like it if he didn't lie on top straight away, but would leave it to me for a while. We had a lot of pleasure from that: we both giggled a little and were a bit nervous. But in the end he really liked it.'

Some men experience women who take the intitiative as 'unfeminine', and therefore unattractive. In *Worlds of Pain* by Lilian Breslow Rubin, a beautiful book which makes very clear how sexual relations follow from the division of labour between women and men, there is a neat example. The man is talking about how his wife once let him know that she felt like making love. 'It isn't that I mind that she let me know what she wanted, but that she was so unsubtle. I mean, if she'd done it in a nice feminine way it would have been OK. But femininity and a bit of subtlety, well, they aren't her strong points.' By which he's saying that women can only look after their own needs by doing it with flattery and *very* carefully.

Many men react very peculiarly if you, as a woman, take the initiative.

'Once at a party I just said to a man with whom I'd been making eye contact for quite a while that I'd like to make love to him. You could see all the colour drain out of his face. He drank up his beer and wouldn't leave the toilet for the next half hour.'

4. ... As you want it

'I never knew when I felt like a fuck, because he always wants it well before me. Then I announced I was going on strike. I didn't want to make love until I really wanted it, and I didn't want any hints about whether I was in the mood, or suggestive hands up my jumper. It wasn't easy to begin with, even though he said he agreed. We both had to get used to it. But when we did make love, it was terrific. We fuck less now, but we make love better.'

'Before we were married I thought making love was wonderful. It was exciting to keep on finding out new ways of giving each other pleasure. I found it extremely moving to notice how happy he was with me. But after a couple of years of marriage, it changed a lot. It was taken for granted, every time the same. More of a habit. He didn't bother any more to wait until we'd made a good atmosphere. "We aren't so young any more, love is for children", he'd say.'

If we've made love in the past better than we do now, it may be a question of the *way* we make love, or of the situation. It's often considered 'mature' to give up cuddling and go straight for the goal. That way we forget to make love with our whole skin, our whole body. An exercise, which is used in sex therapy too, is to relearn how to make love with your whole body: to spend an hour with each other, when everything is allowed except fucking or anything aimed directly at making an orgasm.

'The two of us have begun to do the things we used to do when we were terribly in love. Eat out, dress up. Meet in the city after work. A weekend away, with the car.'

'I would rather concentrate completely on my own orgasm. I just don't make it if I think about him at the same time. What I like best is to come first. Then my vagina is terribly soft and sensitive, and I get a very good feeling if he comes into it. I don't get another orgasm, but I enjoy myself concentrating on him, experiencing it with him. If he comes inside me before I've had an orgasm, it isn't half as nice.'

'Occasionally I have an orgasm when we fuck, but only if I'm really very excited, completely in the mood, and if we wait until I'm close to an orgasm. If we start too soon, it doesn't work'.

5. Difficulties

There are few sexual difficulties which are really 'technical' problems. And even these would be fewer if we didn't cling to the idea of what *ought* to happen.
People's need for sex varies. Often the man has more inclination to make love; sometimes the woman does. In both cases, you can put the other person under pressure, or call them 'sick' (a 'weak' libido) and send them to a therapist. Or you could try not to save up all your sexual needs so as to get rid of the whole lot in one go. You could try to improve your erotic relationship with yourself. Men too can learn to be more friendly towards their own bodies, and not assume that the slightest twitch in their penis means they need a woman's body.
Very occasionally there are physical ailments which make fucking unpleasant. An infection, erosion, or too little discharge can make the vagina oversensitive. Infections and erosions can be cured. Too little discharge can also be a way of telling you that you're not enjoying making love, not excited enough. As you get older, hormone changes may affect the walls of the vagina and make it drier or thinner. There are creams for that, and it's also possible to use spit or a lubricant. (Vaseline isn't good because it isn't soluble in water.) But you may want to consider whether you find fucking the most enjoyable way of making love. As with 'vaginismus', when the muscles of your cunt pull together so tightly that nothing can get in, you might do well to ask yourself

why you should do it if your body tells you you don't want to. There is therapy for vaginismus (see the next chapter), or you can practise by yourself, inserting a finger slowly while your muscles are relaxed, until you aren't afraid any more. But it's also worth thinking whether you really want to fuck.

Even impotence is a problem that has more to do with outside pressures than with physical disability. Many men have learned to see their body as a kind of machine programmed to obey commands: naked woman's body equals erection. Penises are often wiser than their masters; they refuse if the emotions don't fit the commands. Anxiety and desire don't go happily together, and fear of failure leads to failure. So it's no coincidence that there have been more complaints of impotence lately – men who react defensively to women who demand that their needs be fulfilled. If men could learn to make love with their whole bodies and attach less importance to the stiffening of that one tiny area, impotence wouldn't be such a problem, nor would premature ejaculation, or having an erection but no orgasm, or not being able to keep an erection long enough. Because if we stop thinking that a woman has to come via fucking, why should a man need to keep going, or make big efforts to postpone his orgasm, trying to take his mind off it by saying his thirteen times table! Can't he make love in a different way too? Can't we still make love even if a man has no erection, or if he's lost his erection?

You can make love in all kinds of ways, and I don't mean all the different positions, which all come to the same thing in the end – except upside down or back to front! You can also make an orgasm with gentle fingers, with lips, with a tongue. It's sometimes a bit of a struggle if you're used to thinking of 'sex organs' as dirty. Having a bath together helps. Learning to know your own dear cunt so that you know it's nice, not dirty, helps too. Not all women enjoy having a penis in their mouth. Perhaps you'll like it better after a shower. Perhaps it will help if you sit or lie so you can decide how deep it goes in; it's always unpleasant if you get the feeling you're going to choke because you can't control the movements yourself. Swallowing sperm does no harm, and it can't make you fat either. But perhaps you don't like the taste. Most men don't like the taste either – ask him if he'd like to taste his own sperm, and if he pulls a face, you're obviously supposed to enjoy something he'd never do for himself. You can spit sperm out, or make sure that it doesn't go in your mouth. Actually, it's mostly the little part under the glans, where the foreskin is joined with a little bit of skin, that is the most sensitive. By the time an orgasm is close, it's often just enough to stimulate that little part. It doesn't do any harm either to fuck during your period, but perhaps you don't like having your uterus poked at when it's more sensitive. That may also be the case at other times – some women love the feeling of pressure against their uterus; others don't like it at all. If you think it's a terrible mess with all that blood, but you want to fuck, you can use your **203** cap, if you have one, to hold back the blood until after you've made love. Perhaps you love having a penis inside you. A vagina has few nerve endings, certainly not deep inside you, but you can feel the pressure and that can be a specially satisfying feeling, even if you don't get an orgasm from it. But there's a big difference between having someone lying on top of you hammering away at you, and feeling that you can determine for yourself how deep and how quickly, and how strong the movements are. So you could try lying next to each other, or he could support himself on his elbows so that his whole weight isn't on top of you. Some women occasionally enjoy feeling the whole weight of someone on top of them; others are reminded of lying under a steam roller, which isn't so erotic. If you want orgasms from fucking, but don't 'manage' in the traditional position, you can try to find a way in which he could caress your clitoris at the same time – for example, if you lie with your back against his stomach. You can also stroke your own clitoris while you're fucking. You could also show your lover how you orgasm if you do it yourself. As long as we don't forget that it was meant for our pleasure. Not to prove something. Not to achieve something. Not because we 'ought'.

Further reading

I mentioned Lilian Breslow Rubin's book, *Worlds of Pain*, in this chapter. It's a beautiful book about the lives of working class families which clarifies a lot about wife and husband relationships, on a sexual level too (out of print).
There are hardly any books about sex specifically about and for men. In general that's because just about all books on sex are about men, without saying so in so many words. But there are some books about male sexuality coming over from the States now. One with a kind of liberated-sex-therapist approach is *The Male His Body His Sex* by Alfred Allan Lewis (import). It could be a lot worse – it does relate sex to relationships, gives men's personal experience by using quotations and is 'liberal' about homosexuality. It's also 'liberal' about porn – 'part of the art and religion of many great civilisations' (so that's all right then?). And – a tell-tale sign! – there is no clitoris in the index! It tells us that there has been a 'sexual revolution' – which apparently means that nowadays 'foreplay enriches the marital sex experience', and men stay in the vagina about ten minutes longer before ejaculating than they used to three decades ago (not such a revolution for the woman if she doesn't *like* him being in there!). And that 'the contemporary man can be victimised by the liberated woman in her new role as sexual aggressor' (tell that to the women in the local refuge). It's revealing that the author says that 'while writing this book, it was repeatedly brought home to me that I was treating my body with far less concern than I accorded to any other machine that I owned' – what a *male* metaphor! And that before writing it, 'all that I knew about my

sexuality was that, in the main, I enjoyed it'. Not what many women would say, or expect other women to identify with.

Men and Sex by Bernard Zilbergeld (Fontana) is a more radical book, though still written entirely for heterosexuals, with the usual excuse that gay men can use 'much of the material and most of the techniques'. It talks about men 'faking it' – not erections, rarely orgasms, but regularly their feelings. It even says penetration is only *one* way of relating sexually, not necessarily the best – quite a breakthrough! Yet it doesn't seem altogether convinced by this. For instance, it justifies not caring about whether you have an erection by saying that not caring is precisely the way to get one! 'You need to be able to take such situations in stride.'

There are a lot of books around about sexuality – mainly about heterosexuality in fact. Some are mentioned in further reading for chapter five, in relation to orgasm. Kass Teeters' *Women's Sexuality: Myth and Reality* (import) is a lovely book about women's pleasure – neither specifically heterosexual nor lesbian. It's very accessible and beautifully illustrated, with the emphasis on being sensual and playful and having fun.

Treat Yourself to Sex by Paul Brown and Carolyn Faulder (Penguin) absolutely omits homosexuality – mentioning it on the last page, after voyeurism and fetishism! Very couple-oriented, it's based on the work done in the sex therapy clinics run by the National Marriage Guidance Council. Organised in 'sex-pieces' – exercises for couples to do together, along 'put-off-intercourse-until-you-can't-wait-any-longer' lines. Within that framework, some good advice, and some sense of the social context that helps produce 'sex problems'.

Any woman would of course learn a lot about herself and her sexuality from the books on lesbianism too (further reading chapter eight).

Most books about sex aimed at young people are fixated on sex for reproduction, avoiding sex for pleasure. One such – a soft example – is *How a Baby is Made* by Per Holm Knudsen (Piccolo). The woman is drawn with no clitoris – the excuse presumably being that she doesn't *need* one to have a baby; intercourse is shown only with him lying on top, and we're assured that father and mother are making a baby because they love each other so much – and afterwards they're 'very happy because now they are a family'. What about mom and dad making love and having fun, not just making babies and having a family?

Where Do I Come From? by Claire Rayner (Arlington Books), for eight years onwards, goes further than the title would suggest. It even advocates self-examination for little girls! Masturbation and homosexuality are still seen as phases, though.

Most sex education books treat 'sex' as synonymous with heterosexual intercourse – which means female arousal and orgasm can be easily overlooked. Most teenage girls still don't know about the clitoris, and many books still shy away from

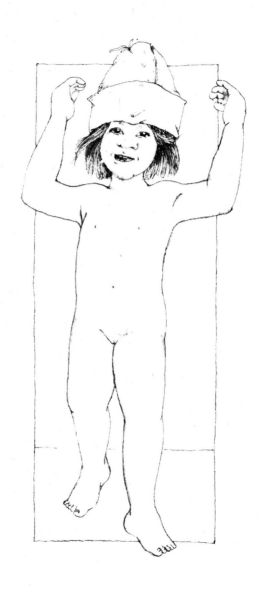

including it on their diagrams of female parts. The 'fucking for babies' approach also makes it easy to ignore homosexuality. *Will I Like It?* by Peter Mayle (WH Allen) has this to say on the subject: 'Nobody really knows why homosexuality develops in some people . . . It's a mistake to assume you're a homosexual on the basis of occasional homosexual feelings, and it's a mistake to push yourself towards homosexuality because of them. Wait until you're sure, otherwise you could cause yourself a lot of unhappiness and confusion.' Can you imagine the same being said about heterosexuality? Just try substituting hetero- for homo- throughout!

In other ways, this book is quite sympathetic, written from the point of view of girls and boys about to go to bed with each other for the first time. Yet ways of making love which are nice for her are still called foreplay or afterplay with fucking the Real Thing. The text is critical about advertising using slim beautiful young people with a toothpaste smile, but the book itself is packed with sugary pictures. It's also a bit hearty, ignoring sexual inequality: 'If both of you feel like raping each other, fine, if not, an over-aggressive rush by either side could lead to an impossibly tense vagina or a lost erection.' Eager to highlight the pleasures of sex, it becomes glib in places, untrue to most girls' experience.

Boy Girl Man Woman by Bent Claesson (Penguin) isn't at all bad. A lot of reliable factual information, and thoughtful about love. But the language is highly unerotic, and it still assumes heterosexuality as the norm – not reproduction-oriented, though. *Make It Happy* by Jane Cousins (Penguin/Virago) has less on relationships, deliberately steering clear of love and emotions and sticking to information. This is clearly presented in an informal but not patronising tone. The author, a feminist, challenges the purely 'sex-for-babies' line and informs girls well about their own sexual response. Even here though, homosexuality is treated briefly, separately, and as if for the education of heterosexuals.

Helen Singer Kaplan's *Making Sense of Sex* (Quartet) is terrible on homosexuality, placing it with sexual variations such as voyeurism, and saying 'psychiatrists are not sure what causes homosexuality' (try substitution again!). It also tells us that 'a woman who needs clitoral play to climax can be a great sex partner' – thanks a million! The book's supposed to be for young people, but it doesn't sound like it at all.

Coventry Women's Education Group managed a very readable style in their pamphlet *Please Yourself – Sex for Girls* (in alternative bookshops). It aims to reinstate the clitoris and stress sexual *pleasure* for girls. If anything, it overreacts against any sensitivity in the vagina. It also covers contraception, 'know your body' and VD – which unfortunately means there's virtually no space actually to talk about relationships, or making love, which is where it could have been excitingly different from so many sex education books.

XV. Help

As soon as we begin to think about sexuality from the point of view of our own needs, our definitions of what we call 'problems' change. This chapter is about the help you can get for 'sexual problems' and about the help you can organise for yourself, together with other women.

1. The medical 'experts'

GPs aren't the best people to ask for help with sexual problems. Few doctors have been taught anything about sexuality during their training – and so they're as ignorant, or as informed, as the next person. Some doctors have acquired some knowledge about it, but the medical approach to sexuality is questionable. In medical ideology, people are regarded simply as bodies which do or don't 'function' well. A GP who decides that your symptoms aren't physical might refer you to a psychiatrist, but this isn't necessarily going to help. Consultants in specialist clinics are obviously going to have more experience in dealing with sexual problems, but the question still is, what kind of experience? It can't be taken for granted that psychiatrists have freed themselves from male or heterosexual patterns and really accept female sexuality from a woman's point of view. You could still fall into the hands of someone who would measure your satisfaction by your 'coitus frequency', and want to give you treatment because you don't come during fucking. Obviously lesbian women run the gravest risk from orthodox psychiatry – you can have your whole sexual identity called into question. For every good experience with seeking this kind of help from the medical profession, you hear of many bad ones. It's as well to be wary.

The trouble with looking for therapy is that it's very difficult to find out beforehand if it's going to be of any use to you. Like the medical profession in general, psychiatrists and therapists surround themselves in a smokescreen of mysterious language. They don't open up their work to discussion; they seldom explain what they do and why, so it's almost impossible to decide if you want what they're offering. In many forms of therapy there's a lot of misogyny – hatred of women – or, at least, a lack of understanding of women's position – which is why we have problems in the first place. If you want to find out more about therapy before you even start looking, read *In Our Own Hands: A Book of Self-Help Therapy*. It describes the different methods of therapy, conventional and alternative, as well as suggesting how you can use therapy techniques without going to the professionals, and it's written by women for women.

2. Where to look

Despite the general gloomy picture, there are therapists working in the NHS who are sympathetic and have an understanding of women's social reality – if only you can find them. And, outside the hospitals, there are a number of organisations which offer a counselling service. They don't always sound the likeliest places to go to – the Marriage Guidance Council is one; others are the Family Planning Association, Brook Advisory Service, the Youth Counselling Service and the local Child Guidance Clinic. The sort of counselling you get depends on the individuals working in your area; you may be lucky and find someone you can really get on with.

How do you set about looking? Possibilities vary so much around the country that local advice is best – from friends with first-hand experience or from a local women's centre if there is one. If you have a well-informed GP whom you know and trust, it's worth asking there. Or you could write to the Women's Therapy Centre in London (address at the end of the book). The Centre offers individual therapy and a variety of group workshops from a feminist point of view, and they can also give information about the rest of the country.

How you make your final choice depends completely on how you feel about the therapist. Can you really trust this person? Can you see both of you working together on the problems you bring? Don't forget that therapy tends to open up more of yourself to be explored than you might originally have thought. In the end, how you feel about the therapist is far more imprortant than what school of thought she or he belongs to, or what methods she or he uses. Don't be afraid to shop around or to say no, if you have misgivings.

3. Conventional psychotherapy

Individual psychotherapy is what you're most likely to be offered (if you're offered anything) if you go through the normal NHS channels. Psychotherapy these days is usually based on a mixture of methods. There aren't many psychiatrists around who make you lie on a couch like Freud did, and whom you'll visit twice a week for years to bare your soul. But many therapists retain something of Freudian psychoanalysis. That means that he (or she, but that's less likely, so I use the word he), if you to come to him with sexual problems, will attribute many of your present problems to your early childhood and the relationship between your mother and your father. We have of course inherited from the past many of the patterns we are now stuck in, and it can do us no harm to work out what, for example, was the effect on us of our mother always suppressing her own needs and making them subservient to the needs of her family, and living out her ambitions via her children; or of our father letting us

know subtly that he would rather have had a son than a

daughter. The trouble with most people who are trained in psychoanalysis is that they accept the power relations between women and men as given, and see problems if the power relationship isn't functioning as it 'ought'. We, on the other hand, are now slowly beginning to realise that the inequality *itself* is the cause of many problems. So a therapist will quickly call a woman 'dominant' if she doesn't constantly allow herself to be put down as a matter of course.

The most infamous piece of rubbish from which the psychoanalytical school starts is the myth of the vaginal orgasm. Rather than helping a woman find a way of making love which is pleasant for her too, or investigating whether the vaginal orgasm really exists, women are 'treated' for 'disordered development', are suspected of unconscious penis envy, or of traumas in their early years. Another well-known crime which the Freudians have on their conscience is disbelieving the stories about incest which their patients told them. They thought that women came to them with fantasies of their unconscious desires to fuck with their father. Most therapists today aren't so crude, but most still work from the premise that a woman ought to desire a man, that she ought to want children, that she ought to find sex (with a man) pleasurable, and that she ought to do it often. The trouble is that it's seldom made clear that these judgements are being passed. Most therapists insist that their own opinions don't count. Meanwhile the questions that they ask, the approval they do or do not show, point clearly in a certain direction. If this isn't a direction with which you agree, you don't benefit from the therapy, and you can find yourself in a situation in which you feel very vulnerable and uncertain, which leads you even further into despair.

I'll be able to afford therapy with all this change...

The disadvantage of individual therapy is that you have no chance to compare your experiences with those of other women, and so are almost automatically shoved back into your feeling that it is, after all, your own personal problem, your fault. That can strengthen the female pattern which gives us all so many problems. So it's very bad that most therapists receive little training in how to perceive the social causes of problems, let alone the problems women have in particular. You may well get a lot from one therapist who *does* have a perception of the position of women and of social causes, and looks with that perspective at your development and what kind of damage you suffered in your youth. But, alas, such therapists are rare.

4. Family or couple therapy

Family or couple therapy is a modern form of therapy sometimes available on the NHS. In this field too, many variations are possible. The best thing about family therapy is that it's based on the premise that problems don't just stem from an individual's development, but that they can start in a relationship with someone else – with the different expectations that people have **211**

of each other, with patterns that develop between them. Many sexual problems are referred to family therapists. So far as it goes, that's fine, because sex is seldom just a technical occurrence. It usually does have a lot to do with the way people interrelate.

But family therapy also has limitations. Most therapists treat a woman and a man as two equals, who have got stuck in their communication with each other. With the help of a specialist, they learn to be more honest with one another about what bothers them, to express their needs more openly, and then to relate to each other. If *she* complains that he always leaves his dirty clothes on the floor, and *he* complains that she shows little interest in sex (with him), then the solution is obvious: in exchange for the fact that she shows more willingness to make love with him, he will tidy up now and then. What such a solution disguises is that it should be absolutely normal that he clears up his own mess, without her having to thank him for it, and that nothing is ever solved by making love if you don't really feel like it. Never. The limitation built into practically all relationship therapy is that it only looks for solutions *inside* the relationship. By definition it doesn't touch most of the real problems. A married couple hardly ever consists of two equals. Men have an advantage because of their social position, and few family therapists take that into account. The division of labour between women and men is seldom seen as the cause of their problem.

Luckily, experiments are taking place here and there with other forms of relationship therapy. For example, it is sometimes accepted that marriage problems aren't just something for the woman and man *together*, but that a woman might have more in common with other women and their problems, and might also get more support and recognition from other women. Occasionally work is done with women's groups and men's groups.

5. Behaviour therapy

This is another therapy used in British hospitals. There are different schools of behaviour therapy, but they all have in common that they don't try to look for a radical solution to a problem. They teach very practically how to get rid of a problem, for example, agoraphobia or alcoholism. The method used is that people learn a specific behaviour pattern by reward, and unlearn another behaviour pattern by punishment. By rewarding desirable behaviour and punishing undesirable behaviour, it is possible to learn new patterns of behaviour. This mostly happens step by step. Someone who has agoraphobia for example is encouraged first to go out with someone else, and then a little bit further each time on their own.

Terrible things can be done in behaviour therapy. People have, for example, tried to teach men to unlearn their homosexuality by showing them pictures of naked men and at the same time giving them electric shocks, or giving them something that will make them vomit. Afterwards they are shown pictures of naked women, accompanied by soft music and lighting.

Behaviour therapy can be very efficient in helping you to get over unpleasant anxieties, but it doesn't get to the *cause* of the problems.

An example of the use of behaviour therapy is in the treatment of 'vaginismus', the contraction of the vaginal muscles so that a penis can't penetrate. You could try to do something about it by finding out if there is any early cause, for example if you once had a dreadful experience with men and are now afraid of a penis. (This isn't at all unlikely if you hear the experiences women do have.) But behaviour therapy tries to make you unlearn the reflex which causes your vaginal muscles to contract automatically as soon as it looks as if you are about to be fucked. *One* behaviour therapist who treats vaginismus puts the woman in a chair with a blanket over her and tells her she must put her own finger into her vagina. If that succeeds, he gives her a cup of coffee and five pence (truly!). If she succeeds in keeping her finger in for a while, he goes on with glass tubes. And if that also succeeds, she has to try it with a real penis. Considering that real penises tend to be attached to men, women who didn't have a regular lover had problems, so the therapist tried to experiment with a volunteer. His experiment failed because the woman in question didn't like seeing the volunteer sitting there and threw him out. Experiment failed. The therapist then suggested that the youth service organise a sort of pool of male volunteers, who would allow their penises to be used for women with vaginismus to practise on. For a fee.

Most women who follow this form of treatment are 'cured', that is to say, ordinary fucking can take place afterwards. But it's a striking fact, according to the therapists, that patients are so little pleased with the result later. This kind of treatment is at least better than the one used in the past, where the vaginal muscles were cut surgically. In later discussion, one or two therapists admitted to having doubts about this treatment. You need to ask yourself for whom the vaginismus poses a problem – for the man who wants to get in, or for the woman who thinks that she is depriving her husband? Perhaps it is *more* a question of the woman needing to get back control over her own vagina?

6. Sex therapy for married couples

One kind of therapy that specialises in sexuality is the sex therapy based on the work of Masters and Johnson – though it is not obtainable everywhere. During this therapy, the woman and the man (it is always done in couples) are given a number of exercises through which they slowly learn to make love pleasantly. At first the couple learn to caress each other without worrying about the results, just to enjoy it. If that works well, they
go further, step by step, and they're allowed to caress the

'genitals' too. All this time there is a prohibition on 'ordinary' fucking. The therapists expect that by the end of the therapy, the people themselves will disobey the prohibition on fucking, and usually that happens. The treatment succeeds if they can 'perform coitus' with each other again, without the man coming too quickly or becoming impotent, and without the woman remaining 'anorgasmic', that is to say, not coming.

The objections against this therapy – as it is usually applied – are that at first it seems to be just about making love pleasantly, but in the end the main goal is after all the ordinary prick-in-cunt sex, with coming as a must. But what if the reason the woman feels bad about sex is because she has more need to be cherished and cuddled than to perform sexual intercourse efficiently? That's dismissed as a side-issue. All the problems that occur in a relationship because of the inequality between the woman and the man just aren't considered relevant. So it usually turns out to be a course in well-adjusted fucking.

7. Alternative therapy

Since the 1960s various other kinds of therapy have flourished, which you certainly won't get on the NHS. They tend to get lumped together and called 'alternative therapy' by some people, 'radical therapy' by others or 'growth movement' by still others, though these terms by no means all mean the same thing. The variety of theories or methods is bewildering – Gestalt, bioenergetics, psychodrama, encounter might be some of the words you've heard. All offer something different from the conventional, analytic, talking sort of therapy, and most of the methods can be used in groups – recognising that 'problems' have as much to do with relationships as with individuals. One advantage they have in common is that they haven't yet been co-opted by the medical establishment, so you're less likely to

find yourself in the usual unequal and authoritarian doctor/
patient relationship, and more likely to be working with people
who have some understanding of women and women's
situation. The disadvantage is that this isn't necessarily so. You
could still find yourself in the hands of someone with very
conventional attitudes towards authority, female and male
sexuality and homosexuality. And don't forget, you'll usually
have to pay for this kind of therapy.

8.   Sex therapy in women's groups

Here and there experiments are taking place with sex groups
intended specifically for women. A group of 'pre-orgasmic'
women (women who haven't *yet* been able to come) usually
have more success than sex therapy groups for couples. Many
women join those groups because they think it's sad for their
husbands that they can't come. So from the start, the women are
still suppressing their *own* needs – that problem isn't solved.
In pre-orgasmic groups, women learn to talk together about
sexuality and to stand up for themselves more in all areas of life.
The first exercises concern a reappraisal of your own body
(many of the principles can be found in the chapters on coming
and making love to yourself in this book). You are encouraged to
take pleasure in your own body, and finally overcome the taboo
against touching your cunt and making love to yourself. The goal
is to learn to enjoy the possibilities your own body offers you;
what you can do with that in contact with other people is only a
secondary goal.
The Women's Therapy Centre may be able to tell you about
existing groups or suggest how to start one. Sometimes groups
advertise for new members in the Small Ads column in *Spare
Rib* – or you might think of taking an advertisment yourself.

9.   Consciousness raising groups

Women can do a lot for themselves. It's certainly *not* always
better to ask an authority. Any woman can get together with
others and organise a consciousness raising group. Sexuality is
one of the subjects talked about in practically every CR group,
but you could decide to make that the main topic if you wanted to.
Six to eight women is the best number for a CR group. Usually at
least one person drops out, but with more than eight, it's difficult
to give everyone equal attention. You don't need a leader to start
a CR group. You could decide that, every time you meet, a
different person should make sure that everyone talks and
everyone has a turn.
You can decide in advance whether you are happier with women
you are already friendly with in the group, or whether you'd
rather have women you don't yet know. It can be good to get
started with people you trust. But it can also be true that you're
more honest with women you don't meet every day. You'll also

have to consider whether you want lesbians and heterosexual women in the same group. On the one hand it can be very good to break through mutual mistrust. On the other hand it's often more pleasant for lesbians to start talking with other lesbians, because you don't have to be so anxious about other women's fears. And you're less afraid of getting a 'well, you see, being a lesbian isn't perfect' reaction if you talk about problems.

CR groups often use techniques from radical therapy. For example, working in a circle, each one giving in turn an answer to a specific question, or everyone relating something about her first sexual experience. Dividing up the time equally is also a tool taken from radical therapy. You can decide that everyone has ten minutes to tell her story, or that at each meeting two women get half an hour. That prevents the ones who don't talk from remaining silent, and the talkers from gossiping through an entire session. It also has the effect that everyone is more restful, because you know that you'll all get a turn. For those who find it difficult to cut a woman short in the middle of an emotional story, an egg timer is very useful!

You can proceed in different ways. A good way to start is for everyone to relate her sexual lifestory, or to write it down.

That usually takes a very long time, and opens up a treasure house of recognition for everyone. Just by talking about it, you encounter many of the things you haven't worked through.

You can work from a list of questions, which you put together yourselves. Questions like:

– What do you know about your parents' sexuality?
– How were you told about sex? Were you just told where babies came from, or also that you can get pleasure from making love?
– How did you learn about menstruation?
– What was your first period like?
– Did you know your cunt when you were a little girl?
– Did you notice that you could make love to yourself?
– What were your first physical experiences with someone else, with a girl, a boy? How did it happen?
– What was your first romance? Woman or man?
– How did you learn to make an orgasm, or how have you tried to make an orgasm?
– What do you like doing best with your body? Do you do that?
– What kind of sexual fantasies do you have?
– What is your dream sexual relationship?
– If you are having a relationship with someone, how would you like to see it change sexually?
– How would you like to change your sexual relationship with yourself?
– What do you find difficult to say to someone else?
– Have you ever faked orgasm?
– Do you ever make love against your will?

It's easy to take up other questions once you've begun. You can also use *contracts*. A contract is a promise you make to yourself, and that you say out loud in the group so that the other women

217

can support you. Such a promise has to be possible to achieve within a certain time. If you promise yourself too much, you will be disappointed. And if you 'achieve' a contract, you can easily make a new one. A example of a contract can be: 'In the coming week I want to talk to Dave about how I want to make love differently', or 'I want to let the woman I love know that I am in love with her', or 'I want to enjoy my own body for half an hour a day, all by myself, with no one around'.

● You can *read* together, this book or *Our Bodies Ourselves*, and then discuss points you recognise. You can use books on therapy because there are methods they use which are also useful to sexual CR groups. *In Our Own Hands* contains lots of exercises and games that can help you talk more easily, and guidelines on how to get the most out of them.

● It's good to leave room for *actual problems*. It usually happens that while a discussion group is in progress, certain things happen to women there which they would like to talk about with other women. You can either let them go first, or make a space for them to talk.

● It's important for us to learn to *listen* to each other, not to give an opinion as soon as someone says something, because you then cut her story short ('yes, that happened to me last week . . .'). It's better to let someone finish talking first, and then ask if anyone has had the same experience. It's also good to realise what we do to someone if we make judgements, or if we say too easily: 'I would never have done that, I'd have thrown him out ages ago.' In order to feel safe so that we can be honest, it's important that we don't look too quickly for the 'best method' or the 'right solution', and that we don't get into competition about who is behaving in the most emancipated way.

● Usually it's clear in a sexual CR group that you aren't just discussing sex in a vacuum, without also looking at relationships, at the rest of your life, at the way in which women are treated and so on. So it's a very good idea to try to sum up at the end of an evening what all the experiences which you have heard about from each other, have to do with the *position* of women. Later on in the CR group you can read literature together which makes clear how our personal experiences are connected to politics. It is also quite possible to see what kind of action can be taken from the point of view of your separate experiences – for example in relation to discrimination against lesbians, or independent mothers or older women – and to see which groups are already doing something about it or to participate in demonstrations, for example for a woman's right to choose on abortion.

10. Women's self-help therapy groups

It isn't always easy to mix 'therapy' with 'discussion'. It's hard to switch from a therapy way of talking – where you concentrate on

uncovering and exploring emotions without rationalising them or drawing conclusions – to discussion – where you *do* try and make sense of things by comparing notes and looking for social/ political explanations. The two activities overlap, but they're not the same thing – it may help to keep them separate. A self-help group works on the same sort of principles as a CR group, but the group concentrates on helping each woman unearth the buried feelings and experiences which interfere with her getting on with or changing her own life. Discussion about what is common in women's experience, and the political issues that arise from that, is kept for a different place.

Further reading

Probably the most useful *and* enjoyable book on therapy around at the moment is *In Our Own Hands: a Book of Self-Help Therapy* (The Women's Press), written for women by Sheila Ernst and Lucy Goodison out of their own wide experience. It's a basic guide to what therapy is about and how to use it, on your own, with a friend and, particularly, in a group. The book contains masses of exercises, ideas and practical information, and goes into broader issues, such as the difference between therapy and more usual consciousness raising, the politics of therapy, and deep worries like, 'Will I feel worse before I feel better?'

Phyllis Chesler's *Women and Madness* (import) and Jean Baker Miller's *Towards a New Psychology of Women* (Penguin) are academic books rather than manuals; sometimes hard work to read, but rewarding if you're deeply interested in the subject.

On the more particular area of sexuality, *Getting Clear (Body Work for Women)* by Ann Kent Rush (Wildwood House) gives many really good exercises for getting back in touch with your body, and Jack Lee Rosenberg's *Total Orgasm* (import) suggests exercises intended to open up the whole body to sexual experience. Wilhelm Reich's *The Sexual Revolution* (latest printing: Farrar, Straus and Giroux, New York, 1979) is the classic book which relates sexuality, emotional and physical, to society and politics, and is well worth reading.

The feminist Women's Therapy Centre (see useful addresses) offers workshops of one or two sessions on a variety of subjects, as well as one-to-one therapy (there's a waiting list for the latter). The women at the Centre will also do their best to put you in touch with other feminist or pro-women therapists, or with self-help groups, or with other women in your area who would like to start a group.

XVI. Not getting pregnant

Every woman who fucks in the classic way – however rarely – has a problem about how to avoid getting pregnant. Most of us have been given a lecture about 'where babies come from'. An awful lot of women are told by their mothers, who were 'taught' in the same way, and sent off into the world with the warning that they should 'watch out for' boys.

'When I had my first period, my mother told me I was a "big girl" now and should "watch out for" boys. When I asked how, she said I should be careful never to be alone with one. I should let a boy walk me home at night, but shouldn't dawdle on the way. It all sounded pretty threatening. I couldn't imagine the boyfriend I had then suddenly jumping on me if I got off my bike – it seemed terribly extreme. But later on, it did happen that I made love to a boy I was crazy about, behind the shed. He said he'd be careful, and at sixteen I was pregnant.'

1.   The battle for control over our bodies

It's not as difficult as it used to be to avoid getting pregnant when you fuck with a man. You can get contraceptives free from your GP, or from family planning clinics, which are part of the National Health Service too. Even a woman who is under age (under 16) can get contraceptives from her GP – though she or he *might* tell her parents. To be more sure of confidentiality, she can go to the young people's advisory service at her local family planning clinic, or to an agency like Brook (see useful addresses), which is especially intended for young people. As a result of these services, fewer young women now give birth in secret and kill the baby – though it does still happen, as there is still so much shame and ignorance surrounding sexuality.

Fewer doctors now refuse to prescribe contraceptives on religious grounds. If yours does, you are free to choose another doctor (look up the Family Practitioners list in your local library or at the local Community Health Council – there's a C next to the names of doctors who do give contraceptives).

Getting sterilised if you want to is not as hard as it once was, and it's rare nowadays for an older woman who's had five children to hear that she can't be sterilised if she's healthy and quite *capable* of having more children. (That's a true story – the woman had ten in the end and only after that, when she collapsed, did she get any help.)

And if a contraceptive fails, many doctors who are normally anti-abortion will be more lenient about allowing you one – after all, you did try.

Perhaps you're thinking we should be grateful to technology and medical science for these modern acts of mercy. So it's worth **221** knowing a bit more about the history of birth control.

It's not new for women to seek ways and means of avoiding an unwanted pregnancy. Throughout all history and in all cultures, women have devised forms of contraception so that they can have children only when *they* want to, or when the circumstances are right. Some of these contraceptives look pretty primitive to us now, but others were really quite effective, the forerunners of today's methods. There were magical medicines, which perhaps worked if you believed in them, but there were technical ones too – like vaginal douches with vinegar or citric juices or other things which we now know do indeed kill off sperm, even if not as reliably as modern methods. Women blocked off their cervix with certain plants, with fat, with gum of arabic, with cocoa fat mixed with sperm-killing substances, with half an orange cleaned out. The douches and the sponges are still used in our society, and the method of blocking off the neck of the womb developed, with the invention of rubber, into the diaphragm or cap. People also used the method of withdrawing, or making love without letting any sperm into the woman's vagina. The only device used by men, the condom, wasn't originally meant as a contraceptive, but as protection against sexually transmitted diseases. There have always been methods of abortion, not always gentle, but sometimes effective. Women themselves kept the knowledge about ways of preventing pregnancy. It was passed down from mother to daughter, or through 'wise women' (the predecessors of midwives). This was *before* the time when medicine was a separate profession practised mainly by men.

Women's right to control whether or not they want children and to have access to the means of doing so has been a cause of strife many times throughout history. In the eighteenth and nineteenth centuries, the medical class (with a very few exceptions, all men) played a less than honourable part. Instead of using their knowledge to make contraception safe and more effective, they used their medical authority to pressurise women into not using any contraceptives, using terrible, nonsensical, medical-sounding arguments. They'd say that a woman's uterus would shrivel up if she wasn't pregnant before she was twenty-five, or that to go against the 'natural' process would lead to hysteria, madness or an early death, or that you would grow old sooner if your womb didn't 'drink' sperm.

Women's right to control their own bodies has always been a political question. The first witch-burnings in the Middle Ages (when around nine million witches were burned and drowned) were largely an attempt to stop women from 'conspiring' and giving knowledge to one another. Of course, this attempt to stop the spread of information about regulating pregnancy was never really successful – a great deal of information remained underground. In the last century it was clearly understood that *one* of the most effective ways of keeping a woman in her place – inside the home – was to make sure she didn't know how to stop getting pregnant, and to make unmarried pregnancy such a scandal that a 'fallen woman' would sometimes end up drowning herself along with her unborn child. The women of the first women's movement, at the end of the last century, saw the right to choose motherhood as one of the most important conditions for women's emancipation, just as it is now in the modern women's movement. They too were accused of being 'over-sexed' and 'man-haters' (how modern that sounds to us today) when they tried to spread information and contraceptives. The cap, which was developed in the Netherlands, really caught on there. Aletta Jacobs set up the first birth control clinic – in America and Britain other feminists followed her example. In America, women were sentenced to prison for doing so, but others carried on. Few women now know that we owe our right to birth control not only to medical technology, but also to these women. The only modern contraceptive which has been developed by science is the hormonal pill.

The right to self-determination is still a political issue. In Britain we still have to be on guard so that our still limited right to a safe legal abortion isn't taken away. In many countries the 'protectors of the unborn child' force women back to the back streets for abortions which often kill them, or make women suffer unwanted pregnancies and constant dread of pregnancy. The legalisation of birth control today has a lot do to with population politics. In the last century, when soldiers were needed, or when there weren't enough workers, abortion was forbidden, and birth control was restricted and made a crime. When a government got scared about the increase in 'unwanted members of the population', birth control was made legal again. In America, for example, clinics were set up in the black ghettos to give advice on birth control, while in the rest of the country there were hardly any clinics, and there are many known cases of Indian, black and poor women being forcibly sterilised, against their will. Poor women were often the first guinea pigs for the pill, and methods like the IUD and Depo-Provera were developed with an eye to keeping down the population of the Third World. In Eastern bloc countries too, a woman's right to self-determination is made subservient to population politics. It seems that women now *want* on average fewer children – one of the reasons being women's double burden of work – but in some socialist countries, it's getting harder to obtain an abortion, because the government fears under-population.

2.   The blessing of science and the medical profession

It's undeniably less risky to regulate pregnancy now than it's ever been before. We now expect almost one hundred per cent reliability from a contraceptive device, something which women could never have hoped for before. It's not all bad that birth control has become a medical matter, and we can certainly be pleased that abortion – hardly a joyful experience – at least no longer involves such physical risks. But the fact that the **223** knowledge and the means have been taken out of the hands of women themselves, and are now the monopoly of doctors and the drug industry, has a lot of unpleasant side-effects.

To start with, the drug industry has other interests besides women. It is interested in profit. Profit on the pill is much larger than on any other device. Most companies have been only peripherally interested in whether hormonal regulation is safe. Sometimes they really have to be pressurised into continuing to do tests and into taking drugs out of circulation if they seem to be unsafe. The first pills were sold on the open market after Puerto Rican women had been used for experiments, often without their knowledge. From the start, women were suspicious of the possible side-effects of hormonal contraceptives, and with hindsight you can see that these fears were certainly not unfounded. One particular morning-after-pill was proved to have caused cancer in female children born when it failed. It was taken off the market. Depo-Provera, the contraceptive injection, is banned in America because in tests it appears to cause cancer in animals. But it's still legal in Britain, though only recommended for short-term use or if it's vital that the woman doesn't get pregnant – after a german measles injection, for instance. In fact it's used disturbingly widely, particularly on working class and black women.

The Dalkon Shield, an IUD sold to women in a blaze of publicity, was one new invention which turned out to be the cause of dangerous miscarriages. It was withdrawn after a number of women had died because of it. Manufacturers of medicines are seldom prepared to give true information about the risks people run if they use their products.

With some exceptions, doctors don't give good information about possible methods of birth control either. This is often because they themselves aren't given good information by the drug companies, and they're certainly not motivated, nor do they have the time, to be familiar with the latest research findings. And many doctors are taught during their training not to give the patient too much information, because she wouldn't know what to do with it. That isn't just true for contraception, but for all information about our bodies. But it's particularly infuriating when it's a question of our having children or not.

Again, not all doctors are equally patronising towards women, but there are plenty who are. Doctors who just prescribe the ontraceptives which *they* think are suitable, rather than allowing women to make the choice.

'My doctor used to say: "Madam, the pill is not suitable for you, the best thing to do at your age is sleep alone." When I went to another doctor, I got the pill really easily. But when it gave me problems, he gave me the IUD, which gave me problems too, without even telling me that there was such a thing as the cap.
224 *When I asked him later why he hadn't told me, he said it didn't*

*seem to him to be a suitable method for me. "All that fussing",
he said, "is more suitable for young people." '*

Some doctors prescribe the pill almost automatically. Only later,
when it doesn't work out too well, do they talk about other
means. One reason for that is definitely that it's much easier just
to write out a prescription than to measure for and check up on a
cap. Luckily the cap has come back into fashion. Many women
don't want to carry on taking the pill and ask for the cap instead. It
is possible to influence doctors if you make sure you're well
informed *before* a visit to the doctor or clinic. You need to know
what you want, even though there are doctors who find this a
tremendous threat to their authority. Sadly, many doctors will
only give women information if they're sufficiently well-informed
to ask for it. This came out in a recent Dutch TV programme
about birth control.

The question was whether you should tell women to whom you
have prescribed the IUD that if it fails, they may well be allowed
an abortion. One authority said to the others: 'You can't say so,
but you'll have to tell them when they ask.' In other words, if you
don't know what to ask beforehand, you won't get to hear about
it. Unless you have a doctor who has a lot of experience with
contraception, and whom you really trust, it's better to go to a
clinic which specialises in measuring caps, prescribing pills and
putting in IUDs.
Some doctors have an extremely patronising manner.

*'My first abortion didn't work because I had a kind of double
chamber in my womb. So, very sadly, I had to go back when I
noticed I was still pregnant. This time he said: "Why don't you let
it be – after all, it's not sporting to shoot at the same hare twice."'*

*'When, despite the IUD, I got pregnant, I wanted an abortion. I
was scared the child would be deformed. But the doctor said:
"Madam, you can love an unhappy child too." And refused.'*

Few doctors give honest information about the side-effects and
risks of the pill. Often they have the idea that women panic if you
tell them there is a higher risk of, for example, thrombosis.
Apparently, if there happens to be an article in the paper about
newly-discovered risks of the pill, a wave of women stop taking
it, without taking any other precautions instead – with more
unwanted pregnancies as a result. But this can only happen
because women aren't properly informed from the start about
the arguments for and against the pill. So quite understandably
they get a terrible fright if they read something about it in the
paper. To prevent panic, women don't need *less* information, but
more.
Another argument doctors use to justify giving very little
information to women is that they don't want to give women
flimsy excuses for avoiding sexual intercourse. The 'sexual **225**

avoidance syndrome', they call it. Certainly women were once able to use their fertility as an excuse for saying no now and then – since the development of the pill, they're less likely to have this excuse. But we *should* say no if we don't feel like sex. It's quite scandalous for doctors to decide that women are only allowed 'time off' if they have a good excuse (headache, stomach-ache, unable to take the pill), and they don't want to provide us with one.

Women do sometimes use their contraceptives badly. One reason for this is that if you don't feel like making love, it's more of a nuisance to have to take the pill every day or to put in your cap every time. But the solution to this is *not* to dish out contraceptives to women with optimistic stories about how they will improve their sex lives, or to put them under pressure to enjoy sex. The solution is rather to encourage women to make their own choices, to take their own decisions. To say no to what they don't want and yes to what they do. And to give information that's as honest as possible. Most contraceptive methods need to be used by women – the pill, the cap with spermicide, the IUD. Only the condom is used by men. On the one hand that is understandable because it's still true that the consequences of an unwanted pregnancy weigh more heavily on women than on men. A woman would have to have absolute faith that her lover had taken his pill – if there were such a thing – and hadn't forgotten, or wasn't lying when she asked if he'd taken it. Otherwise a male pill would only be useful to us if it made the man's ears turn green or something like that to prove beyond a shadow of a doubt that he *had* taken it. So women usually end up carrying the responsibility more or less alone, because then at least they're sure it's in good hands. However, this means that men don't learn to be responsible too. And when the methods have unpleasant side-effects, it's absurd for women to have to suffer them alone when it's for their *shared* pleasure.

This is even more true in fact for sterilisation. Until recently, this was a much less complicated operation for men than for women, although in the last few years sterilisation for women has become almost as easy. Yet all the same, more women than men let themselves be sterilised. Many men are afraid of having their bodies messed about with, and would rather it were done to their wife (after all, she's used to it). What's more, they connect their fertility to their feeling of virility, so that even if they don't *want* children any more, they still want to hang on to the idea that they *could* have them.

A survey on contraceptives for men other than the condom has shown that many men would still rather leave the responsibility to women. Opposition from both doctors and men in general seems to be exceptionally strong. Many men want a male pill – as long as other men swallow it, not them. Suddenly arguments are put forward such as that it would be unnatural to swallow hormones for years on end – though that's what women have **226** been doing for years. One pill which was developed had as a side-effect that it lowered the 'libido', the urge to make love. That didn't seem such an enormous problem, particularly as it's known that in permanent relationships, it's usually the man who feels like making love more regularly than the woman. But for the researchers, it was a good enough reason never to put the pill on the market. The fact that the women's pill also most probably has the effect of lowering the libido has never been used as a reason for not marketing it.

A man's reproductive organs are more easily reached from outside than a woman's. So, in principle, it's less of an intervention to make the sperm cells unworkable before they reach the egg. A researcher tried to develop a harmless contraceptive based on what's already known by hearsay – that heat temporarily de-activates a sperm cell. One method would be for a man to sit in a hot bath every day for three quarters of an hour, which seems pretty time-consuming! But the researcher persevered and invented a kind of underpants which would keep a man's testicles warm. Cheap, absolutely harmless, without any bad effect on his potential fertility, and nice and warm in winter. The experiments were stopped because they couldn't find enough men to act as guinea pigs.

The best argument against developing better contraceptives for men was given by a French doctor, who said that he thought it was sad to attack a million sperm cells when it was only necessary to attack one egg once a month. That a whole woman surrounds that egg, and that she has to bear the consequences, is obviously considered less important.

3.   How to avoid pregnancy

If you want to make love to a man, there are various ways of making sure that you don't get pregnant if you don't want to. The first, safest, but least known or popularised method is MAKING LOVE DIFFERENTLY. If you make love to a man who also enjoys other ways of making love, you don't have to worry about unwanted pregnancy or the side-effects of contraception. It's also possible to change around – for example, to fuck 'normally' now and then using a cap or a condom; and another time to make love with hands and lips without the penis getting into the vagina.

But watch out – making love differently is NOT the same as 'leaving the church before the blessing' or the so-called 'being careful'. During lovemaking the penis does sometimes discharge some moisture before the actual ejaculation, and in that drop there can be quite enough sperm to allow conception to take place. So making love differently is only reliable if you really don't allow the penis to get into your vagina, not even a little way. And you must also be careful not to get sperm on the outside of your vagina, for example, carrying it to your cunt with your fingers. If your vagina or the lips of your cunt become wet through excitement, sperm can manage to swim in from outside. **227**

The ideal contraceptive doesn't yet exist. It would have to be a kind with which you'd think about *getting* pregnant, instead of thinking about *not* getting pregnant. With some methods, the IUD in any case, and to a lesser extent the pill, it does seem a bit like that. If you are using these methods and want to get pregnant, you have to take out the IUD, or stop using the pill. But unfortunately they are also the methods with the most side-effects. With a method like the condom or the cap, you have to make up your mind afresh each time as to whether you want to use it – many women don't like that at all.

Although contraceptives are widely available, women still have unwanted pregnancies. Some groups of women are especially at risk.

● Young women, girls. Often they are given too little information on the grounds that they shouldn't be doing it yet. In practice it seems that most girls don't start using contraceptives until they have already fucked at least once. They can't usually ask their parents for advice, and many girls are afraid that the family doctor will tell their parents. Many clinics – and all Brook centres – will give advice to girls who are under age without the parents permission (and rightly so), but not all girls know that. There is a double morality involved. In some schools you are thought childish if you don't fuck, whether you want to or not. But it's the very boys who do their best to seduce a girl who are generally not so keen on girls who show enough independence to make sure about contraception in advance. When it's known that a girl takes the pill, she may be regarded as 'easy'. Although the *average* number of unwanted pregnancies has gone down in the Netherlands, the number of unwanted pregnancies among young girls is rising, and the girls involved are getting younger. *So it is not an unnecessary luxury for our young women to learn to stand up for themselves and for boys to begin to realise that when a girl says no, she means no.* The girls who have the biggest problem with unwanted pregnancies are those who are raped by people they know or by their fathers. It's hard to ask your mother for help if your father is abusing you, and the whole situation is already so dreadful that you're unlikely to be able to think about protecting yourself against pregnancy if you can't even manage to defend yourself against sexual violence. The girl is often so ashamed that she daren't ask for help outside the home. It's these girls in particular who came to the clinic for an abortion when it's already too late to have one.

● Older women who are close to menopause often have problems with irregular periods. Sometimes you have no blood for months, and then it seems as if there won't ever be any more. Then suddenly it comes again. It's difficult to find out whether you're pregnant too, because it's often not easy to spot the difference between pregnancy and the period which fails to appear. If you're on the pill, you have no idea whether you have reached menopause, and after you come off the pill, menstruation can be irregular too. Contraceptives should be **229**

the female sex organs

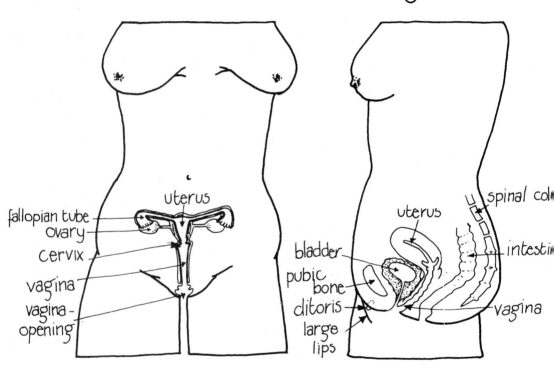

fallopian tube
ovary
cervix
vagina
vagina-opening

uterus

bladder
pubic bone
clitoris
large lips

uterus

spinal col
intestin
vagina

used for a year after the last period, but in exceptional circumstances, it has been known for an egg to ripen even after that.

● Women who have sex with men irregularly. Women who experience their sexuality in a regular relationship with a man don't find it so difficult to fit into that relationship a method for not getting pregnant. But it's much harder for women who don't always know in advance whether they are going to make love. Not all women feel like taking the pill for that rare occasion when they do meet someone they fancy, and taking your cap with you wherever you go seems to be overdoing it. It seems unspontaneous too if, when you do meet someone and get into bed with him, you suddenly produce condoms from your bag. Here too the double morality plays a part: not every man is pleased to discover that a woman might perhaps have thought about the possibility of going to bed with him or with some other man. And as long as it isn't usual to make love in a different way when you have no contraceptives, that kind of situation will lead to unwanted pregnancies. Unless you are quite sure you can say no to a man who likes only *one* way of making love – fucking – and hasn't provided contraceptives himself, there is no alternative but to look after yourself properly and take something with you.

● Women who still don't know how to get and use contraceptives. Although the Netherlands make use of immigrants to do the work Dutch people no longer want to do, health care for women from, for example, Turkey, Morocco or Suriname is, on the whole, exceptionally bad. Many doctors don't bother to think that you can't just shove a piece of paper with the address of a clinic at a Moroccan woman who doesn't speak Dutch or who can't read or write. Luckily there are women's groups busy working on this problem. The same is true for women from Suriname who don't yet know their way around the Netherlands, and often miss the support of their own women around them – support they were used to at home. They too are forming their own groups. And, of course, the male double standard applies for them too.

Another problem is that devices aren't always used properly, sometimes because a doctor in a hurry hasn't given enough information, sometimes because we didn't dare ask questions. We also have a resistance to some or all contraceptives. It's a good idea to find out what our objections are, so that we can choose a method accordingly.

4.   Objections to contraceptives

Many of us have been brought up with the idea that sex is sinful, and that you have to pay for your pleasure by taking upon yourself the risk of pregnancy. The wages of sin, as they say. The idea that you can have pleasure without pain still sounds too egotistical for many women. As if sexuality isn't for pleasure. When we get into arguments about abortion on demand, that's often what we end up arguing about – if there were no pain, women would be immoral and frivolous, chaos would come and everyone would do just what they liked! As if sex isn't about doing what you like. All research so far has shown that there is no question of women becoming 'loose' if they use contraceptives or if abortion is more easily available. On the contrary, as women have more choice about what they *don't* want, they are more conscious about choosing what they *do* want. They're less likely to see sexuality as a fate that you just have to accept. Not all women are brought up with this strict idea that you have to bear the consequences of doing something 'wrong', but it's still worth considering whether you yourself don't have any traces of that 'punishment' idea.

We have learned that sex is something which happens spontaneously. A rose-coloured cloud – they look at one another and violins starts playing. It doesn't match with that image of sexuality to say: 'Darling, I left my cap in the drawer', or to point out that you've just stopped taking the pill. And there are still gentlemen who promise to be 'careful', and women who think vaguely that perhaps it's their infertile time because they've just had their period. And we tend to think of ourselves as cold and calculating if we carry a contraceptive in our bag. For most women – unless they choose to follow a career – the future depends on getting married. In the past, when women were divided into two kinds – the chaste ones, whom you married, and the whores, with whom you 'did it' – promising him sex after marriage was a way of hanging on to him. Nowadays that's hardly the way. There's still the old tradition that says if a man gets a woman pregnant, he should marry her. Not that it always happens, but the idea lives on. Men, especially when they are young, often experience marriage as a trap – bondage which they put off for as long as possible. For a young woman in a lousy job, or who'd like to leave home, marriage still looks like a solution. A pregnancy, especially if it's a 'mistake', can be a way of getting a man. So there are quite a few 'mistakes' – half wanted, half unwanted. None of that is very pleasant of course, because it often has nothing to do with wanting a child, but everything to do with getting a man. And beginning a marriage with a baby is not the best guarantee of a happy future. But as long as women are so dependent on men for their future, these situations will occur.

Some of us would of course want a child if we lived in different circumstances. Feeling a child grow can be a beautiful erotic feeling, and a physical relationship with a child can be very satisfying. Many women make a rational choice not to have a child, considering ourselves to be still too young, feeling that it doesn't fit in with our image of the future, thinking our economic situation is too bad, or having a man who doesn't like children, or no man, and not wanting to choose to bring up a child alone. But sometimes our emotions, our gut feelings, tell us that our choice not to have a child is wrong. In fact we *would* like to have one.

232 The effect of that can be that you are careless with your pill, or with your cap, become pregnant and then feel as if fate decided for you. So it's good to become conscious of the contradictions most of us feel in the choice for or against having a child. Then you can take them into account if you notice yourself taking too many risks.

Some of us don't much enjoy sex with the man with whom we are having a relationship, but don't dare say no, or can't imagine saying no. If you don't feel like fucking, you probably also don't feel like putting in the cap, or taking the pill every day. A careless use of contraceptives can point out that you are making love against your will. The best way of not getting pregnant in such a situation is to learn to say no.

5. Information about contraceptives

This book can't go into detail about all contraceptives; there isn't room for that. We have included something because it is still very difficult to get reliable information which doesn't only give the medical side, but also the practical: is it pleasant to use? There is usually something about 'safety' in most information about contraceptives. What's misleading is that it isn't always clear if safety means that it isn't harmful to *you*. What's more, the risks of taking the pill are swept under the carpet with inexact comparisons. For example, I've read that you have to weigh the risks of thrombosis against the risk of pregnancy, if you are taking the pill. But this isn't true, because you don't choose between the risks of the pill and pregnancy, but between the risks of different contraceptives – the real question is whether the pill compares well with other methods. Another comparison which is often made is between the pill and other medicines, which also have harmful effects – even aspirins. But the pill isn't a medicine we swallow to cure an illness. It is taken daily by completely healthy women, for years on end. Again, the only proper comparison we can make is between the different contraceptive methods. And if you don't feel like making love in a different way, you have to make a choice, taking into consideration how reliable the method is, how safe for your body, and how pleasant to use. Unfortunately, there is no method which scores the same on all these points. It's still a question of weighing up the different drawbacks.

a. The cap

What it is: A small soft rubber dome with bendable metal in the rim, so that you can squeeze it together to get it into your vagina.
What it does: it acts as a barrier across the mouth of the womb, or cervix, stopping sperm entering the womb. Its main purpose is to hold spermicidal (sperm-destroying) cream in place – it is only effective if you have contraceptive cream or a pessary inside it. (If you have a cap, you can also use it if you want to make love during a period, and want to hold back the blood while doing so.) **233**

Use: You have to be shown how to put a cap in. Usually women are shown at a family planning clinic or by their GP. After you have practised a few times, you'll find it easy to get the cap in and out of your vagina. It's a good idea to practise using it *before* you use it when you want to fuck. The cap must be in your vagina before the penis goes in, not when you're half way through fucking, or when he thinks he's about to come. The usual way to use it is to spread contraceptive cream or jelly round the edge and in the middle of the cap. Another way is to put a contraceptive pessary into your vagina, holding it for a minute against your cervix with your middle finger to make sure it spreads over the correct area – this is slightly trickier and so perhaps not quite so effective. Some women find it easier to take pessaries out with them than a tube of cream. You can also use foam with an applicator – you fill the applicator with foam, put that in, put in the cap and then put more foam in. Cream or jelly in the cap is probably the simplest.

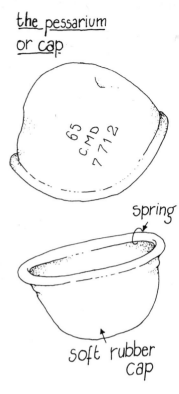

the pessarium
or cap

spring

soft rubber
cap

The cap should remain in position for six to eight hours after fucking (six is enough; more won't hurt so long as it's not *too* long – no more than about twenty-four hours – or it could harbour germs, or the rubber could rot). If you make love again before six hours are up, *don't* take the cap out – put more spermicide into your vagina before fucking and leave the cap in for another six hours.

Reliability: Depending on how carefully you use it, this is a safe or a moderately safe method. If you have any resistance to putting it in, for example if you don't like putting your finger in your vagina, or if you don't feel like fucking and so aren't very motivated to put it in, there is a chance of twenty to twenty-five pregnancies per every set of a hundred child-bearing years. If you like using it, and put it in in time, and never leave putting it in too late because it's around your 'safe days', its reliability comes close to that of the pill or the IUD.

Safety: Of all the methods, the cap and the condom seem to be least harmful for your body. They also offer some protection against VD. Their safety is the reason why, during the last few years, when we have become more attentive to our general health, the cap has become more popular again. Very occasionally a woman is sensitive to rubber, or to contraceptive cream. The cap doesn't affect our fertility at all. It can't really be used by women with a dropped uterus (though they can use a special vault cap, or a cervical cap – a tiny cap, also used with spermicide, which fits over your cervix). If you haven't yet fucked, there is no *medical* reason not to use the cap, though you might find it a bit awkward; you'll also need to have it checked regularly, in case the size of your vagina changes. You need a cap which fits you, so you should anyway have a new one measured if your measurements change, if you have been pregnant or have gained or lost more than ten pounds. When you are first given a cap, you should have it checked after a week. After that, you should get it checked every six months.

spermicide
applicator

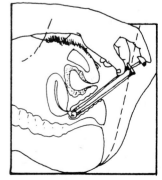

putting the cap in place

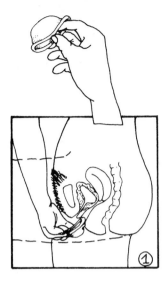

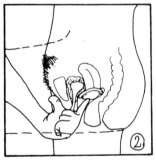

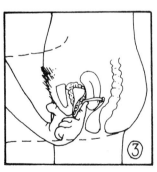

You can check it for holes every time you use it, by holding it against the light.

Maintenance: Wash it with warm water and a mild soap. You can powder it with cornflower (better than talcum powder which doesn't dissolve in water and which you shouldn't get into your vagina). Keep it in a dark place. Don't boil it. You can get a spare cap to keep in reserve.

Experiences: The cap can be a pleasant method if you are familiar with your body. In a regular relationship, you can get used to putting it in before you go to bed, whether you are thinking of making love or not. That's not such a big step as having to get up and put it in. Opinions vary on how pleasant it is to use:

'I got the feeling that he was looking to see whether I had put it in. If I didn't, he looked relieved, as if to say: "Well, then, we won't." If I did put it in, it was like a kind of signal for: "Come on, on top." If I did it secretly, he got confused. I found it very unpleasant.'

'At first, I found it difficult to get up and walk right to the other end of the house to the bathroom to put it in. Now that I'm more familiar with my body, I don't mind any more if he sees. After all, he should be glad that I always take the responsibility! I don't feel at all like hiding it in a ladylike manner.'

'With the cap, it's possible to take turns. One time I use the cap; the next time he uses a condom.'

b.   The condom (or sheath)

What it is: A thin rubber sheath, which fits over the man's penis. Some have plain, round ends, and some have a teat at the end to allow a space for the semen. Some are dry, some ready-lubricated. There are also some which are ribbed, because women are supposed to enjoy that, but that's mostly male fantasy. The sort of carnival condoms with additions and pompoms which you find in sex shops are unusable as contraceptives.

What it does: It holds back the sperm.

Use: Condoms are easy to use, but you must know how. A condom is rolled over an erect penis before it goes into the vagina – *not* just before ejaculation. When it is rolled on, a little space should be left at the tip, with no air in it, so there is room for the sperm. Otherwise it might split. It can also tear if your vagina is too dry. If it is, you could use a condom with a lubricant, or a contraceptive cream. You could also ask yourself if you're actually enjoying making love. When the man withdraws, the condom should be held at the edge to stop it slipping off. He should withdraw immediately after ejaculation. You could check for **235** leaks beforehand by blowing it up, and afterwards by filling it with water – but you don't need to.

Reliability: Used with cream or pessaries – for additional security – this method is certainly no less reliable than the cap, and it comes close to the cap and the IUD. When it is used carelessly, you run the risk of fifteen to twenty pregnancies in a hundred child-bearing years. With careful use, the risk is three pregnancies in a hundred child-bearing years.

Safety: It does nothing to your body except in the very rare instances of someone reacting badly to rubber (in which case, try to find condoms made of sheep guts).

If the condom packet carries the British Safety Institute's sign – a kite mark – they should be safe. You can get them free from family planning clinics, or from Brook centres, though ridiculously enough, GPs are not allowed to prescribe them on the NHS! You can buy them from chemists, including Boots, but not in most supermarkets – they say the customers and staff would be embarrassed! You should throw away condoms which have been kept in the drawer for over two years, or ones you've been carrying round for a long time in your bag.

Maintenance: Throw them away after use.

Experiences: The condom is at present the only device used by men, except the definitive step of sterilisation. Some men don't like them, and neither do some women:

'My boyfriend said he felt like he was getting into the bath with his socks on! I don't find it that terrific either. How can you get into stroking and licking when you feel like it, if you have to put up with a rubbery thing like that!'

'I don't make love very often. And if I do make love, I don't fuck very often. I feel safe if I have condoms with me, because when the moment occurs, you can decide whether you want to do something about it. And it's such a small thing to take with you – not an apparatus that you have to go to the doctor for.'

'A doctor advised us to use a cap and condoms. With all that rubber we got the feeling that we were rubbing each other out!'

c. The pill (contraceptive pill, also Depo-Provera)

What it is: The pill is a series of tablets. There's the combined pill which you take every day for three weeks, then take seven days off and start again, and the mini-pill, which you take continuously. Depo-Provera is a three-monthly injection.

What it does: The combined pill contains two artificial hormones: oestrogen and progestogen. It works by suppressing the development of the egg, and no fertile egg is released. Because the different hormones have different side-effects, experiments are still being made with different combinations. The sequential **236** pill (high dose) was withdrawn from the market because it

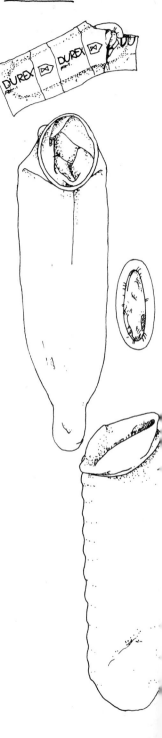

seemed to be linked to cancer of the uterus. There are now triphasic pills which vary the dosage of each hormone at different times during the month. The mini-pill and the injection contain only progestogen. If you want to find out more, you can read the relevant chapter in *Our Bodies Ourselves*, so that if you take the pill, you can choose the one which has the least nasty side-effects.

Use: Simple – keep taking the pills!

Reliability: The pill is the best method if you are just looking at the risk of pregnancy. If you take it according to instructions, you have a risk of pregnancy between a tenth, and two to five, per hundred child-bearing years. Just as with other methods, its reliability is dependent on your motivation. If you don't really want to fuck, or don't like taking a pill every day, you often forget to take it.

Safety: People haven't yet stopped debating the safety of the pill. It is a method which works constantly on your body. Fears that the pill causes cancer are not proven, but there is an extensive list of other side-effects and risks. Many doctors don't tell us much about them, but according to a survey, a lot of doctors would not prescribe the pill for their own family. Many women give up the pill during the first year of using it – figures on this show that between thirty and fifty per cent give it up.

Side-effects: Nausea and headaches, especially when you start taking it, weight gain, painful breasts. The pill probably also influences your mood and your desire to make love – it's not possible to measure this, as so many other factors have to be taken into account. It's logical that it would, if you think about it, as we also have a change of mood with menstruation and menopause, when our hormones change spontaneously. Some women get high blood pressure from the pill and that has to be controlled. Women who have a tendency to diabetes can have trouble with it. Cancer growths already present on your breasts can grow faster if you are on the pill. There is a higher chance of thrombosis. If you have ever had jaundice, you run the risk of liver problems. The pill can affect the degree of acidity in your vagina, and there is a greater chance of infection, sexually transmitted diseases and also kidney infection. Probably our chance of a heart attack is greater, certainly in combination with smoking. The pill can make asthma and epilepsy worse. If you have a tendency to one of these illnesses, you shouldn't take the pill. The same applies to illnesses which are related to circulation and to liver infections. If you have had cancer of the womb or if you are breastfeeding, steer clear of the pill. You should watch out if you have a tendency to diabetes, migraine, epilepsy, asthma, varicose veins, or are liable to depression. If you are over thirty-five, the risks are much higher and you should ask yourself if you wouldn't rather be sterilised or try another method. Don't do that suddenly though, because stopping the pill without using another method is a well-known cause of many unwanted pregnancies. There is also a recent survey which

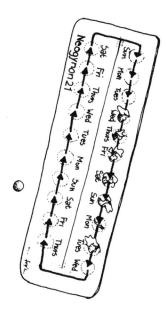

the pill

shows that the risks of heart disease are much greater depending on how old you are, how long you have been on the pill, and whether you smoke. So choose either the pill or smoking. Girls who haven't yet developed fully should also not take the pill. A pleasant side-effect is that you have the chance of less heavy periods, and that you know exactly when they are coming.

The mini-pill: This is less heavy and so has fewer side-effects. On the other hand, it is also less reliable, because it has to be taken precisely on time. If you forget the traditional combined pill at night, you can still take it next morning, but between the taking of two mini-pills, there should only be a gap of twenty-six hours. With the mini-pill you sometimes have an irregular loss of blood. That can be nasty if you are scared that you are pregnant.

Depo-Provera: This is not a pill but an injection, which is given at ten or twelve week intervals. The advantage is that you don't have to think about it again. This is the reason why doctors like giving it to foreign women, whom they clearly don't think are capable of swallowing a pill every day. A disadvantage is that you can't easily stop it: you sit for months with the stuff in your body; and if you don't like the side-effects, you still have to put up with them, and it can really upset your fertility afterwards. You might not get periods for some time afterwards. Depo-Provera, which is the brand name, is banned as a contraceptive in America because it has been shown to cause cancer in animals. That ban means a lot if you realise all the things that have to happen before a drug is taken off the market. Before using DP, you should have a very good reasons why other methods aren't suitable for you. If you choose the pill, it is good to have more information than is given here. You can find it in *Our Bodies Ourselves.*

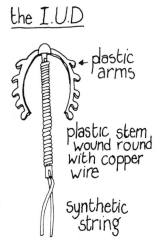

the I.U.D

← plastic arms

plastic stem wound round with copper wire

synthetic string

'I took the pill because it seemed so simple and clean. But I just didn't feel good with it. Blown up and lethargic. The doctor said that was subjective and I was fine. But I still didn't like it. Then I changed to the cap. I felt much better. That might just be suggestion. But what does that matter?'

'I had a pill which gave me headaches. The next kind made me fat. Then I got the mini-pill. Once I forgot to take it, and had to take a morning-after-pill. Vomiting and nausea. Then I'd had enough of that lot. I had an IUD fitted. My sister is on the pill too, but she hasn't had any problems with it.'

d. The IUD

What it is: A small pliable plastic shape, which is inserted in your womb with a sort of reed. In the diagrams you can see the different shapes. The Dalkon Shield has turned out to be dangerous and is no longer used. If you remember that is the shape you have, you had better ask to have it taken out. The

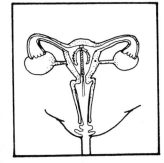

the IUD in the uterus

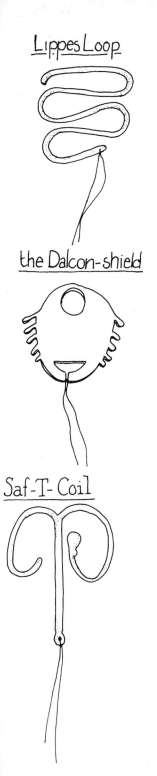

Lippes Loop

the Dalcon-shield

Saf-T-Coil

IUDs in the shape of a T or a 7 aren't shown here, and there are other shapes. The copper T and the copper 7 have copper wire around the plastic, and there are also IUDs with a reservoir for progesteron.

What it does: It is still not known exactly how it works. The theory is that it disturbs the fertilised egg from attaching itself to the uterus by changing something in the uterus membrane. The most plausible explanation is that it precipitates the manufacture of the kind of cells which 'get rid of' bacteria and therefore of the egg too. That effect seems like a permanent infection. It probably means that if you are taking antibiotics for an infection at the same time, you run the risk of getting pregnant. Such cases are known, and in any event, if you are using antibiotics, it's a good idea to use another method as well to make sure you don't get pregnant.

Use: A doctor inserts the IUD. It's best to go to a doctor who is experienced, for example at a family planning clinic, because she or he is then used to doing it. Insertion can be very painful, but some people have had one put in without even noticing it. Strings hang down, which can help you check that it's still there (though sometimes they curl round the cervix). Men seldom have problems with the strings, unless they are cut off too short. At first you might get cramps, from menstrual cramps to genuine bellyache. Really bad bellyache might be a sign of infection – go and see a doctor. It's dangerous to let yourself be put off with the story that bellyache is normal with an IUD! In the first months you also run a great risk of your womb getting rid of this foreign object on its own. In the first three months you'd be well advised to use a contraceptive cream as well. The copper IUDs need to be changed every three years, the progesteron coil every year.

Reliability: The IUD is between the pill and the cap. You have a chance of six pregnancies per hundred child-bearing years.

Safety: There is a very slight risk of perforation, that is to say that when the IUD is inserted, it can go right through the uterus wall. But if someone experienced does it, this seldom happens. You have more chance of infection, and sexually transmitted diseases are more dangerous, because they can easily penetrate to your womb and ovaries. It's important to get yourself tested for sexually transmitted diseases and infections before an IUD is inserted. If your doctor doesn't do that as a routine, ask for it, or make sure that you have yourself tested somewhere else. If you get gonorrhoea while you have an IUD, it may be necessary to have it removed in order to be cured. You will probably get more discharge and heavier periods. If you already have heavy periods, an IUD is probably not a good method for you. If you have a tendency to anaemia, the heavy periods will just make it worse. So: if you have infections of the womb or the vagina, or if you often have trouble with them, the IUD is not so suitable. If you have sexually transmitted diseases, or heavy periods, or a tendency to anaemia, try another method. **239**

There are smaller IUDs for women who haven't had children, but there is a greater chance that they will be rejected.

'I didn't like it when the IUD was inserted. After that I was very happy with it for a couple of years, I never thought about it again. Then I got a discharge and an infection. I am trying out a copper IUD now.'

'In the end the periods were too much for me. I missed the pill, where I knew exactly when I would menstruate. I still don't know what I'm going to do now.'

'When I had the IUD put in, it went fine. A little tummy-ache. A few days later it was a very bad tummy-ache. I rang the doctor, who said it was normal, and would go away. I'm not much of a complainer, so I went to bed with my tummy-ache. The next day I had a high temperature, and I was so giddy that I hardly knew what was happening. My boyfriend called an ambulance. It seemed I had an infection which had affected the ovaries.'

The method of periodic celibacy (working out 'safe' days) is not reliable and is not discussed here. The chance of getting pregnant decreases with this method, but it isn't reliable. If you want to use it, you can read about the way the menstrual cycle works in *Our Bodies Ourselves*. We can thank the withdrawal method for a large part of the population of Europe. Because it's so risky, it isn't discussed here, just as we don't discuss the other unreliable methods, like using contraceptive creams etc without using the condom or cap at the same time.

6. Sterilisation

One way of making sure you don't get pregnant is to get sterilised. It's not easy to get it done if you don't live in a 'normal' marriage, if you haven't 'completed' your family (minimum of two children), if you aren't over thirty-five years, or if you go without your 'partner's' permission (though it's sometimes forced on black women against their will). But there are some doctors who believe that adult people can decide for themselves what's good for them, and who will perform a sterilisation if it seems that is what you want. You'll be asked stereotyped questions like: 'Wouldn't you be sorry if your partner were to die, or if you divorced and the other partner were awarded custody of the children?' Mostly it's assumed that sterilisation is a decision you should take together with a partner. But you might decide that you'll never have a child together if *you* don't want a child, which makes it *your* decision. Of course *he* can make a decision like that too. It's a good idea to think whether you might want a child under different circumstances. Sterilisation can be carried out on men as well as women. It's less of an intervention for men than for women, but even for women it's no longer a big

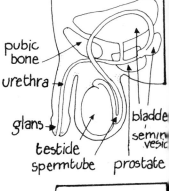

sterilisation for a man

pubic bone
urethra
glans
testicle
spermtube
bladder
seminal vesicle
prostate

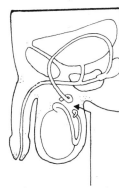

place where the tubes are cut.

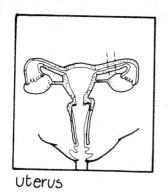

uterus

operation (though there have been problems later: heavy periods, a possible increase in hysterectomies). The choice of *who* should be sterilised would have to depend on what each of you wanted to do with your lives in the future. Sterilisation is certainly an individual choice for each person: 'Do *I* want any more children, then *I'll* do something about it.' So in some couples, both the woman and the man get themselves sterilised. When men are sterilised (vasectomy), two small pieces of the tubes (the vas deferens) are cut away or clamped together with a kind of staple. The operation takes place through two small incisions in the testicles. It's a very small operation done under a local anaesthetic. It usually lasts less than fifteen minutes, and the man can go home immediately afterwards. After ten or twelve ejaculations, when all the old spermazoids are used up, he is infertile. That is tested. There are methods being developed with a kind of tap – these will be reversible, but they are not yet in use. For the moment, you start sterilisation from the

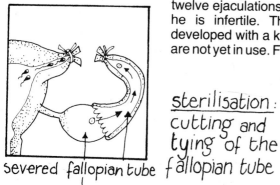

severed fallopian tube

ovary

sterilisation: cutting and tying of the fallopian tube

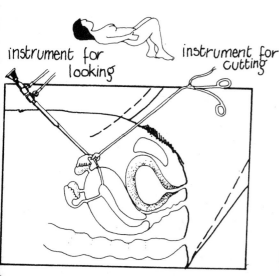

instrument for looking

instrument for cutting

Laparoscopy

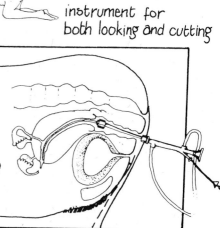

instrument for both looking and cutting

Culdoscopy

premise that once the operation is done, it is irreversible.

With sterilisation, the risks to the body are minimal. Sterilisation is NOT castration, it changes absolutely nothing except that there is no sperm present in the ejaculation, which is normal in every other way. There can be psychological problems for men who haven't completely thought through their emotions before they allow themselves to be sterilised, or who have been badly informed. They can become temporarily impotent because they *think* that might happen – with impotence, the psychological component is much stronger than physical. Other men have heard that the operation will make them randy, so they become randy. Men who are a bit worried that they'll become less virile may get the feeling that they have to prove their virility by fucking more often. To prove their masculinity, some men have been known to develop an inability to do the dishes – an unpleasant 'side-effect'.

Sterilisation of women: This can be performed in different ways. One is by 'laporoscopy', in which a small quantity of gas is pumped into the abdomen through a small incision under the navel. Afterwards a very small telescope is put into the same incision so that the doctor can see exactly where the ovaries are. After that, at the edge of the hair on your cunt, a second incision is made through which a small forceps is inserted. The fallopian tubes are then either cut and tied (known as tubal ligation) or closed together with small plastic clips. That takes twenty to thirty minutes altogether. Sometimes the tubes are lifted out through the incision, and the work is done outside. Depending on whether you have a local or a general anaesthetic, you can go home immediately or you have to stay a while. With the 'culdoscopy', the operation takes place through your vagina. You don't lie on your back for it, but sit on your knees and elbows with your bum in the air. Not very comfortable. In both cases you are immediately sterile.

Just as with an abortion, you'll be asked questions beforehand about your motivation. This is justifiable, because no one should allow such an intervention to happen under duress. It's a good idea to talk about your feelings about sterilisation beforehand. Many of us have mixed feelings about whether or not we want to have children. Some women, although quite decided about taking the step of not having any more children, still have a sense of regret. Sometimes it's good to mourn the children you won't be having, even if you are very certain about what you are doing. The doctor who decides whether you can have a sterilisation or an abortion may get the impression that you are still in doubt, that you aren't really motivated. Those who have the power to say yes or no are perhaps not the people to help us when we have conflicting emotions.

'In my women's group I cried for the daughter I would not have. It was as if I had to say farewell. Having a child was one of the possibilities I had, a direction I could follow in my life. I chose for

other things which I would have had to give up. Although I made a very definite choice, there was still anger in me, and sorrow. After all, we're still in the position where children are a crazily heavy responsibility, and you have to carry the biggest share of the burden yourself. If I could have shared it more with other people, I wouldn't have had to choose between a child and other things I found important. I was pregnant then. And that was painful, that I would never know the child I could have had. After the mourning, I asked for sterilisation. I have no regrets. It was good for me to work through the decision emotionally at the same time, instead of putting it off all the time until I was too old.'

7. Methods for after you may have conceived

a. the morning-after-pill

The morning-after-pill isn't *one* pill, but a series which can be taken within seventy-two hours of fucking (at the very latest – the earlier the better). You can take them if you have reason to believe that you are pregnant – if for example a condom has torn, or you didn't use any contraceptive. Any doctor can provide it, though not all will. You must complete the course, or you could damage the foetus if you don't then have an abortion.

The morning-after-pill alters the lining of the womb, and makes it inhospitable for an egg to implant. The safest method is to take two high dose ordinary pills, and then another two twelve hours later. This *has* to be done early, and it has to be the highest dose pills (50, not 30). It's highly unlikely that you'll have these, so you have to get them specially. A lower dosage won't work. This method seldom causes nausea, and there is usually no bleeding until your normal period comes.

A more old-fashioned method – still prescribed by many student health centres and doctors – is the five day high oestrogen treatment. In 15-20% of women, this causes bleeding straightaway – most don't start bleeding till some days later. With this method, you can be terribly sick for a couple of days, and if you are on holiday, or having a romantic new love affair, it can certainly sour the whole thing. Ask for pills to help nausea to take with these morning-after-pills. On top of all that, it's a horse medicine. In one swallow you take as much oestrogen as you would normally take in two years on the pill. If you think of the number of objections being made to the pill, it's clear that this isn't a method you should use every now and then, or that doctors would casually give to anyone going on holiday.

The advantage of the morning-after-pill is that you never know whether you were pregnant. The disadvantage is that you are swallowing horse medicine when it's perhaps not necessary.

b. The morning-after-IUD

The IUD works by making the uterus hostile to an egg settling. **243**

So if you put one in within 72 hours of fucking without contraception, or with faulty contraception, it will probably stop the egg implanting. This is just an ordinary IUD but inserted with a different motivation. It might be difficult to find a doctor to do it with that motivation – and without it, it might be hard to get it put in quickly enough. Don't put one in too late – it could damage the foetus. Clinics who provide this, and the morning-after-pill, are listed at the end of the book.

c. Menstrual extraction

It is possible to suck out the contents of your uterus in order to get a period over in one day instead of five – this is sometimes known as 'menstrual extraction' or 'menstrual regulation'. It is also possible to do this if you think you might be pregnant – even *before* pregnancy is confirmed. This is known as 'pre-emptive abortion' or 'endometrial aspiration'. In the Netherlands it's often called 'overtime treatment', and is fairly widely available.

This is the safest and least disturbing form of abortion. It gets it over quickly, before your body has begun to make many changes, and saves the tension of waiting. If you have it done before you know for sure whether you are pregnant, it saves you the emotional and other decisions about whether to terminate the pregnancy if you are. (On the other hand, you might feel you *want* to face up to those decisions.)

A small flexible tube is inserted into your uterus, usually without any dilation of the cervix. The contents of the womb – the lining plus a little foetal tissue if you were pregnant – are very gently sucked out, with a hand syringe. This takes a few minutes, and can cause brief cramps. A local anaesthetic is seldom used. It can be done up to about fourteen days after you should have started your period.

This method should be generally available, but isn't. It is rarely used officially in Britain. In America it is used widely by women's self-help health groups. It is in fact quite an easy technique for women to learn. If 'menstrual extraction' is done when you are *not* pregnant, it is probably not illegal, though it is still a grey area of the law. But if this method is used as an abortion before pregnancy is confirmed, you are bypassing the Abortion Act. So you are unlikely to find a professional who would be prepared to do it without confirmation of pregnancy.

With an ordinary pregnancy test (such as you get from your doctor or family planning clinic, from Brook, some chemists and some Women's Liberation groups), this means that by the time you have got confirmation of pregnancy, and permission to have an abortion, you are probably already too late to use this method. These tests are done when your period is about two weeks late.

However, there is now a pregnancy test which is accurate ten days after conception – which may be before you have even

missed a period! This test is more expensive than the ordinary one, and is not yet widely available. You can get it at PAS and Marie Stopes (addresses at the end of the book). With this test, there would still be time to have a very early abortion – if you can get your forms filled in quickly enough, and if you can find a place that does it. Now this test is available, there is no *legal* reason for clinics licensed to do abortions not to use this very early method. It's worth at least asking your local hospital.

d. Abortion

Until you actually need one, you perhaps imagine that abortion is entirely legal and freely available in Britain. Sadly, such freedom exists only in the minds of the anti-abortion lobby. The facts are that pregnancy can only be legally terminated under certain circumstances. Two doctors, usually a GP and a hospital consultant, have to agree that one or more of the following conditions exists:
1) there's a high chance that the baby would be born badly handicapped;
2) there's a grave risk (which would be greater if the pregnancy continued than if it didn't) either to your life, or to your physical or mental health, or to that of your existing children. These are conditions, not rights, and legally you don't have any say in the matter. Nonetheless, it's worth knowing the legal grounds in case you really have to argue your case for termination with a doctor. Your chances of getting an abortion quickly and easily on the National Health Service depend entirely on where you live, which is very unfair. Some doctors interpret the law rigidly and will only consent if you're at death's door; others are very liberal. Your local doctor could be at one of those two extremes, or anywhere in between. It's hardly surprising – though a national scandal – that as many as half the women who want abortions have to go outside the NHS to get them.
(In Northern Ireland, the situation is far worse, as the 1967 Abortion Act, which widened the grounds for abortion, does not apply there. Most women who need abortions have to travel to England, bearing the expense of the operation and the travel themselves. The Ulster Pregnancy Advisory Association (see useful addresses) arranges for women to go to non-profit-making clinics in England.)

Where to look

If you think there's even a slight possibility that you want an abortion, you should start looking at once, because the NHS referral process can take a long time – certainly long enough for you to make up or change your mind. Although even late abortions carry less risk than childbirth, they're more difficult to get later on (they are rarely done after twenty weeks), and the methods are more drastic. Early abortions are always easier on you, physically and emotionally. Remember that doctors calculate pregnancy from the first day of your last period, so by the time you've missed a period, you're already four or five weeks pregnant in their terms.

Go to your GP first. A sympathetic and well-informed doctor should help you decide without putting pressure on you, answer questions about what actually happens and refer you to a hospital consultant with a liberal attitude to abortion. The GP also has to sign your 'green form', a legal requirement for any abortion. Of course ask around among friends to see what their experience of local facilities was like. If they can't help, try a women's centre if there is one. Any woman who's been through an abortion is bound to know things about the hospital and its staff that the GP doesn't. If you have bad luck and the GP won't help, or can't help because the local hospitals are known to be anti-abortion or have huge waiting lists, you'll have to think about 'going private'.

There are various organisations that can arrange for you to have an abortion privately. Beware of the commercial money-making concerns which will rip you off. Look for the non-profit-making charities which will arrange a termination at the lowest possible cost and without pushing you into it. The two biggest are the British Pregnancy Advisory Service (BPAS) and the Pregnancy Advisory Service (PAS) – central office addresses and 'phone numbers at the end of the book. The law is the same as for the NHS (they'll get your 'green form' signed if your GP is hostile,

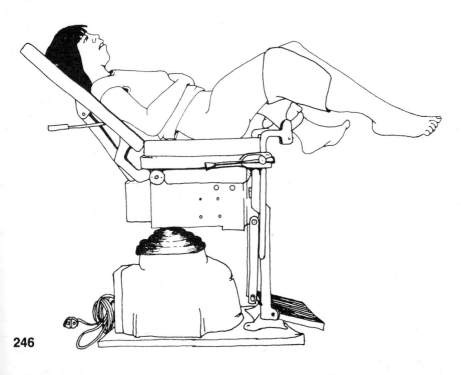

though they like to be in touch with your regular doctor), but there are distinct advantages. They offer a counselling service if you want it; if you go into a clinic, the other patients are in the same situation as you; and, above all, it's quick – about ten days from first consultation to finish. The NHS can take weeks. The big disadvantage is the cost: at the time of writing, about eighty pounds for a straightforward early abortion.

Medical procedures

Out-patient day units are the most sensible and economical way of organising the majority of early straightforward abortions: they save you the stress and domestic upheaval of being admitted as an in-patient and they save the NHS scarce resources. Nonetheless, they are few and far between. The few there are risk being deluged with patients, so they tend to stick rigidly to

Abortion using the vacuum aspiration method

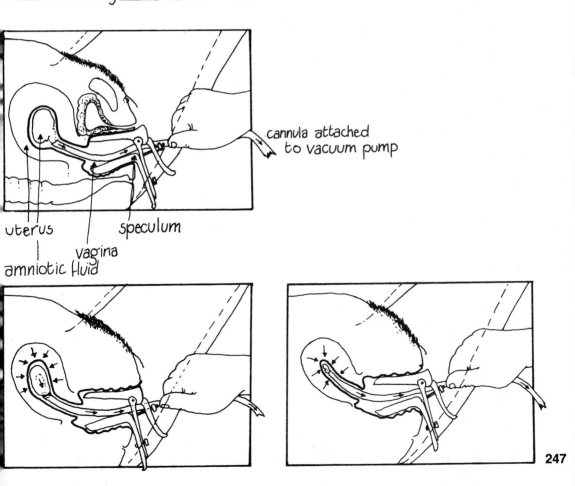

cannula attached
to vacuum pump

uterus   speculum

vagina
amniotic fluid

their 'catchment area' – that is, you have to have a local address. BPAS and PAS have day units, but you're quite likely to have to stay in twenty-four hours; in NHS hospitals, forty-eight hours.

The different ways of doing terminations are described in detail in *Our Bodies Ourselves*, with accounts of what it actually feels like. It's a good idea to read these. Nurses and junior doctors don't often volunteer information, either because they're too busy or it's against hospital policy or they simply don't know the consultant's intentions. The most usual method (up to twelve weeks after the start of your last period) is by Vacuum Suction: with a local or light general anaesthetic, a slim tube is inserted through the dilated cervix, and the contents of the uterus drawn out by means of a gentle suction machine attached to the other end of the tube. This method has largely replaced 'D&C' (dilation and curettage), where the contents are loosened and removed with instruments. D&Cs, though, can be used up to fifteen weeks and would be preferable to Induction (the method always used after sixteen weeks). Induction means that you are injected with a fluid that makes your womb contract – in effect you go into labour and have a miscarriage. It's long-drawn-out, painful and emotionally harrowing. Try to get a D&C if you're not much over twelve weeks.

Attitudes and feelings

Finding your way through the NHS maze to arrange and have your abortion can be disturbing enough, even if you meet the kindliest doctors and nurses. Given a hostile staff, the experience can be awful. You might be heavied about your life-style or about contraception, or even pressured to accept sterilisation as the price of your abortion. It's a good idea to take somebody with you to appointments for moral support. If that's not possible, try to talk the whole thing through with friends before you go for your first appointment, so that you're as clear as you can be about what you feel and want. Afterwards, some women feel fine about their abortion; others are miserable, even if they didn't expect to be. Most of us have mixed feelings. Deep, lasting depression is rare. Again, talking things out will really help – so long as friends don't try to tell you that you 'ought' to be feeling differently from the way you do. If you feel angry about how difficult it is to get an abortion, you could contact an organisation like the National Abortion Campaign (NAC), which campaigns to defend and improve abortion services – address at the end of the book.

Further reading

I firmly believe that the most reliable source of information on contraceptives is still *Our Bodies Ourselves*. There is plenty of other information about contraceptives, but I can find nothing
else as good. It also has a long list of more detailed books if you

should need them. A new one out since *Our Bodies Ourselves* is *The Birth Control Book* by gynaecologist Howard Shapiro (Penguin). The information is pretty thorough and reliable, though there's nothing about the experience of using the different methods.

Birth Control by Michael Smith (a *Woman's Own* guide, published by Hamlyn) is more of a question-and-answer routine, and so perhaps easier to use. But some of the questions are very glibly answered – 'How long will it be before the male pill is widely available?' 'How long is a piece of string?' By the honorary chief medical officer of the FPA, it's also too comforting about Depo-Provera. *The Pill* by John Guillebaud (Penguin) is detailed and fairly objective.

If you're interested in finding out about natural birth control, there's a pamphlet by a group in Sheffield called *Birth Control by Observing Natural Cycles* (from alternative bookshops). It shows you how to observe your mucous and chart your temperature. If you don't want to risk it as a form of contraception, it will anyway help you to understand more about how your cycle works.

An excellent historical book about birth control is Linda Gordon's *Woman's Body, Woman's Right: Birth Control in America* (Penguin).

On abortion, there's a lovely pamphlet by 'Brent against Corrie' called *Mixed Feelings* (from alternative bookshops). Ten women write about their own experience of pregnancy and abortion. On similar lines, but not so good, is Linda Bird Francke's *Ambivalence of Abortion* (Penguin). Personal feelings and political demands were well-blended in an article in *Spare Rib* issue 87 – 'Abortion, the Feelings Behind the Slogans' by Eileen Fairweather. About the politics of the abortion campaign, there is *Abortion in Demand* by Victoria Greenwood and Jock Young (Pluto). And there are plenty of leaflets and pamphlets available from the National Abortion Campaign (see useful addresses).

XVII. Conclusion

We haven't got there yet, with this new sexuality of ours. A great deal still needs to happen.

We are learning to stick up for ourselves, to take ourselves seriously, to find out our needs and to see that we get what we want. We are learning to say no and to say yes. We are learning to like ourselves again. We have learned that sexuality isn't just about orgasms and technique. We want different relationships, not just different positions. The right to our own sexuality means the right to control our own bodies, to control our own lives. So all the things that need to be changed are connected and interconnected: better contraceptives and a better health service, abortion on demand, no discrimination against lesbians, against older women, single women, mothers. We want to strip off the mask and show the underlying hatred of women disguised in porn. We want an end to sexual violence inside and outside marriage. So: crisis centres for raped women, self-defence, Women's Aid refuges for battered women, a better legal system. Everything is connected and that's why it's important that lesbians take part in an abortion demonstration and heterosexual women march for gay liberation.

And it's vital that we make sure that our sexual revolution doesn't turn into a farce like the one men achieved: the relationship between women and men must be radically changed. Men have to change, they should no longer dominate as a matter of course simply because they are breadwinners. And we need to be economically independent: equal pay, the right to go out to work, the right to education. And we need collective facilities which will take from us part of the burden of our housework: good childcare, good housing, pulic transport.

If you think about sexuality from a woman's point of view, you inevitably come to the conclusion that almost everything has to change. That won't happen just like that, and so the liberation of our sexuality won't just take place overnight. But changing sexual relationships can be just as good a place to start as trying for a more honest division of housework, campaigning for non-sexist children's books or demonstrating against cuts in child benefits.

Women need each other. We need each other to give us confidence, to support each other in all the risks we take whenever we try to change our lives, to find out what we want, to start campaigns when we know what we want. And just for a cuddle.

To us!

Books

If you're interested, here's a list of a few titles of books and articles I found useful, which haven't been mentioned at the end of the chapters.

Nancy Adair and Casey Adair, *Word is Out*, New Glide Publications, San Francisco, 1978

Ti-Grace Atkinson, 'The Institution of Sexual Intercourse', from *Amazon Odyssey*, Links Books, New York 1974

GM de Bruijn, *Over opwindig en bevrediging bij vrouwen, twee diskussiepunten uit de sexualiteit van vrouwen*, Nisso 1975.

Lörenne Clark and Debra Lewis, *Rape: the Price of Coercive Sexuality*, The Women's Press, Canada, 1977

Gina Covina and Laurel Galana, eds, *The Lesbian Reader*, Amazon Press, USA, 1975

Susan Griffin and Diana Russell, 'On Pornography: Two Feminist Perspectives', from *Chrysalis*, no 4, Los Angeles, 1977

Nancy M Henley, *Body Politics: Power, Sex and Nonverbal Communication*, Prentice-Hall Inc, New Jersey, 1977

Stevi Jackson, *On the Social Construction of Female Sexuality*, 'Explorations in Feminism', no 4, Women's Research and Resources Centre Publications, London, 1978

Helen Singer Kaplan, *The New Sex Therapy*, Penguin 1978

Susan Lydon, 'The Politics of Orgasm', from *Sisterhood is Powerful*, Robin Morgan, ed, Vintage Books, 1970

Norbert Ney, *Sterilisation des Mannes, das geringste Übel*, Verlag Frauenpolitik, 1978

Red Collective, *The Politics of Sexuality in Capitalism*, Red Collective/PDC

Alice Ruhle-Gerstel, 'Die Weibliche Sexualität', from *Zür Psychologie der Frau*, Gisela Brinker Gabler, Hrsg, Fisher, Verlag, 1978

Gunter Schmidt and Volkmar Sigush, *Arbeiter-Sexualität*, Luchterhand, 1971

Alix Shulman, 'Organs and Orgasms', from *Woman in Sexist Society*, Vivian Gornick and Barbara K Moran, eds, New American Library, New York, 1972

Dr Emily L Sisley and Bertha Harris, *The Joy of Lesbian Sex, A Tender and Liberated Guide to the Pleasures and Problems of a Lesbian Lifestyle*, Crown Publishers Inc, New York, 1977

Carol Smart and Barry Smart, eds, *Women, Sexuality and Social Control*, Routledge and Kegan Paul, London, 1978

Elke and Thomas Schmidt, *Sexualerziehung in der Grundschule*, Raith Verlag, 1974

Jos van Ussel, *Afschied van de seksualiteit*, Bert Bakker, 1970

Jos van Ussel, *Intimiteit*, Van Loghem Slaterus, 1975

Claudia von Werlhof, 'Sexualität und Ökonomie, Über den Zusammenhang zwischen Frauenmisshandlung und Klassengesellschaft' from *Konfliktfeld Sexualität*, Ignatz Kerscher, hrsg, Luchterhand, 1977

DJ West, C Roy and FL Nichols, *Understanding Sexual Attacks*, Heinemann, London 1978

Useful addresses

A few years ago it was still possible to list all useful addresses on ONE page. That's no longer possible, and we'd have to print hundreds of addresses. Not only do addresses go out of date, new ones are added. This is a selection. If you want all the addresses of women's centres and many other organisations, you can buy the women's diary published by *Spare Rib*. Or you can contact *WIRES*, the national Women's Liberation information service – that's at 32a Shakespeare St, Nottingham (0602-411475). *WIRES* is also a fortnightly newsletter, for women only, which will keep you up to date with feminist events and ideas. *WIRES* can also put you in touch with local women and health groups. It's also worth reading *Spare Rib*, a monthly women's liberation magazine – you can get it from newsagents or from 27 Clerkenwell Close, London EC1.
Send sae when writing to any of these organisations.

Books

Many of the books marked 'import' in the further reading lists – and a lot of the others – are on sale in your local radical bookshop or women's centre. If they don't have them, you should be able to get them from *Sisterwrite*, 190 Upper St, London N1, or *Compendium*, 234 Camden High St, London NW1 or *Grass Roots*, 1 Newton St, Manchester 1. These three bookshops all do mail order. The *Family Planning Information Service*, 27/35 Mortimer St, London W1, also does a lot of these books by mail order – send an sae for their booklist.
Sisterwrite, a women's co-operative, produces a catalogue of women's books in print. They are constantly updating it. You can get a copy from them, address above.
At the same address, there's the *Women's Research and Resources Centre*, which has a lending library, a reading room and a newsletter.

Battered women

Women's Aid houses are refuges for women and their children who are being battered or threatened. The addresses are kept secret, but you can get in touch with your local refuge through the *Women's Aid Federation (England)*, 374 Grays Inn Road, London WC1 (01-837 9316), or *Scottish Women's Aid*, Ainlee House, 11 St Colne St, Edinburgh 3 (031-225 8011), or *Welsh Women's Aid*, Incentive House, Adam St, Cardiff (0222-388291), or *Northern Irish Women's Aid*, 12 Orchard St, Derry (Derry 67672).

Rape

There are now *Rape Crisis Centres* all round the country, to counsel and support raped women. The only 24 hour lines are in Birmingham (021-233 2122) and in London (01-340 6145). There are also centres, operating part-time, in a lot of other towns – get the number through Birmingham or London. There are also groups called *Feminists Against Sexual Terrorism (FAST)* – contact c/o 37 Chestnut Ave, Leeds 6 – and a national network called *Women Against Violence Against Women*, c/o AWP, 48 William IV St, London WC2.

Contraception

If you can't get what you want from your GP or local family planning clinic, try the *Family Planning Information Service* (address above – phone 01-636 7866) or *Brook Advisory Centres* – find your nearest through 233 Tottenham Court Road, London W1 (01-323 1522 or 580 2991). Brook is particularly for young people.
You can get the morning-after-pill and morning-after-IUD at *Brook*, at the *Pregnancy Advisory Service*, 40 Margaret Street, London W1 (01-409 0281), and at the *Marie Stopes Clinic*, 108 Whitfield Street, London W1 (01-388 4843).
There's also a *Campaign Against Depo-Provera* at 374 Grays Inn Road, London WC1, a *Pill Victims Action Group* at 3 Eney Close, Abingdon, Oxfordshire. and a *Dalkon Shield Association* c/o 16b Elvaston Place, London SW7.

Abortion

If you can't get an abortion on the NHS, you can try the *British Pregnancy Advisory Service*, Airsty Manor, Wootton Wawen, Solihull, West Midlands (05642-3225). They can tell you your nearest branch. In London there's also the *Pregnancy Advisory Service (address above).* Both organisations also do pregnancy testing. *PAS* does a very early test, reliable ten days *after conception.* If you need an abortion in Northern Ireland, contact the Ulster Pregnancy Advisory Association, 338a Lisburn Road, Belfast (Belfast 667345). They can also help you arrange a pregnancy test.
Campaigning for a woman's right to choose, there is the *National Abortion Campaign*, 374 Grays Inn Road, London WC1 (01-278 0153). At the same address is the *International Contraception, Abortion and Sterilisation Campaign.* And there's a *Northern Ireland Abortion Campaign* c/o Women's Centre, 16-18 Donegall St, Belfast 1.

Sterilisation

If you can't get it on the NHS, try *BPAS* (above) or the *Marie Stopes Clinic* (above).

Drinking

The main organisation is still *Alcoholics Anonymous*, 7 Moreton St, London SW1 (01-834 8202). They'll put you in touch with your local group.

Compulsive eating

There are now several groups working according to the ideas in *Fat is a Feminist Issue* by Susie Orbach. Contact them through *Spare Tyre Theatre Company*, 100 Fortess Road, London NW5.

Anorexia

Anorexia Aid has self-help groups – find your nearest through Alison Cork, The Priory Centre, 11 Priory Road, High Wycombe, Bucks.

Therapy

There are various kinds of therapy being done now by feminists. Find out more about it through the *Women's Therapy Centre*, 6 Manor Gdns, London N7 (01-263 6200/6209).

Lesbians

There are now several phone lines for lesbians to ring who want to talk, get support or information about what's going on. Try *Lesbian Line* 01-837 8602 or *Lesbian Link* 061-236 6205.

Women with disabilities

A general organisation (for both women and men) is the *Disability Alliance*, 1 Cambridge Terrace, London NW1 (01-935 4992). *Gemma* is a specifically for lesbians with disabilities – BM Box 5700, London WC1V 6XX. And there's an organisation called *Sexual Problems of the Disabled* at 27/35 Mortimer St, London W1.

Pre-orgasmic

There are usually a few groups going – ring 01-452 9261 or the *Women's Sexuality Workshop* 01-794 2838. They may know of groups in your area.

Men

If you have a friend or husband who would like to get involved in something, you can pass on the following addresses: *London Men's Centre*, c/o Bread and Roses, 316 Upper St, London N1; *Achilles Heel*, a men's magazine, 7 St Mark's Rise, London E8, and the *Anti-sexist men's newsletter*, c/o Misha, 12 Terrapin Road, London SW17.